I0109716

THE OCTOPUS ORGANIZATION

THE OCTOPUS ORGANIZATION

*A Guide to Thriving
in a World of Continuous
Transformation*

PHIL LE-BRUN • JANA WERNER

HARVARD BUSINESS REVIEW PRESS
BOSTON, MASSACHUSETTS

HBR Press Quantity Sales Discounts

Harvard Business Review Press titles are available at significant quantity discounts when purchased in bulk for leadership development programs, client gifts, or sales promotions. Opportunities to co-brand copies with your logo or messaging are also available. For details and discount information for both print and ebook formats, contact booksales@hbr.org or visit www.hbr.org/bulksales.

Copyright 2026 Phil Le-Brun and Jana Werner

All rights reserved

Printed in the United States of America

10 9 8 7 6 5 4 3 2 1

No part of this publication may be reproduced, stored in or introduced into a retrieval system, or transmitted, in any form, or by any means (electronic, mechanical, photocopying, recording, or otherwise), without the prior permission of the publisher. Requests for permission should be directed to permissions@harvardbusiness.org, or mailed to Permissions, Harvard Business School Publishing, 60 Harvard Way, Boston, Massachusetts 02163.

The web addresses referenced in this book were live and correct at the time of the book's publication but may be subject to change.

Library of Congress Cataloging-in-Publication Data

Names: Le-Brun, Phil author | Werner, Jana author
Title: The octopus organization : a guide to thriving in a world of continuous
    transformation / Phil Le-Brun and Jana Werner.
Description: Boston, Massachusetts : Harvard Business Review Press, [2026]
Identifiers: LCCN 2025027600 (print) | LCCN 2025027601 (ebook) |
    ISBN 9798892791403 hardcover alk. paper | ISBN 9798892791410 epub
Subjects: LCSH: Organizational change | Organizational behavior
Classification: LCC HD58.8 .L41626 2026 (print) | LCC HD58.8 (ebook) |
    DDC 658.4/06—dc23/eng/20250829
LC record available at https://lccn.loc.gov/2025027600
LC ebook record available at https://lccn.loc.gov/2025027601

ISBN: 979-8-89279-140-3
eISBN: 979-8-89279-141-0

The paper used in this publication meets the requirements of the American National Standard for Permanence of Paper for Publications and Documents in Libraries and Archives Z39.48-1992.

CONTENTS

PART 2

INCREASING OWNERSHIP

PART 3

INCITING CURIOSITY

ANTIPATTERN #36

PRETENDING TO INNOVATE   291

Ideas of any size, from anyone, anywhere create
real value.

CONCLUSION

BECOMING THE OCTOPUS   297

A BETTER WAY TO OPERATE

This is a book about what great organizations do to thrive, which is to behave like an octopus. More on that soon, but first we need to talk about what most organizations *actually* do, which is behave like the Tin Man.

This insight—not the metaphor—came to both of us, separately, as we worked with hundreds of companies and witnessed them making the same mistakes repeatedly. Together we developed the metaphor as we began sharing field stories with each other and we recognized the same frustrations with the behaviors we were witnessing. We began to see these organizations rather like the "Tin Man" in *The Wizard of Oz*. He was a rigid and clumsy character—slow to move and slow to react, lacking heart and struggling with empathy. He could take instructions but showed little initiative. His tool of choice was a blunt axe. When Dorothy found him, he had completely rusted up and needed her to fetch him some oil.

Blunt tools. Rusted joints. Missing a heart. Yearning for oil. Tin Man wanted to feel and move freely but simply couldn't—just like the organizations we encountered, stuck in rigid structures, lacking a unifying purpose, and constantly searching for external fixes to help them operate more fluidly.

To be sure, no organization or leader sets out to be a Tin Man. In fact, we believe that this model is so prevalent today because, for a long time, it worked so, so well. The Tin Man organizational models that dominate most businesses today are, in essence, still factories. For decades, this model—built on standardization, specialization, control, measuring individuals' performance, compliance, mass production, and predictable outputs—achieved immeasurably great results.

But it's a rusting construct—now more than a century old. We work with some businesses using the factory model that are beautifully engineered, humming with efficiency. But they're churning out *average output*.

Tin Man orgs can't get beyond average because they're not structured to allow it. They're built on a foundation of *permission*. Permission to innovate, permission to speak up, permission to even *care*. They're designed to minimize risk, eliminate variation, and create efficient, predictable outcomes. This works if you are making bushings or building boats.

But the world has changed since these models were invented and perfected decades ago. You're probably not making bushings or building a boat, and even if you are, competitive pressures aren't as forgiving as they once were. The Tin Man's design, optimized for an era of mass production and linear control, becomes his undoing in a complex world where success is adapting and discovering.

Today, success depends on building genuine trust-based relationships with customers, employees, and broader sets of stakeholders. Work is less transactional. Customers have more choice and so do your employees. They don't want to be told; they want to be *heard*. They don't want to be managed; they want to be *inspired*. Creativity cannot be commanded. You can't mandate passion. You can't org chart your way to exceptional. Traditional organizations are beautifully engineered for a world that no longer exists. They're not *bad*; they're just . . . *inadequate*.

The Transformation Trap

What strikes us when we work with customers and leaders—people—stuck in Tin Man operating models is that many of them *know* that how they operate is working against them. And in response to the pressures rising from the mismatch between Tin Man models and the demands of customers and markets, they have sought an escape through *transformation*—large-scale initiatives designed to modernize operations, embrace digital technologies, and cultivate adaptability and nimbler operations.

But despite trillions invested in transformations over the past two decades, the results are most often underwhelming. The litany of failure statistics could fill a book themselves. Lowlights include:

- Less than 12 percent of transformations create the expected sustainable performance gains thirty-six months into a program of work.[1]

- Less than a third of organizations realize anticipated revenue benefits, and just a quarter achieve the cost benefits anticipated from their transformations.[2]

- Anywhere between 70 and 90 percent of digital transformation initiatives end in failure depending on whom you ask.[3]

Beyond the staggering financial waste, the greater cost is often less invisible: years of lost opportunity, the erosion of employee trust, and the departure of your most passionate and innovative people who grow tired of watching good ideas wither in the face of bureaucratic inertia. This is how a company's passion, problem solving, and sense of possibility quietly erodes.

Transformations don't really work. And they don't work, ironically, because organizations *use a Tin Man approach* to their transformation. Traditional transformation methodologies mirror the structures they seek to overhaul. They're rigid and linear. Top-down. Measured with simple metrics. Conventional approaches frequently focus on changing the optics and artifacts of an organization—implementing specific technologies, reengineering discrete processes, or changing the org chart, hoping that behavior will follow. It's an approach that treats the organization as a machine to be fixed through targeted interventions, rather than a complex, living system requiring a more holistic, engaging, and adaptive evolution.

But true change doesn't come from artifacts—it comes from how people see the world and from changing *behavior*, not structures. Otherwise change becomes bolted on and ephemeral, overridden by fear and biases that we're all subject to. Beliefs and feelings make the behavior change *hard*. For example, trust is required for effective change, but paradoxically trust plummets when a massive change is declared, because it feels threatening when you have no agency over it.

It's a cruel irony: to escape their Tin Man roots, organizations engage in a transformation that represents the apotheosis of Tin Man behavior.

Introducing the Octopus Organization

This book proposes a fundamentally different organizational paradigm: the *Octopus Organization*. We are inspired by the remarkable adaptability, distributed intelligence, fluid movement, and innate curiosity of this remarkable sea dweller. And, okay, it's also beautiful. Some important traits of the octopus pertinent to our conversation: It has an absurdly sophisticated ability to adapt to its ever-changing environment, through camouflage, shape-shifting, and other physical gifts such as the ability to change the texture of its skin (skin that it also uses both to see and to breathe). It is designed to explore and has a remarkable capacity to learn, easily solving puzzles and mazes humans created. Two-thirds of the neurons in the octopus's body are not in the brain;

they are in the eight incredible arms that can think and act for themselves, but also coordinate with the brain to think and act as a team.

You get the metaphor. The Octopus way of thinking offers an approach to building organizations that thrive in complexity and embrace continuous change. They tap the intelligence of people and teams distributed throughout their organization, coordinating complex efforts as gracefully as the arms of the octopus. They sense subtle signals and learn and adapt instantly to navigate uncertainty.

And complexity. At the heart of the need for Octopus Organizations is a shift of focus from *complicated* business environments to *complex* ones. Understanding the distinction between the two is crucial to grasping why traditional organizational models are faltering and why the Octopus Organization offers a more viable path forward.

Tin Man operating models are rooted in a worldview that sees the world as fundamentally complicated. Complicated systems are not always easy to understand, but they are governed by predictable cause-and-effect relationships that follow clear rules, with no inherent uncertainty. If I do X, Y will happen. Complicated problems can be broken down into smaller, more manageable components and managed through centralized control. Solutions to those problems are built with defined blueprints and assembled linearly in a tightly managed, efficient process.

Complicated systems are brought to heel through efficiency, specialization, control through hierarchy, and standardization, through projects with a defined start and end date, aimed at "fixing" or "upgrading" the machine.

Conversely, complex systems are like, well, octopuses. They're governed by emergence—outcomes from interactions that are not linear or predictable through analysis of the system's components. If you take the welder out of the boat-making factory, you can guess what happens. Try to understand, then explain, what happens if you grab one arm of an octopus. Complex systems are managed through learning, resilience, and collaboration. Octopus Organizations prioritize adaptability, decentralized ownership, interconnectedness, and continuous learning and experimentation. In an Octopus Organization, running and changing the business are mutually reinforcing aspects of a single, continuous dynamic. Change is built into the fabric of the organization. See table I-1.

The Octopus Organization is a fundamental rethink of what it means to be a successful organization, a shift from metal suit to living organism, from the programmable machine to the adaptable animal. It's about building organizations designed to thrive in complexity, not futilely manage the complicated. It's about choosing breakthrough performance over average

TABLE I-1

From complicated Tin Man to complex Octopus

Tin Man	Octopus
Efficiency: Cost reduction, maximizing output	**Adaptability:** Experimentation, resilience
Control: Centralization, hierarchical command, adherence to process	**Connection:** Collaboration, teams with ownership, relationships
Standardization: Consistency, average market needs, good enough	**Distinctiveness:** Differentiation, individualization, uniquely valuable
Tasks: Output, following plans →	**Problems to solve:** Learning, growth
Permission: Control, lack of trust, passivity	**Agency:** Ownership, initiative, passion
Silos: Distinct functions, departmental optimization, specialized expertise	**Ecosystems:** Cross-functional collaboration, holistic problem-solving, collective intelligence
Short-term focus: Quarterly targets, simple metrics, risk minimization	**Long-term vision:** Thinking big, responsible risk-taking
Run or change the business: Activities focused on one or the other, and the latter is a task to serve the former	**Run and change the business:** Delivery and change are not distinct; running is changing and changing is running

results, connection over control, and agency over permission. It's about shedding the Tin Man's welded body and embracing the gorgeously fluid movement of the octopus.

Practically, the difference between the Tin Man and the Octopus Organization looks like this: In a Tin Man organization, a strategy meeting will be driven by presentations. Each speaker adheres to a preset agenda, delivering carefully prepared slides, sticking to their allotted time. Questions are reserved for the end, and they are often perfunctory. There's a sense of *controlled information flow*, of *structured communication* to inform. The meeting is efficient. Participants are primarily receivers of information.

The Octopus Organization strategy session will look, sound, and feel completely different. A diverse tenured and functional group from across the organization gathers around a whiteboard to talk about a well-defined topic such as "How might we approach this market?" Leaders encourage people to throw out ideas rapidly and ask provocative questions, and the people in the meeting feel safe doing so. Contributors build on and challenge each other's curiosity and ideas. Conversation flows organically, tangents are explored, and unexpected connections emerge. Participants are active cocreators of ideas, their interaction driving innovation. There's a sense of *constructive conflict*, of *emergent thinking*. The energy is palpable. *The feeling is one of unleashed, collaborative curiosity, energizing, and generative.*

Or let's go to the Tin Man call center, where reps stick to scripts and decision trees dictated by an algorithm. The agent is a process executor held to metrics that reward volume of resolutions. Over at the Octopus call center, agents *own* the customer's problem. They actively listen, empathize, and tailor solutions to the individual caller. Perhaps they even have a discretionary budget to use to ensure a good outcome for the customer. There's a sense of *human-centered problem-solving*, of *genuine connection*. The interaction might take longer but results in more satisfied and loyal customers. The agent is a problem-solver and relationship builder, looking beyond narrowly defined job definitions to identify new customer needs and to automate away repeated problems.

Innovation is similarly transformed. Tin Man organizations tend to segregate innovation in labs or groups physically and culturally isolated from the core business, populated with "innovation experts," who develop ideas in isolation, then hand them off (along with all the integration and real-world challenges they haven't accounted for) to the business for implementation. *The feeling is one of artificial innovation with limited real-world impact.*

Octopus Organizations make innovation a responsibility and capability of *everyone*. It's embedded in daily work. Ideas are encouraged to come from anywhere, experimentation is fast and decentralized, and learning from it is shared across the organization. Innovation emerges organically from countless customer interactions, collaborations, and experiments happening everywhere. *The feeling is one of pervasive progress, quick to execute, fueled by the collective curiosity and distributed intelligence of every employee.*

Most of all, Octopus Organizations are deeply customer-centric. They don't just pay lip service to customers (as you'll see in many antipatterns). Nearly every change you make to be more like an Octopus involves shifting your focus to what any given behavior means to *customer value*. And when you get there, the rewards are great. Research shows that customer-obsessed companies can be more than three times as likely to lead their industries in revenue growth.[6]

For many leaders, even imagining these ways of working will feel foreign, possibly uncomfortable. But we suspect that whatever discomfort the Octopus organizational model creates, it also creates an equal dose of intrigue. We find that most leaders sense they are operating Tin Man organizations and would like to develop more octopus-like qualities—the ability to make fast decisions, adapt quickly to changing conditions, and harness collective intelligence across decentralized teams.

Amazon Prime, you may be surprised to discover, did not start as a gigantic strategic bet. It began as an idea of one person, but it developed into something delivering massive customer value through the collective intelligence of the organization.

We deeply believe the Octopus Organization is a better way to run businesses. Organizations that shift their ways of working to the Octopus approach intuitively are set up better to succeed than those that don't. They are more adaptable, more innovative, and more resilient to shocks and downturns. They engender more customer and employee loyalty.

And we are going to show you how to shed your metal straitjacket and become something better. Something more alive.

Breaking the Antipatterns

The journey to becoming a more adaptable organization begins by identifying what's holding you back. In our careers leading large-scale transformation—working with executives and frontline teams across hundreds of organizations, most of them *Fortune* 500, driving major initiatives, and re-architecting entire systems of work—we've discovered that most companies aren't stuck because of unique problems. Instead, they make the same predictable mistakes again and again, repeating patterns we've witnessed in conversation after conversation, initiative after initiative.

In all that experience, we've seen the same struggles and mistakes repeatedly. Quite a few of the mistakes are so remarkably predictable that we were able to document and categorize them. We call them *antipatterns*: conditioned, formulaic responses to complex challenges that, despite good intentions and surface-level appeal, consistently make things worse. They are solutions that feel right but are fundamentally wrong for creating an adaptive, innovative organization.

You can think of an antipattern as a sort of worst practice that we're here to fix. In the next three sections, the heart of this book, we will identify and describe Tin Man antipatterns that emerge with stubborn persistence across so many organizations we have worked with, creating the most significant ripples of dysfunction. While countless antipatterns exist, these represent the ones with the greatest systemic impact. Then, drawing on our experience working with a select set of companies that are more like Octopus Organizations, we'll describe how Octopus Organizations behave to escape the antipattern. The behaviors we'll describe that you can develop in place of

Tin Man behaviors are *not* transformations, but they are transformative, simple changes in mindset, practices, and behavior. Finally, for each antipattern we'll give you "levers" to pull—concrete, actionable advice on things you can try right away to start attacking your antipatterns. (In systems theory, a lever is a point of intervention where a small shift can produce disproportionately large changes throughout the entire system.) They're not every possible lever you could pull, but they are the most common ones we see organizations turning to, and they will inspire you to come up with your own as well once you see the general structure of them.

We've grouped our antipatterns and advice for escaping them into three broad categories:

- Creating clarity

- Increasing ownership

- Inciting curiosity

Why clarity? Traditional Tin Man organizations breed obscurity—a bureaucratic fog that naturally emerges from layers of management, vague strategies pronounced from on high, and siloed information. Octopus behaviors create clarity—shared understanding of why the company exists, where it will play (and crucially, where it won't), what truly matters now, who it serves, and what to solve for.

This isn't a detailed map for every step—that would stifle curiosity and ownership. But it cuts through the bureaucratic fog, providing the context and focus people need to enable them to move with speed and confidence, and understand what to solve for.

Why ownership? Traditional Tin Man orgs and their rigid processes can inadvertently treat people as interchangeable capital—just do your job, keep quiet, and follow orders. But in the modern connection economy, people crave agency. They want to matter. Ownership is responsibility plus authorship. It's about feeling like you're building something, not just turning a wrench. When people own their work, when they feel responsible for an outcome, not just a task, magic happens. They bring their whole selves. They problem-solve. They care. In Octopus Organizations, ownership isn't delegated; it's ignited. And it's contagious. Without it, you're left with a workforce of clock punchers waiting for Friday and constantly asking for permission, not innovators hungry for Monday.

Why curiosity? Tin Man organizations gravitate toward certainty and predictability—it feels safer and more controllable. But this creates a dangerous comfort zone where companies optimize what they already know while becoming blind to emerging threats and transformative opportunities. Without curiosity, organizations don't just stagnate; they calcify, slouching toward irrelevance. Curiosity, in the Octopus world, is the continuous current of adaptation and bold reinvention, a relentless humble posture of learning over knowing, questioning sacred assumptions, and asking "what if" about everything taken for granted. Curiosity emerges in a culture of learning, not just knowing, where failure is feedback and leaders are positively discontented with the status quo. Curiosity drives deep customer empathy and the exploration of what's possible with emerging technologies, allowing organizations to invent their future rather than simply manage their present.

Clarity, ownership, and curiosity form a virtuous cycle. Clarity enables ownership because it creates a common *clear* understanding of what problems to solve. This agency in turn creates curiosity. Let me *own* a challenge and I'll experiment and learn my way through it based on my strengths and preferred ways of working. The learning that results from curiosity swings around to increase clarity, which in turn increases ownership as people understand what to do and can get on with it, and the virtuous cycle continues.

So clarity, ownership, and curiosity are the fundamental traits, the DNA of Octopus Organizations. They're the antidote to the factory mindset. They're the ingredients for organizations that don't just survive but thrive.

In all, we've included thirty-six common antipatterns in these three categories for you to discover and dismantle. Think of these not as chapters, but more as *entries*. We fully intend, and hope, that this book will be used modularly. You *could* read it straight through, but we believe most will want to scan the contents and look up the antipattern that gets them excited to read about because they just know their organization suffers from it. When we mention antipatterns in keynote addresses and other workshop sessions, we always see heads start nodding eagerly or hear involuntary chortles when we mention an antipattern that absolutely resonates.

So, attack any antipattern that resonates with you. They've been written to stand on their own. You will notice, the more antipatterns you explore, that there is some repetition of ideas and levers. There's a beneficial reason for this overlap. For one, we don't know the path you'll take through the book, so we're ensuring you get the ideas you need when you arrive. Secondly, as you explore more antipatterns, you'll see themes emerge—about iteration, about agency, about safety, and about learning. Some antipatterns share common root causes. You will start to get a sense not just for the actions you need to take to become an Octopus Organization but for the *types of behaviors* that are hallmarks of Octopus Organizations.

When you do choose an antipattern, dog-ear it, mark it up, add your own antipatterns and levers. We suspect you'll want to share specific antipatterns you recognize all too well with colleagues or leaders. Do it. This book is intended to become a reference of sorts that you can come back to. At the end of each entry, we've also included a few links to related antipatterns, so you can roam through the book. We've designed this book not to be read but to be *used*. We've designed it to be an octopus-like experience, and in using the book this way, you're already starting, in a very small way, to be an Octopus. You're feeling ready to adapt the content to your needs. To work with it the way that helps you learn and solve problems. You are taking ownership and approaching it with curiosity. That's a good start.

Developing Octopus DNA

The Octopus Organization is a model whose concept we've seen many leaders embrace immediately. But then, quickly, they want answers: "How do I do it? What's the framework? How can I get there? Who should I hire?"

You will not find those answers here. Indeed, the search for a recipe, a process to follow, an end state to reach—these are the very Tin Man mindsets we're trying to help you overcome. Some leaders think what we're describing is just a different way to talk about transformation. Let us be clear: it is not. We are not here to force a transformation on you; transformations (with a few exceptions) generally don't work.

But in seeking these kinds of answers, leaders are betraying that they need to learn their antipatterns. There is no recipe or playbook for a onetime Octopus transformation. This is about patterns, not plans. There's no date when you'll say, "We're done. Now we're an Octopus." Many people out there will try to sell you such a thing, but unfortunately, we have never seen such approaches to fundamentally altering your organization work and stick.

What we've provided instead is a concluding chapter that gives you a guide to starting and maintaining momentum to develop Octopus DNA. It's a how-to for attacking even one antipattern, for understanding how to think about and use the levers we provide in each entry. It's designed to be deeply practical and should jump-start your journey to adopt an Octopus approach, but you should think of it as a compass, not a map.

The reality is that an organization doesn't become an Octopus in a linear, tidy fashion. True change comes from how people see the world and from changing *behavior*, not artifacts. Like building a strong marriage or family, it's a messy process that involves doing a few things simultaneously, making mistakes, making incremental progress on specific aspects of your challenges; and it must be tended to constantly to be preserved.[7]

The ocean is always moving, but an octopus learns to thrive in the turbulent flow. Our aspiration is that this book helps you in a similar way—that it changes how you solve problems, how you decide which problems you solve. We want to help you, and your teams, change behaviors and your culture to achieve great things. Start your journey here, and you'll find your organization can learn and adapt as quickly and gracefully, as playfully and *intelligently* as the ceaselessly amazing octopus.

Now, head back to the table of contents, pick an antipattern to explore, and let's get started.

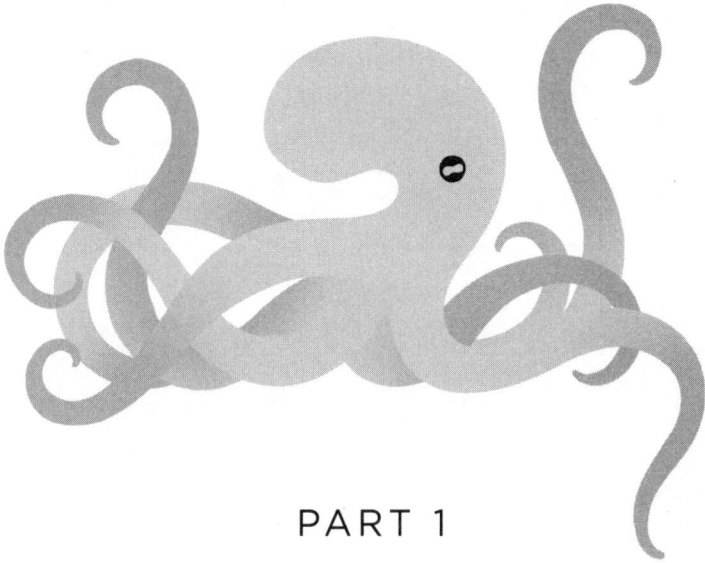

PART 1

CREATING CLARITY

T he first cluster of antipatterns that are holding Tin Man organizations back from becoming Octopuses focus on what makes it hard to create *clarity*.

Clarity is the shared understanding of an organization's purpose, values, priorities, and what success looks like. It creates the context for decentralized action, free from top-down mandate. Clarity means individuals and teams understand which problems are worth solving and can confidently make decisions because they understand not only *what* needs to be done but *why* it's important. The vagueness in the many organizations that don't create this clarity hinders their people from having agency—the power to take initiative and own the outcome.

Creating clarity requires building grounded, shared mental models—which are our internal maps to make sense of complex situations, predict outcomes, and decide how to act. This is about understanding markets, customer needs, data and insights, technology trends, as well as how work gets done. These models also contextualize generic terms so that they make sense to *your* organization—terms such as "digital" or "product." It requires repeated communication of these concepts and opportunities for people to wrestle with these ideas, to question them, and ultimately, to *choose* to adopt and internalize them as their mental models. In doing so, clarity is cocreated, not just delivered by fiat.

Creating clarity isn't a onetime task; it's an ongoing process of trying to be clear, collecting feedback, and adjusting. Most leaders tend to grossly overestimate the degree to which there is a shared understanding of what the organization is there to do, and how. In our discussions with them, CEOs like Benedikt Böhm (Dynafit), Benedetto Vigna (Ferrari), and Dame Julia Hoggett (London Stock Exchange), all of whom you'll hear from in the following antipatterns, understood that a key part of their CEO roles was to drive ongoing clarity. To do this, General Stanley McChrystal writes, requires "radical information sharing and ensuring common understanding across the entire organization . . . pumping information *out* to empower people at all levels."[1]

When it's created and maintained, clarity provides a common context to decide when and where not to invest energy. There's no wasted time deliberating and negotiating on those points. The up-front and ongoing investment in creating clarity produces a good tension between where we are and where we've committed to go. This tension pulls exceptional work out of people. Problem-solving, decision quality, and speed improve. More decisions are driven into teams closer to customers, safe in the assurance they are being made with shared values and intent. A Formula One pit team has great clarity. It can change tires with perfect synchronicity and a minimal amount of communication; a choreographed dance in the face of numerous challenges secure in the knowledge that they have a clear and common goal.

With a common understanding, constant communication, and speed, Octopus Organizations lay the groundwork for giving people ownership and inciting their curiosity to learn and innovate. They can improvise like a jazz band, where what seems random actually relies on performers intensively communicating in real time with one another and doing so with few specific rules but pure clarity on the structure around what they're doing.[2]

This clarity demands intense focus, especially when making hard choices or operating in a difficult environment. Take mountaineers climbing above twenty-six thousand feet, where the air is so thin that climbers need oxygen tanks to stay alive. Carrying these tanks weights them down, resulting in a longer ascent, decreasing chances of a successful summit as weather conditions can change quickly. Instead of carrying such speed-stifling weight, climbers like Benedikt Böhm, who is also a CEO you'll meet, become manically focused on carrying a sixth of the equipment traditional climbers take, allowing them to ascend and descend much faster. They cut their shoelaces and hair, obsessing about every gram that might slow them down. They ski down to speed up the descent. Böhm openly describes weight reduction as an obsession to bring absolute clarity to the task, in the same "drastic, uncompromising style" with which he brings clarity and speed to his business. It's the same ruthless clarity Octopus Organizations strive for in defining what truly matters, and ensuring everyone understands how to contribute effectively, what will create success, and how to contribute innovatively (like skiing instead of walking down a death zone mountain).

Two words of caution: Don't mistake marketing or sloganizing for creating clarity through communication.[3] Grand dynamic proclamations of a desire to "transform" do not create understanding of how and why you want to transform. Secondly, your organization's clarity isn't found in your mission statement; your employees and stakeholders find it in what they experience. They find clarity in the last difficult decision a leader made and how it made sense given their understanding of the business. They find clarity in the project that got funded (and those that didn't) and how it matches the mission as everyone understands it. They find clarity in the last person who got promoted because they operate in a way that reflects desired values. These *actions* are the signals that communicate "what matters here." If your stated clarity contradicts these lived realities, the slogans are worthless.

. . .

The following antipatterns show the behaviors that companies typically engage in that hold them back from creating and maintaining the clarity they need to become an Octopus Organization. Look for the behaviors that you believe most affect your organization and pay close attention to what you can do instead to bring clarity to your organization.

RELYING ON JARGON

Clear language creates collective
understanding and a shared purpose.

THE TIN MAN BEHAVIOR

Defaulting to vague, impressive-sounding language, avoiding the
rigorous work of creating genuine, shared understanding and having
difficult conversations

THE RESULTS

- Confused workforce pulling in many directions
- Disunity and wasted resources
- Leadership seen as evasive, manipulative, dishonest

How Octopus Organizations Behave Instead

- They speak in clear, plain language to create transparency and
  understanding.
- They understand that facts tell but stories sell, and create emotional
  connections, buy-in, and action.
- They are mindful of language's impact, using language that invites
  ownership and curiosity.

The Tin Man Behavior

The words we use matter, perhaps more than we allow ourselves to believe.
Consider these common corporate pronouncements, straight from our interactions with companies:

> "In light of the dynamic and unprecedented economic landscape,
> we have implemented a multifaceted strategy to right-size our core
> competencies, resulting in enhanced operational efficiencies and
> a strengthened market position poised for future success."

"By harnessing the power of integrated and disruptive technologies and embracing an end-to-end paradigm shift in our business model through a game-changing digital transformation, we will unlock unprecedented value creation opportunities, setting the stage for sustained growth and prosperity."

"By leveraging cutting-edge AI-driven solutions and fostering a culture of agile innovation, we're pivoting toward a data-centric ecosystem that will revolutionize our customer engagement strategies and propel us to the forefront of industry leadership."

Many of us, if we're honest, might have penned something similar, perhaps on a slide with some stock art of a rocket taking off. Born from a desire to sound strategic, or to gently navigate difficult truths, or even to conform to an expected "executive" vernacular, this language of *corporatese* may seem harmless. It may even generate nods of approval. *We all understand each other.*

But it rarely generates the frank discussions, or engagement, that you need to adapt, learn, and innovate.

Orwellian management-speak is often a symptom of deeper issues: perhaps a genuine lack of clarity among leaders, an ingrained fear of vulnerable, direct communication, an individual's attempt to mask intellectual insecurity with impressive-sounding phrases, or simply the path of least resistance in a culture where such management-speak has become the expected dialect. Mostly it's a symptom of a desire to *hide* or *blend in* rather than to truly *lead* or *connect*.

"Vision 2030," "NextGen" System, "Manufacturing 2.0," and "Org of the Future" stir the imagination with general notions of a different, better future, but they say nothing about the behaviors and concrete intentions to deliver tangible value. Their very vagueness can also serve to diffuse accountability; if the goal itself is ill-defined, then who is truly responsible for achieving it? Down the line, this vague aspirational language often manifests as the "nodding heads, blank stares" phenomenon in meetings—outward agreement masking internal bewilderment and cynicism from those expected to do something with these vague visions. The absurdity is clear if you imagine a leader approaching an employee: "What are you working on today, Ida?" "I'm embracing an end-to-end paradigm shift in our business model." Many of us have likely caught ourselves defaulting to such "yogababble," as Professor Scott Galloway calls it—maybe out of habit, a momentary lapse for more precise words (which, as our editor constantly reminds us, takes considerable effort!), nervousness about delivering uncomfortable news plainly, or simply because certain phrases become so ingrained we don't even register them as jargon until our children start giggling when we tell them we'll put a pin in that question until after dinner.[1]

Generic, jargony language is endlessly interpretable, too. "Fusion teams," "agile," or "data-enabled" roll off the tongue yet often mean ten different things to ten different people. Try it right now. Go find five colleagues and ask them what "data-enabled" means. We promise you'll get at least three distinct interpretations. This ambiguity isn't just a semantic quibble; it fuels confusion, even confrontation, as differing interpretations collide. It creates operational overhead, fosters misunderstandings, and can contribute to expensive failures.

The in-vogue jargon as we write this is "AI transformation" and "agentic AI." One CEO we spoke with was candid enough to share with us that there was little behind the words, but the *perception* of it being *something* had added $5 to the stock price. No doubt that bump will disappear, and then some, when millions of dollars go away with no meaningful transformation occurring, as happens, some estimates report, in 80 percent of projects.[2]

Some jargon inevitably emerges as somewhat useful shorthand (like OpEx and CapEx in finance, or SLA in IT). But getting to the point where people use a high density of obscure language can create cliques: there's us, who use leverage, circle back, and close the loop, and them, the ones who don't.

Some words betray that we work in Tin Man ways. Words like "cascade" and "roll out" reflect "top-down" processes, creating hesitation or even fear in workers of what is being done *to* them. Management guru John Kotter talks about how the words "consult" and "train" irk him because most people know more about their own organizations than outsiders do.[3] Language that suggests employees are merely recipients of information or instructions ("marching orders," "delivery team") rather than active participants and owners of change, is counterproductive to creating a sense of ownership.

Most pernicious is the corporatese developed to soften, mask, or plain lie about bad news. "Rightsizing" is a classic that means many people are getting fired. Even worse, "cost avoidance"—yes, you're a cost—or "unallocated" or the laughably delusional "promotions outward." "Headwinds" are effectively an admission that leadership failed to foresee challenges, and "it is what it is" mostly translates to "I have no intelligent way to talk about this." There's a tinge of cowardice in all this, an inability to be vulnerable and say the hard thing.

Ultimately, jargon is often just . . . boring. It pulls organizations to a blunt mediocrity, making them sound like everyone else, and it squanders the opportunity to galvanize people around a shared, clearly understood purpose. As a senior banking leader quoted in *The Guardian* newspaper wryly observed: "Jargon was the gift of the person desperate to get on without having any more talent than their peers."[4]

What Octopus Organizations Do Instead

Let's take the low-hanging fruit offline and circle back on this. Do I have your buy-in? The antidote to corporatese is so obvious. **Octopus Organizations speak in plain words.** Octopus Organizations know that true understanding isn't about sounding smart or exclusive, it's about being clear and inclusive. They eschew euphemisms, opting for simplicity. They don't "face headwinds"; they didn't "anticipate challenges that are pressuring profitability." They don't say, "We have high confidence in our back-to-green plan;" they say, "The project is off track and we're building a plan to try and get it back on track." This directness stems from a culture that values truth over comfort and believes that a shared, unvarnished understanding is the fastest path to effective solutions. Cultivating trust and transparency starts with the words we use, and the words we use are emulated and embedded by others.

Crucially, **Octopus leaders consistently ground initiatives in their purpose, explaining the *Why* before detailing the *How* or *What*.** When the underlying intent is clear and compelling, the subsequent plans become more understandable and the jargon naturally falls away. When it is not possible to make connections between the *why* and the *how*, they take this as a symptom to dig deeper, to clarify and align people's understanding.

Octopus Organizations avoid unnecessary technical jargon, internalizing Albert Einstein's wisdom: if you can't explain something simply, you don't understand it well enough. Leaders in these environments strive to distill complex ideas into digestible, relatable concepts. Steve Jobs famously avoided jargon, communicating with a clarity and passion that made his vision resonate broadly and forged an emotional connection with his audience.

Octopus Organizations do not hide behind words. They don't present negatives as positives through euphemism or prioritize marketing spin over substance. Let's revisit those opening examples and illustrate the stark difference (table 1-1):

Octopus Organizations use storytelling. Humans are narrative creatures. Storytelling is fundamental to our ability to understand and use ideas. Good storytelling can be learned and naturally resists jargon. Those who have mastered the skills capture people's imagination and supercharge their efforts and energy. When we spoke to Robert Barrios at E&J Gallo Winery, we were struck by the stories he told and the metaphors he used. The emotion in his voice, the tempo he used clearly communicated his passion for his company and its opportunities. It inspired us and we don't even work there!

TABLE 1-1

Comparing the jargon of Tin Man orgs and Octopus Orgs

Tin Man orgs say	Octopus Orgs say
In light of the dynamic and unprecedented economic landscape, we have implemented a multifaceted strategy to right-size our core competencies, resulting in enhanced operational efficiencies and a strengthened market position poised for future success.	We're acing challenges. We should have anticipated some of these market shifts sooner, and now we need to make tough decisions, including layoffs. For those remaining, we'll need to work differently to achieve our goals.
By harnessing the power of integrated and disruptive technologies and embracing an end-to-end paradigm shift in our business model through a game-changing digital transformation, we will unlock unprecedented value-creation opportunities, setting the stage for sustained growth and prosperity.	We're investing in new practices and technologies with the help of external experts. Our aim is to find new ways to serve our customers and improve how we work.
By leveraging cutting-edge AI-driven solutions and fostering a culture of agile innovation, we're pivoting toward a data-centric ecosystem that will revolutionize our customer engagement strategies and propel us to the forefront of industry leadership.	We invested in AI software that, while complex to implement, we believe has strong potential to improve our productivity, enhance customer engagement, and keep us competitive. There will be a learning curve.

Storytelling is inherently social, too, aligning with the collaborative nature that Octopus Organizations strive for.

Levers

^ **Conduct writing and storytelling workshops.** While we all think we are proficient writers, writing clearly and concisely is difficult. Find your good writers and have them review your documents, or run workshops on how to express ideas clearly. Who tells good stories in or to your organization? How do they go about this? How do they include customer anecdotes to make a story real? Find these individuals and have them talk through their mental process and an example story.

^ **Hunt down corporatese and reward its elimination.** Build a living list of jargon and challenge yourself and others to replace these terms with everyday words, or, better, data. Gamify this with a "bullshit bingo" game card to make people more conscious of their words.[5] Have people select a non-word of the week that triggers charitable donations when used.

^ **Connect every initiative to a concrete customer or business outcome.** For any new project, strategy, or technological adoption, refuse to proceed until its impact is articulated in simple, tangible terms. Instead of "leveraging AI for enhanced ecosystem optimization," define: "We will use AI to reduce customer support wait times by 20 percent by Q4." This clear statement grounds abstract concepts in measurable reality, forcing substance over spin.

^ **Build a "clarity checklist."** Create a simple checklist of questions to run through before sending any important communication: "Could this be shorter?" "Would my message be clear to someone outside my team?" The World Health Organization developed their communication protocols this way, ensuring critical health information is universally understood.

^ **Run "the toddler test" for all key messages.** Before communicating a complex idea, mentally (or literally) explain it to a curious young person. If you can't convey the essence without resorting to jargon or overly complex terms, it's not ready. This simple exercise forces a profound distillation of thought.

DISCOVER MORE

ANTIPATTERNS TO READ NEXT

#2: Whiffing on Purpose Statements

#3: Making "Everything" the Strategy

#7: Declaring Superficial Principles

WHIFFING ON PURPOSE STATEMENTS

An authentic, specific, practical purpose improves performance.

THE TIN MAN BEHAVIOR

Using buzzword-laden purpose or vision statements that lack conviction, authenticity, or meaning to inspire performance

THE RESULTS

- Strategic drift and indecision
- Culture of compliance not contribution; employee disengagement
- Erosion of trust and brand integrity

How Octopus Organizations Behave Instead

- They craft a simple authentic purpose that guides the entire organization on a mission beyond profit.
- The purpose inspires people intellectually and emotionally, igniting intrinsic motivation and engagement.
- They embed their purpose into daily work as a means of connecting every action to meaningful outcomes.

The Tin Man Behavior

The wisdom of the cheaper-than-a-management-consultant Cheshire Cat in *Alice in Wonderland* applies perfectly to this antipattern: "If you don't know where you're going, it doesn't matter which path you take." Many organizations, like the Tin Man on his own journey, operate without a true heart—a deeply felt and understood purpose. They may have words. They may have put them on a wall in the lobby, but unbeknownst to leaders, their generic wisdom doesn't make a difference to their people.

Generic purpose statements lack clarity and sincerity. They send employees running off in conflicting directions based on their own interpretations, or they are simply ignored. Either way, teams are not inspired and less productive. In *No Rules Rules*, Reed Hastings, CEO of Netflix, describes how a manager made what he considered an awful decision, but upon investigation, Reed realized that the manager had made a very sensible decision given the information available to him.[1] The root cause was insufficient context—a lack of clarity about the overarching purpose that should have guided the manager's decision. Without a clear lived purpose, organizations resort to Tin Man mechanisms: purely extrinsic motivators (compensation) and rigid controlling structures to command what they failed to inspire.

Since Peter Drucker's 1970s exhortation to "describe the business you are in," Tin Man organizations have gotten busy creating buzzword-laden values and purpose statements. They're often designed to appeal to everyone and offend no one. Ranjay Gulati in *Deep Purpose* calls this "convenient purpose"— superficial statements that "sound good and feel right" but fail to prompt meaningful action or trade-offs.[2] This way of crafting purpose statements has turned the exercise into creating vacuous, performative marketing with pretty but useless sentiment most employees either don't remember, ignore, or mock.

Here are a few real examples, disguised to protect the guilty:

- "The future, powered by generative AI" [Thanks for the answer, what was the question?!]

- "Advancing what matters" [the alternative being . . .]

- "Tomorrow starts today" [er, no, it doesn't]

- "Undisputed marketplace leadership" [an aspiration, but not a purpose]

- "To leverage synergies and optimize core competencies to achieve impactful stakeholder value in a dynamic global environment" [if we work at decoding this magnificently dense jargon, we think it means "to run a business"]

None of these communicates what an organization does, is driving toward or stands for, why employees should be excited, or even why a customer should be drawn to the organization beyond a mere transaction.

These word-salad statements permeate organizations but, as Daniel Coyle highlights in *The Culture Code*, they're rarely truly understood. He found that despite 64 percent of executives believing their employees knew and understood their organization's purpose statements, in truth it was—get ready—2 percent.[3]

One survey saw 52 percent of leaders acknowledge that their purpose statement was seen more as a brand and marketing play than something useful to guide behavior.[4] This isn't just a communication failure; it's a failure of authenticity. Purpose must clarify what the company stands for and *how* it will make a difference.[5] Vague statements achieve neither. Worse, these statements are often inconsistent with an organization's actions. Another study found nearly one-third of employees think their organizations lie about their purpose.[6]

Such hollow purpose statements provide nothing in terms of unity of direction, motivation, or a higher meaning. Gallup declared that only about 21 percent of employees globally are engaged, feeling a strong connection to their company's purpose and priorities.[7] At a macroeconomic level, the resulting low engagement costs 9 percent of global GDP annually.[8] Entrepreneur and academic Scott Galloway goes as far as to show an inverse relationship between the "degree of bullshit in these organizations' statements and the long-term share price of companies."[9] This suggests that a lack of genuine purpose isn't just bad for morale, it's bad for business.

Why does this happen? Many executives, influenced by business school training and workplace experiences, create a self-fulfilling prophecy.[10] Tin Man environments have taught them to see the relationship with employees as contractual, both sides trying to minimize expense and effort for the maximum output. Leaders consequentially see incentives and controls as the prime motivators for behavior, not purpose statements. In doing this, our innate need for meaning or purpose is downgraded in importance. Many leaders also haven't had a chance to do the hard work of actually *determining* their organization's purpose on a resonant intellectual and emotional level. They themselves see it as marketing for Wall Street and PR.

What Octopus Organizations Do Instead

Octopus Organizations work to create meaningful purpose statements. Even if Tin Man organizations have let him down, Peter wasn't wrong to suggest you should describe the business you're in. We don't need to get hung up on whether it's a purpose, or a vision or mission statement; the point is to create one that is specific, authentic, and provides a clear direction for how the company and its employees will contribute value.[11] It should be meaningful, and long-lived, something that unites and inspires. Such a statement is extremely powerful. Simon Sinek calls this a "just cause"—a noble, often customer-centric or society-centric reason for existing that rallies the organization and customers. "People don't buy *what* you do," he says," people buy *why* you do it."[12] A good purpose answers the fundamental question that Dame Julia Hoggett, CEO of the London Stock Exchange (LSE), asks: "Profit is important . . . *but in service of what? . . .* Profit is a consequence of serving this cause, not the cause itself." Economist Alex Edmans emphasizes that companies that deliver genuine value to society ("growing the pie") ultimately deliver greater long-term profits.[13]

You can start crafting a good purpose by answering three questions:

What is your reason for existing?

What value are you giving your customers?

Why is your organization uniquely capable of providing that?[14]

Octopus Organizations create a purpose that resonates intellectually and emotionally taps into our intrinsic motivation. As Daniel Pink explains in *Drive*, humans have a deep need for mastery, autonomy, and purpose.[15] Ranjay terms this "moral motivation," where employees are driven by a desire to contribute to something meaningful. Intrinsic motivation is more powerful than extrinsic motivation like bonuses or job titles. It leads to higher engagement, a sense of belonging, heightened trust, and a willingness to invest discretionary effort. The likely apocryphal but illustrative story of JFK asking a NASA janitor about his role in 1963, and the janitor replying, "Well, Mr. President, I'm helping put a man on the moon," captures this perfectly. How incredible is a purpose that aligns and motivates every member, making clear how their work fits into the bigger picture? This connection between daily tasks and a larger purpose is crucial.[16] The knowledge that your individual effort matters in turn inspires bigger thinking.

Octopus Organizations make their purpose simple, honest, inspirational, and jargon-free. Consider these examples:

- Starbucks: "To inspire and nurture the human spirit—one person, one cup, and one neighborhood at a time." [Focuses on human connection and experience]

- Mastercard: "Connecting and powering an inclusive, digital economy that benefits everyone, everywhere."

- Merck: "We use the power of leading-edge science to save and improve lives around the world." [Societal impact through innovation]

Each of these statements hearkens to an origin story of the company and is consistent with the organization's behavior.[17] They also serve as a guide to what the organization doesn't do or is willing to trade off. Merck's purpose led the company to withdraw profitable drugs that they concluded didn't improve lives. It also led the company to freely distribute ivermectin, a cure for river blindness in impoverished areas.[18]

Consider IKEA's—"Create a better everyday life for the many people." It's a clear statement of what they are for and who they serve. It's an origin story. Their "why" has guided their decisions, translating purpose into action by gaining deep insights into how people live and creating affordable, flat-pack products. Founder Ingvar Kamprad established IKEA to serve those with modest means, whose only way to have furniture was to make or inherit it. He stayed true to this purpose, even when competitors pressured him to raise prices; instead, Ingvar brought production capabilities in-house and sought new manufacturing sources to keep costs low.[19]

Octopus Organizations use purpose as their transformation catalyst. With needed skill sets changing so rapidly, a meaningful purpose is the best way to attract, hire, motivate, and align a workforce that has a deep-rooted desire to learn. Dame Julia tapped into the three-hundred-year history and purpose of the LSE, which, while doing the same job for centuries, needed to adapt how its job was done today. This created a transformation "pull" by making it clear that "not changing would be illogical." The proposed changes seemed natural to fulfill the purpose. Purpose can also drive hard decisions on workforce reduction, automation, and helping employees to move to other roles with integrity.[20] It drives an understanding of who an organization's customers are, how to evolve and transform to provide value to them, what data is needed to gain insights into customers, and what technology and operational capabilities are required to deliver on the purpose.

Octopus Organizations bring purpose to life; they cascade and reinforce the purpose in *all* communications, watercooler chats, and shareholder reports. They arm leaders with talking points on the purpose to use regularly in staff one-on-ones, bringing clarity to goals and inciting curiosity to advance the organization.

Levers

^ **Diagnose your current purpose.** Honestly test your purpose to inform a leadership discussion on its efficacy. Ask about:

- Inspiration. What emotions does it evoke? You want to hear about pride, belonging, being part of something bigger, empathy.

- Connection. Does it make people feel they are part of something meaningful?

- Simplicity and memorability. Is your purpose simple and jargon-free? Can people recall it? Ask customers, partners, and employees.

- Authenticity. Does it reflect your organization's actual behavior and history? Or does it feel like a lie?

- Specificity and guidance. Does it clearly articulate *how* your organization creates unique value? Does it guide strategic choices and help in making trade-offs?

^ **Rediscover or refine your purpose.** Look inward and outward, as Ranjay suggests in *Deep Purpose*. Explore your organization's founding ideals, unique capabilities, and the genuine needs of your customers and society. What unique value can you bring? What problem are you uniquely positioned to solve?

- Involve stakeholders: While purpose shouldn't be designed by committee, involving diverse voices in the discovery process can build ownership and uncover richer insights.

- Aim for "deep purpose": Strive for a purpose that is not just aspirational but also operational, informing strategy and willingly embracing necessary trade-offs.

^ **Bring your purpose to life.** What story will you tell in company forums that illustrates how your purpose is meaningful and what it means to you and your day-to-day decisions? How does your purpose connect to your organization's origin story, if it exists?

^ **Make it a tie-breaker.** Use the purpose to make a difficult decision. Talk about how it guided the choice. Encourage leaders to weave the purpose into the fabric of their day to frame team goals, justify difficult trade-offs, recognize great work, and coach their people.

^ **Change the language.** If words like "purpose" and "mission" are getting in the way of really communicating about what your organization stands for, create a pride or ambition statement. What makes you proud to work for your organization? What ambition do you hold for it? How can you use language to connect the purpose emotionally with people?

DISCOVER MORE

ANTIPATTERNS TO READ NEXT

#1: Relying on Jargon

#4: Pursuing Fluffy Goals

#24: Mismanaging Incentives

ANTIPATTERN #3

MAKING "EVERYTHING" THE STRATEGY

A sharp focus on just a few durable customer needs creates unique value.

THE TIN MAN BEHAVIOR

Trying to be great at too many things or pursuing a strategy with too many priorities and without making necessary trade-offs to succeed

THE RESULTS

- Fragmented, conflicting direction
- Resources spread thin, inability to adapt
- No clear vision of success

How Octopus Organizations Behave Instead

- They choose where to play and, crucially, where not.
- They prioritize long-term, durable needs over just short-term wins.
- They embrace trade-offs and actively stop work that doesn't align with chosen paths.

The Tin Man Behavior

Do you want to "deliver value to your customers" or "achieve sustainable growth" or "be the number one choice for employees"? We bet you do. We see these phrases, sometimes verbatim, in the strategy documents of companies we work with. They sound nice, but they all lead us to the same question: "Can you be more specific?"

You'll deliver value to whom exactly? What constitutes sustainable growth? You will be the strategic supplier of choice how? You want to be the best? Great. At what?

The catchphrases we come up against could apply to almost any company in any industry and mean little to employees or customers. They say little about the things companies *won't* do and the customers they *won't* chase. Tin Man organizations create strategies that sound like they want to do *everything*, serve *everyone*, win *everywhere*. We call this the Tina Turner approach to strategy from companies that just want to be "simply the best" at everything.

Instead, their generic, unclear strategies create a higher chance of failure. If you want to know if you're susceptible, see if your strategy passes the McDonald's test: If someone found it left behind at a table at a McDonald's and handed it to a competitor, would it cause major harm to your business?

If not, you have strategy work to do.

Tin Man orgs can end up here because of how they create strategies—with a cast of dozens weighing in on the ambitious plans. Ideas and opinions are poured into a strategic melting pot and boiled down to broad, inclusive statements to ensure everyone feels their voice was heard and feels confident they will get a piece of the operational action. Strategies become a conglomeration of compromises that include competitor imitation, new technologies that sound interesting, conflicting business unit priorities.

Many of these strategies are born apart from "the work." A two-day offsite followed by three months of leadership review and management consulting disconnects strategy from execution and creates a sense that strategy is something you set once and then turn to execution, which is not optimal.

What's produced from this inevitably includes customer centricity, operational excellence, financial prudence, sustainability, and, of course, every business's "most important asset"—people. All the good words are put on a PowerPoint–friendly "house-shaped diagram" supported by pillars and with some general foundations, such as data and technology.

Maybe you want to stand out, so instead you use a hub-and-spoke, or interlocking circles, but it's the same high-level nothing, answering the question "What should we do?" with generic notions like "deliver the most value to the customer." Even more prescriptive strategy ("Win the market with first-class customer service!") remains generic and dissuades people from experimenting with ways to solve meaningful problems. Instead, discouraged workers take a "wait and see" attitude. "Let me see what leadership wants and then let's see if we're serious about it in six months."

Many of these strategies end up gathering dust. One MIT Sloan report highlighted that only 28 percent of executives and middle managers with execution responsibilities could name three strategic priorities.[1] Even at the C-level, only 51 percent could. At the edge of the organization the results were dire, with a mere 13 percent of supervisors, the very people who are supposedly executing the strategy, able to name three priorities.

All of this is not surprising. If there were one correct way to set strategy, we'd all know it by now. Gary Hamel, one of the world's leading strategic thinkers, said, "The dirty little secret of the strategy industry is that it doesn't have any theory of strategy creation."[2] At the same time, there's no shortage of advice on strategy creation, much of it contradictory: strategies should be set for one year, no three, no, wait—ten to fifteen years; every business unit needs their own strategy, or no, you need one grand strategy; be a fast follower, or find where you are unique and double-down on that; you can't really develop business strategies in an ever-changing world, but you can, and you should.

The sheer availability of frameworks means you can find a methodology that feels safe and comfortable. But a comfortable strategy with poor aspirations and small thinking or generic, please-everybody platitudes delivers small results. The classic case is railroad companies, which, when air transport came along, found themselves stuck because their strategies generally and safely defined them as "being in the road industry." Such generic strategies lead to missed opportunities and threats, higher risk, decline, and existential threats that executives fear. In one global CEO Survey, 45 percent of CEOs stated that they do not believe their companies would survive more than a decade if they remain on their current path.[3]

What Octopus Organizations Do Instead

Octopus Organizations deliberately choose where to play and how they'll win. Benedetto Vigna, CEO of Ferrari, puts it simply when we ask him what strategy is: "Strategy equals choice." Implicit in that choice, but explicit in action, is the choice of where *not* to play: "The greatest business failures often come not from playing the game poorly, but from continuing to excel at things that no longer matter."[4] When you choose, you immediately start having more specific conversations. Winning by "achieving sustainable growth" then becomes a conversation about where that growth comes from, what capabilities are needed, what percentage of growth is sustainable, where, over what time, how, and what exogenous factors will cause us to revisit our definition of sustainable. Questions we find useful when considering a strategy include:

- Who are we here to serve?

- What is the change we seek to make?

- What resources do we have?

- What do I need to learn to make this work?

- Who do I need to work with?[5]

Successful Octopuses vigorously and continuously debate conscious trade-offs they must make to allow their strategy to work. They show courage in pruning markets they operate in, customers they serve, or strategic initiatives they take on. Trade-offs could include what industry changes to anticipate and focus on, technology advancements that might be beneficial, and customer needs the company will respond to, while avoiding distractions and maintaining the company's distinctiveness. Good trade-offs lead to better results as fewer resources are wasted.

Netflix's pivot to a massive investment in original content required trading off billions in short-term profit and incurring significant debt, a deliberate choice to control their destiny and differentiate their offering rather than solely rely on licensed content.[6] More recently, the decision to crack down on password sharing was a difficult trade-off between subscriber growth velocity and revenue maximization from its existing user base—a strategic adjustment in response to market maturity.[7]

Octopus Organizations recognize "strategic inflection points" or major shifts in the business landscape before they fully hit. Rita McGrath, in her book *Seeing Around Corners*, highlights this as a critical skill.[8] It requires leaders to cultivate "peripheral vision" and actively look for weak signals on the edges of their current market.

Octopus Organizations support activities that deliver a unique value. This enables them to stay away from generic, safe, imitative strategies under which their hope is that they can out-execute competitors. Dollar Shave Club (DSC), for example, disrupted the razor market with a direct-to-consumer (D2C) subscription service—totally unique in consumer-packaged goods when they launched, a strategy that led to an eventual acquisition by Unilever.

Octopus Organizations focus on durable customer needs over current trends and local challenges. Seth Godin calls strategy a philosophy of asking yourself, "Who will we become?" and "Who will we be of service to?" Here strategy is a compass, not a map, a plan choosing what to do today to make tomorrow better and working with the system instead of fighting it.

The heart of Amazon's long-term strategic thinking, for example, is based on the idea that no matter what the current or future market is, customers will never want to pay more for their products, have less selection, or wait longer for their deliveries. As Jeff Bezos noted, "If everything you do needs to work on a three-year time horizon, then you're competing against a lot of people. But if you're willing to invest on a seven-year time horizon, you're now competing against a fraction of those people, because very few companies are willing to do that."[9]

Focusing on durable needs fuels innovative thinking. Take Bill Height, who oversaw the $10 billion R&D budget of Johnson & Johnson's Janssen pharmaceutical division. In 2012 he began to look beyond treating diseases to think about the durable need to prevent diseases. This decision was informed by his belief in the convergence of life sciences and devices with biosensors that can intercept diseases like lung or colon cancer.[10]

Octopus Organizations use clear and specific language to communicate strategy, not PowerPoint "houses." This gives a strategy a chance for adoption and success. Jargon invites cynicism. General statements are interpretable. Bill at J&J didn't talk about a strategy focused on leveraging our people to be a market leader in treating diseases. He spoke of the convergence of biosensors and life sciences to prevent disease.

Octopus leaders take charge of strategy communication. An Octopus CEO like Benedikt Böhm at Dynafit says that 80 percent of his job is to create strategic clarity. "The amount you invest is the speed you save when it comes through in the action," he says, "and it's the most rewarding thing because everyone understands." Rather than hand off this work to comms teams, he works with his leadership team to distill key messages and a storyline that connects with people.

Octopus leaders listen. When Ferrari's Benedetto became CEO, he connected with more than three hundred individuals across the organization, asking them what is and isn't working and what they would do. He also signed more than seven hundred non-disclosure agreements, affirming the importance to look outside his organization to identify new trends and technologies and bring diverse voices in. He visited China, Korea, and Japan to gain deeper insight. He then integrated what his curiosity had helped him learn with his own thinking, along with input from other CEOs in his network. Contentious points of the forming strategy were reviewed with a small group. Benedetto asked them to write what they would do because "brain writing is better than brainstorming, taking into account introverts for instance." He was fast, and fast to change when what he heard demanded it. Once he formed a view, he himself communicated the strategy at all levels.

Levers

^ **Anchor on durable problems.** Write down with your leadership team what you believe the durable needs of your customers will be over the next ten years. Compare perspectives and debate differences in opinion to develop a shared set of needs. Prioritize where you play and how you win against these needs.

^ **Make your strategy accessible.** Write a two-page narrative that describes your strategy in simple language. Test it with employees. Use the feedback to iterate on clarity of your thought, your content, and your language.

^ **Communicate continuously.** Make it a goal that every employee knows your top three strategic priorities. Hold monthly sessions where teams share their interpretation of the strategy, and challenge it against what's happening. You might say, "Our top priority is to increase customer satisfaction by 20 percent." Some people on your team might accept that. But others might want to challenge it: Where does that leave employees? Wasn't cutting costs the priority last month? We say that, but we never get any investment to mean it.[11] Make a habit to ask employees in these sessions to draw a line from their daily work to the company's strategic priorities (a "golden thread exercise"). Notice where they struggle, and focus on improving strategy and communication there.

^ **Write "this over that" statements.** Each statement should explain how your strategy values one thing over another. If these trade-offs do not cause strong debates and create defensible opposites, you don't have a strategy.

^ **Test strategy specificity with a "competitor swap" exercise.** Try removing your company logo from your strategy document and replace it with a competitor's. Test with your leadership team whether the strategy still makes sense. If it does, it's not differentiated. Iterate until the strategy sounds absurd coming from a competitor.

DISCOVER MORE

ANTIPATTERNS TO READ NEXT

#4: Pursuing Fluffy Goals

#27: Using Proxies for Customers

#28: Mortgaging the Future

PURSUING FLUFFY GOALS

Goals connected to customer impact guide growth.

THE TIN MAN BEHAVIOR

Announcing ambitious goals that are vague and lack clear connections to the organization's purpose and the ability to guide people's work

THE RESULTS

- Teams struggle to know what to work toward.
- Projects lose momentum when teams can't connect work to outcomes.

How Octopus Organizations Behave Instead

- They anchor goals in purpose and strategies.
- They diagnose core challenges and define a clear approach to achieving the goals.
- They commit to a set of coherent, coordinated actions, ensuring teams are working in concert to achieve the goals.

The Tin Man Behavior

Tin Man organizations tend to have the *machinery* for goal setting—rigorous, annual processes that churn out goals, budgets, and performance metrics for the upcoming fiscal year. The machinery appears sophisticated and well oiled—structured planning cycles, resource allocation models, cascading objective frameworks—yet it lacks the vital essence that translates strategic choices into focused, actionable goals that lead to a commitment to coherent action. *That* requires human judgment, strategic insight, and leadership, not just mechanics. The machinery itself can only create oversimplified, abstracted, or vacuous goals that lack heart.

Examples abound. In 2015 General Electric announced a plan to become a top ten software company within five years. Quite ambitious. But how? What kind of software? *Why?* Despite a $4 billion investment, the goal failed to gain traction.[1] The next year, Ford set the ambition to become a "mobility company," and that was similarly derailed by vague goals.[2]

It's no coincidence that in one week, three CEOs from three different industries shared similarly vague goals with us—all three variants of "We're going to double X in five years by doing Y." We asked why "double" and why "five years"? Why not triple in four? And what do you mean by "Y" (typically a mix of "digital" and "transform")? They were bemused by the questions, but when we asked their employees about the consequence of these goals on their work, most stared at us blankly. These weren't just faces of confusion but reflections of frustration as they couldn't figure out how the goals tied to their daily desire to do meaningful work.

Goals that lack anchoring to purpose, strategy, and specific challenges are what Richard Rumelt in *Good Strategy, Bad Strategy* calls "bad strategic objectives" or "fluff."[3] This fluff often stems from skipping the crucial step in goal setting to identify the core challenges the organization must overcome executing its strategy even if the strategy itself is sound. (If the strategy is also vague, the problem is compounded.)

The result of fluff goals is one or more of these common pitfalls:

- **Ambition masking as strategic goals** like "expand into one hundred new cities by 2025" or "become number one in the market" without diagnosis of current obstacles or competitive landscape, appearing like wishful thinking detached from reality

- **Ambiguous goals** like "improve customer satisfaction" without defining why, how, measurement, or magnitude

- **Cosmetic goals,** often public responses to trends or pressure that rely on jargon like "AI transformation" that mask the absence of a clear problem and fail to resonate with or mobilize those meant to execute

- **Incoherent or conflicting goals** that pull the organization in different directions like wanting to "achieve market leadership" while the whole organization is simultaneously given aggressive cost cutting targets

- **"Blue sky" goals** like "dominate the global enterprise market within three years" without any credible plan or unique capability to make this plausible

This fundamental error—substituting aspirational goals for robust strategy—often leads to a predictable failure pattern we've witnessed repeatedly over years. See if you can pinpoint where your organization might be in this cycle.

First, a leader is brought in who has succeeded with some ambitious goal elsewhere. That person struggles with gaining support as an outsider and a lack of tacit knowledge about "how things really work here"—the informal networks, unstated cultural norms, and institutional memory that dictate real operational flow. The company doesn't know this yet, but the failure rate for ill-defined ambitions led by external recruits exceeds 40 percent, with an average tenure for roles such as chief digital officers a mere 2.5 years.[4] The very existence of this role subtly allows the rest of the C-suite to abdicate their own responsibilities.

Next comes planning, with tweaks and changes as various departments attempt to align the vague goals with their own interests. High-level roadmaps in slick PowerPoints create a false indication of momentum while consuming significant time and energy. Then come experiments to prove the case, often isolated from the core business. Local success and learnings rarely permeate the broader organization due to the lack of clear linkage to the vague overarching goal. Different departments, interpreting the grand vision through their own lenses, launch a flurry of disconnected "initiatives" pulling in different directions.

We're a few years in now and about to hit the "oh shit" moment, when time constraints force frenetic activity, teams compete for resources, dates become targets, not valuable outcomes, and failure looks increasingly certain. The person brought in to achieve the ambitious goal quietly exits.

This pattern yields dire consequences: Resource allocation becomes political. Employees, unclear how their daily work contributes, disengage. Energy is consumed trying to interpret and "align" under ambiguity. Projects fail, resources squandered. If you made a big public deal of the goal at the outset, that may come back to invite investor skepticism as well. Most crucially, the opportunity cost of time spent chasing mirages instead of pursuing specific objectives swells.

What Octopus Organizations Do Instead

Octopus Organizations make a clear diagnosis to understand the "why" before setting goals. Instead of jumping to setting targets like "double revenue," *relevant* goals are defined, rooted in strategy. Octopus Organizations dive deep to understand the specific operational or market challenges and opportunities to realize that strategy.

Octopus Organizations connect goals to the "why." This is framed through customer-centric causes. For example, they develop a compelling rationale on why the goal benefits customers and stakeholders and why it matters to those executing it. This intrinsic *why* translates into a *what*—measurable outcomes articulated in simple language (and communicated regularly).

Octopus Organizations set specific, understandable, and public goals, guiding progress without trying to prescriptively define how to achieve them, allowing learning to happen. As Jeff Bezos noted: "We are stubborn on vision but flexible on detail." When Satya Nadella became Microsoft's CEO, his clear diagnosis was that the company needed to pivot to the cloud (a major strategic choice). His "cloud-first, mobile-first" strategy led to specific transformation goals without trying to prescriptively define how they should be achieved: increase cloud revenue to $20 billion by 2018; 75 percent of server products delivered as cloud services by 2020; and double cloud enterprise customer base annually for three years.[5]

Octopus Organizations back goals with coherent actions—specific, coordinated activities and resource commitments. They might map a goal against annual objectives and quarterly initiatives, and assign responsible teams or individuals. They make this map transparent and a living document. McDonald's 2017 "Velocity Growth Plan" epitomized this approach.[6] Diagnosing customer retention and growth as critical within the company's existing strategic framework, CEO Steve Easterbrook set a guiding approach of rapid modernization and customer convenience. He then set audacious short-term goals: deploy e-commerce in twenty thousand restaurants, launch home delivery in eight thousand, and reimagine the customer experience in thousands more, all within a year. These coherent actions forced new, agile ways of working and laid the groundwork for subsequent programs like loyalty and personalization.

Octopus Organizations foster clear ownership for goals with regular reviews (for instance, weekly or monthly check-ins), and create *feedback loops* that focus on current challenges, cross-functional support needs, and ensuring the goals remain a living, collective responsibility. Dame Julia Hoggett, CEO of the London Stock Exchange, practices this with weekly meetings that bring diverse players together to share updates and tackle issues collaboratively, going around the room to see what's on people's minds and where the blockers are.

Octopus Organizations use goal frameworks thoughtfully. We can't close a topic like goals without talking about the widely adopted objectives and key results (OKR) framework, originating at Intel under CEO Andy Grove, and introduced to Google in 1999 by his protégé John Doerr.[7] In this goal framework, an objective is a broad, qualitative goal—what you aim to achieve. Key results are specific, quantitative metrics that track (typically quarterly) progress toward that objective—the *how* you'll know you're succeeding. Key results measure *outcomes*, not outputs or activities. OKRs do many of the things we think good goal setting should do. They help to focus on priorities, promote transparent cross-team alignment (as teams can see each other's OKRs), and encourage ambitious "stretch" goals along with more specific ones.

However, a warning: OKR implementations are often prone to becoming mechanistic exercises in goal setting and performance tracking or setting output style metrics that don't get to the goal. The key is to ensure OKRs reflect genuine strategic priorities and drive desired outcomes, not just activity as former Google Development Director Chris Butler highlights.

Daniel Pink's work on motivation signposts the importance of this antipattern. When people have the clarity that helps them understand the purpose behind goals and their importance, and how their work directly contributes to meaningful outcomes, they can buy into them and deliver results.

Levers

^ **Diagnose before prescribing goals.** Don't jump to targets. Rigorously diagnose the actual challenge or opportunity. Ask your people and key stakeholders:

- What is the most critical problem we must solve or the single most important opportunity we must seize?

- What are the main obstacles blocking us or the key factors that will enable our success?

- What are our unique capabilities that give us an edge or what disadvantages must we mitigate?

^ **Define an approach and coherent actions** based on diagnosis and in alignment with strategy. Define a small number of critical goals that support this approach, then outline a set of coherent actions for each goal: specific, coordinated activities, resource commitments, and changes to ways of working. For major actions, identify critical paths and key cross-functional dependencies—overall success is limited by the weakest link in these dependencies.

^ **Foster understanding and alignment.** Create a one-page narrative that communicates why a goal matters to customers and the company's purpose, how it delivers toward your strategy, defines measurable outcomes that signal success, and outlines a high-level approach. Test this narrative with frontline teams and refine until it broadly resonates.

^ **Prioritize and ruthlessly sequence initiatives.** Based on diagnosis, make hard choices about which strategic initiatives to pursue and which to forgo. Focus on near-term successes to validate the approach, build confidence, and sustain effort for longer-term, more audacious goals. Early wins must be meaningful steps in your action plan. Regularly conduct a "stop doing" review: challenge ongoing activities by asking if they directly support the current diagnosis and approach to your goals. Decommission or deprioritize ones that don't.

^ **Experiment with OKRs.** Translate priorities into qualitative objectives. For each, establish quantitative key results measuring outcomes. Implement regular (quarterly) OKR reviews with transparent communication, fostering honest assessment, learning, and adaptation. Train teams on OKR *thinking* (impact, learning), not just mechanics. Experiment with aligning incentives to support goals and collaborative behaviors. Encourage both "committed KRs" (expected) and "aspirational KRs" (stretch), differentiating them in reviews and incentives.

^ **Shift focus to controllable input metrics.**[8] Identify goal metrics that teams can directly influence that drive achievement of broader goals (for example, customer contact frequency, experiment velocity, cycle time for a key process, adoption rate of a new tool). Review these metrics regularly. Doing so provides more immediate feedback and allows for quicker course correction than relying on lagging output indicators.

DISCOVER MORE

ANTIPATTERNS TO READ NEXT

#2: Whiffing on Purpose Statements

#3: Making "Everything" the Strategy

#5: Misusing Metrics

MISUSING METRICS

Measures connected to value and purpose
supercharge learning.

THE TIN MAN BEHAVIOR

Becoming disproportionately obsessed with quantification as a
solution in itself that dictates strategy and decision-making

THE RESULTS

- Focus shifts from creating value to hitting numbers.
- Proliferation of vanity metrics and gaming the system
- Valuable innovation that resists metrics is ignored.

How Octopus Organizations Behave Instead

- They use metrics for learning and driving positive change, focusing
  on *intent* over hitting absolute targets.
- They prioritize outcome-focused metrics linked to purpose and
  cross-organizational impact, and avoid misleading proxies.
- They foster a culture where metrics are used for diagnosis and
  improvement, not blame.

The Tin Man Behavior

We'd be naive to suggest metrics don't matter; they are crucial for tracking, decision-making, and creating focus and clarity. However, as Richard Chataway observed in *The Behaviour Business*, "Organisations have become disproportionately obsessed with measurement and quantification."[1]

The problem is that not everything that matters is easily quantifiable. Nobody would think of measuring the value of a friendship by the amount of time spent together or the cost of presents exchanged, yet metrics obsession forces similar reductions in thinking on business issues. Customer-brand affinity isn't something that can be determined by time spent on a website. What if customers are spending all that time fighting a bad user interface, feeling less and less affinity by the second?

In fact, easy-to-measure things tend to drive out harder-to-measure ones, and, you guessed it, the stuff that resists easy quantification is usually more important. Strategy author Igor Ansoff says: "Corporate managers start off trying to manage what they want, and finish up wanting what they can measure." For example, under pressure to improve measurable waiting times, the UK's National Health Service hospitals reduced patient waiting times, but the death rate following emergency heart-attack admissions substantially increased. Emergency heart-attack deaths were not tracked and therefore not managed. Hospitals likely "cut services that affected [heart-attack] mortality rates, which were unobserved, in order to increase other activities which buyers could better observe," creating the perverse outcome where managing to measurable targets actually increased deaths.[2] Hospitals obviously didn't intend that trade-off, but the cliché often attributed to Peter Drucker, "What gets measured gets managed," has costs associated with *not* managing what's not measured.

Easy metrics that organizations become obsessed with come in many forms. Some of the most common you might recognize:

- **Vanity metrics.** Impressive-looking measurements that attract attention but provide little insight on performance. Two million registered users sounds fantastic until you dig deeper and find that only three hundred are active. Adding ten features per quarter is impressive until you notice it's killing the user experience.

- **Proxy metrics.** Indirect measures for outcomes that are difficult to measure directly (such as number of patent applications for "innovation" or time on website for "engagement"). They are useful if strongly correlated to the desired outcome. Otherwise, they can turn into wasted work. Using patents filed to incentivize innovation could lead to spurious applications being filed with no chance of being granted, or big-bet innovations being pursued at the cost of smaller, impactful innovations. Increases in customer dwell time in retail sound great until you consider less flattering explanations: harder-to-find merchandise, longer checkouts.

- **Perverse metrics.** These are technically correct metrics that drive bad decisions and behavior. Economist Horst Siebert's *Cobra Effect* illustrated this issue with the example of the British government's effort to rid Delhi of cobras. The Crown offered a bounty for every dead cobra turned in. So people began breeding cobras to turn in and collect rewards. When the government found out, it ended the program and all those breeding cobras were released, leaving *more* cobras in Delhi than when they started. Athens tried to curb pollution by mandating driving on odd or even days based on license plate numbers. Wealthy people just bought a second car.[3]

- **Absolute target metrics,** which create endpoints for those striving for them. Service level agreements (SLAs) are notorious for this problem: when 99.9 percent reliability is achieved, teams often redirect focus elsewhere until problems emerge. Maybe you hit your absolute target of number of patients seen in a month and then coast rather than seeking further outcome improvements.

All these metrics create an artificial burst of dopamine. An upward curve on a graph has a warming effect, a pretty proxy for progress, compounded by the high sense of "facticity"—or feeling of being objectively true—that statistics possess. But once you become obsessed with metrics, they work against what the company is trying to do. Resources become misdirected, work becomes fragmented as teams pursue different metrics or interpretations of the same metric, and focus shifts to hitting numbers instead of delivering value.

Remember two laws that expose problems with metrics obsession. First, Campbell's Law: the more important a metric is in social decision-making, the more likely it is to be manipulated—like the cobras in Delhi. Second, Goodhart's Law: when a measure becomes a target, it ceases to be a good measure. An extreme example of this is the infamous 2017 United Airlines incident. Aggressive efficiency targets, including filling flights to capacity, led to overbooking flights, then asking for volunteers to bump themselves in exchange for a voucher. If nobody volunteered, an algorithm would randomly select passengers. Dr. David Dao was selected to be bumped, but the sixty-nine-year-old doctor refused, noting that he had patients to see the next day that needed him. David was physically dragged from the plane past rows of horrified passengers, bleeding and unconscious. Metrics obsession, at the root of Tin Man thinking, hearkens back to the comfort with deconstruction of work into standardized, measurable steps that could be improved with metrics. Metrics are seen as the objective drivers for productivity and efficiency.

Tin Man organizations are not set up for creative problem-solving, work that resists simple measure. Their shorter-term focus leads to chasing metrics that can look good for a while but erode long-term value—like cost-cutting that boosts profits short-term but outsources advantages or cuts R&D, ignoring brand building, or losing valuable knowledge.

What Octopus Organizations Do Instead

Octopus Organizations understand that there are few standard and no single silver-bullet metrics. A common request we get is for *the* metric(s) that will help assess and improve an organization. We frequently disappoint on this front, because we answer that effective measurement is nuanced and context-dependent. Instead we challenge leaders to think about the underlying mental model that provokes this question. How are you operating if you think there's a standard answer that solves your problem, when Octopus Organizations know learning and adapting are the only answers?

Octopus Organizations do not focus on absolute targets. Their metrics serve their overall purpose and strategy. Foremost, the metric's *intent* is the focus, not targets. Stephen Brozovich, a seasoned Amazon leader, advocates thinking like a doctor: vitals are good metrics, but they don't replace the doctor's *intent* to help you live well. Use metrics for observability and to change behavior for the better. Netflix evolved from tracking total subscriber numbers to also focusing on metrics indicating intent to renew, like total time viewed per subscriber and genre mix.

Octopus Organizations avoid proxy measures where possible, using outcome metrics instead. It's easy for a leader to say, "Let's cut the number of managers" as a decisive approach to reducing bureaucracy (a good thing!). But number of managers is a proxy for poor performance. Measuring the *actual* problem—decision speed, employee autonomy, or time to complete standard processes—is more beneficial. A better metric might be the number of managers that need to approve a role backfill.

Octopus Organizations measure the right things, *not just what is easy.* Zappos goes way beyond simple, traditional metrics like response times and call times for customer service. It tracks "WOW" experiences created during customer interactions. Most companies make call center numbers hard to find to keep calls and costs down and chase a simple metric—minimizing call center calls. Zappos makes its number easy to find.[4] They invest in understanding what truly matters to their purpose and customers, even if it requires developing less conventional ways to measure.

Octopus Organizations experiment with metrics to find what truly matters. To tackle engineer turnover, Amazon hypothesized that disruptive on-call pagers were a key factor. Amazon piloted a "developer pain" metric, assigning points for emergency pages based on time of day (for example, nighttime calls were three points, evening two, daytime one). This experiment allowed them to correlate high-pain scores with attrition and the cost of that turnover. The learning from this new measure led to a new goal of reducing developer pain by 20 percent, which yielded new engineering best practices and increased retention and customer satisfaction.

Octopus Organizations resist premature judgment when introducing new metrics. When Amazon starts tracking a new metric, such as hardware spend, leaders initially avoid judging the numbers or setting immediate targets for what is "right." This uncertainty creates space for learning what constitutes good performance. Jumping to judging what the numbers mean can also lead to more gaming of the system. One team we talked to had a pattern of watermelon reporting—statuses that looked green on the outside but were red on the inside—to meet the metric. It turned out their leader had the wrong mindset, making the team feel at fault when they reported delivery challenges through amber or red statuses. It took a new leader six months to help the team realize she was not there to fire them, but to support them, and get them to report true status, not fake green to the point green can no longer be faked. A leader does not need to look at 85 metrics that are green, if they are truly green, but focus on supporting teams with the ones that are not.

Octopus Organizations tend to focus on input metrics over output metrics. An input metric focuses on resources, efforts, or activities put into a process and quantifies what goes into producing an output or achieving a goal, rather than measuring the result itself. Amazon's Stephen says, "There is a flaw in mostly creating output metrics as there are so many variables that affect the output that you can no longer have deterministic actions." It also leads to internal blame games when the metric turns up bad news. For example, teams can't directly control customer acquisition (output), but they can focus their efforts on controlling inputs like the number of relevant ads placed or referral program promotion frequency.

Octopus Organizations then connect input metrics to outcomes. In the early days of Amazon Prime, Stephen tells us, a success metric was inventory items in-stock (an input) that could be ordered on Prime. But adding one thousand items to inventory that no one ever buys is not good, so the team connected the input metric to outcomes like: Could customers get the right things, when they wanted them?

Finally, **Octopus Organizations consider when to depreciate metrics.** When is the cost of measuring no longer sensible? We work with many customers that measure things because they always have. When you ask them why, they're often not sure. Can you go from reviewing a metric every week, and turn it into something that gets monitored but you only get notified if it breaches a threshold?

Octopus Organizations recognize that metrics are tools to guide learning and adaptation, not rigid targets to be mechanically pursued. This mindset helps avoid the pitfalls of Goodhart's Law, where once a metric becomes a target, it risks losing its value as a true measure of performance.

Levers

- **Trial a relative metric mindset.** Take absolute metrics (such as SLAs or customer satisfaction) and create relative ones. Instead of aiming to hit a target, pick one metric and focus on trends and deltas, then discuss what caused improvements or declines. Use the metric for learning and improvement, fostering experimentation.

- **Abolish some metrics.** Ask "So what?" three times for metrics you habitually collect and disseminate. If you can't connect the metric to a meaningful outcome or decision by the third "So what?" discard it. Assign review dates to new metrics for continued utility.

- **Conduct metric postmortems.** When a project or initiative fails, examine which metrics you were tracking and which ones *could* have been tracked to identify blind spots.

- **Cocreate metrics with those accountable for them.** Instead of imposing your ideas of the right metrics, have teams propose what their metrics should be. The dialogue will bring clarity to the purpose of the metrics, ownership, and, ultimately, the outcome of the work being done, and buy-in by those accountable for the work.

- **Embrace qualitative data.** Actively seek and integrate qualitative feedback—customer stories, employee interviews, observations—to enrich context and challenge quantitative assumptions. Remember that metrics tell a story, but not always the whole story.

^ **Lead by example.** Leaders should question metrics, admit when they don't fully understand them, share the intent behind data requests, and visibly use metrics for learning and adaptation rather than blame. Your approach to metrics shapes the culture.

DISCOVER MORE   **ANTIPATTERNS TO READ NEXT**

#4: Pursuing Fluffy Goals

#24: Mismanaging Incentives

#27: Using Proxies for Customers

WORKING TOGETHER BUT NOT AS A TEAM

Executives committed to collaborating with their peers jointly deliver enterprise-wide value.

THE TIN MAN BEHAVIOR

Operating at the top of the organization as a collection of specialized experts who are more beholden to their functions than the enterprise's success

THE RESULTS

- Conflicting agendas and turf wars that create organizational drag
- An inward focus that undermines customer value
- Hampered decision-making

How Octopus Organizations Behave Instead

- They cultivate a "first team" mentality that makes the top leaders' first allegiance to the entire enterprise.
- They make decisions through the lens of enterprise-wide impact rather than departmental optimization.
- They use common incentives to drive cross-functional collaboration.

The Tin Man Behavior

When we work with C-suite leadership groups, we can quickly detect if we're engaging with a truly cohesive leadership team or just a collection of leaders who are well intended, highly accomplished individuals focused more on their departments than the customer and business as a whole.

We're observing the latter with increasing frequency, for many reasons. For one, C-suite roles inherently carry intense individual accountability for delivering exceptional results within their specific domain. This bright spotlight can inadvertently draw their primary allegiance inward, knowing that success there is what will get them celebrated—and compensated. Additionally, for many, their role in top leadership represents a personal and professional summit. There can be an understandable, but often unstated, inclination to safeguard the hard-won authority and distinct identity of their domain.

The sheer cognitive load of mastering an increasingly complex functional area can result in the elevation of executives coming to the job with more specialization (and thus less understanding and empathy for other functions) than ever. Also, traditional organizational dynamics can pit functions against each other in a subtle competition for resources. And diverse strategic time horizons—a CFO is thinking in quarters while an innovation officer might be thinking in years—make it hard to coordinate and collaborate.

All these factors make it almost natural for leaders to prioritize their own vertical. It reminds us of what management professor John Kotter heard from an executive: "We are aligned on the things we need to be aligned on. The other stuff . . . we don't play in each other's sandboxes."[1]

Consider a common enterprise goal of "becoming more customer-centric." In an organization operating with a "collection of leaders" rather than a leadership team, this laudable objective can splinter into conflicting departmental missions:

- Finance: "We'll cut costs to keep customers' prices down."

- Operations: "We'll open more stores to meet customers where they are."

- Engineering: "We'll make new products that address customer needs."

- Marketing: "We'll reduce the number of products we sell to reduce customer confusion."

There's simply no way to reconcile these different approaches. Conflict ensues when finance and operations start battling over costs and engineering and marketing fight over product lines, deepening organizational fiefdoms.

Even in organizations that manage to get the C-suite working as a leadership team, their alignment drifts over time if they don't actively maintain it. Circumstances change; new technologies emerge; leaders move on, or up. Any small thing can kick their alignment out of whack. It is a perspective that one study supported, showing that "leadership teams generally agree that aligning on their purpose is critical, but only 60 percent of organizations' team members reported that they were actually aligned."[2] Leaders may tolerate imperfect alignment, thinking they're still "mostly aligned," but that's not sufficient, just as "mostly aligned" wheels on a car aren't sufficient.

Less overtly, but just as critically, Tin Man organizations, with their preference for defined structure over fluid collaboration, fail to cultivate the collective intelligence essential for tackling the complex, multifaceted problems of the modern era. A lack of executive cohesion ultimately reverberates throughout the company, impacting overall performance—from profitability and employee engagement to resilience, adaptability, and, crucially, the ability to seize opportunities for innovation and growth.[3]

What Octopus Organizations Do Instead

Octopus Organizations cultivate a true leadership team—a cohesive unit whose primary allegiance is to the customer and organization, transcending individual departmental loyalties. This isn't accidental; it's the result of intentional design and consistent practice.

Octopus Organizations make the executive group each leader's first team, an idea famously articulated by Patrick Lencioni.[4] While accountability for their functional areas remains critical, their overriding responsibility and loyalty lies with the collective success and health of the overall organization. "My success is inextricably linked to our success" becomes every member's mantra.

Octopus Organizations anchor in shared purpose and clear strategy, and engage in ongoing, deep dialogue to ensure every leader not only understands but can articulate and champion the organization's core purpose, overarching strategy, and key priorities. This shared understanding becomes the bedrock for all decision-making. When the *why* and *where* are deeply shared, the *how* (departmental execution) naturally becomes more aligned. This also helps reconcile potentially conflicting functional goals such that the earlier example of different functions pulling in different directions on customer centricity is replaced with a singular, coherent approach. It can often start with written definitions of terms like *customer-centric* and *controlled growth* so there's a shared understanding of what the terms people use mean.[5]

Octopus Organizations develop shared mental models through robust debate, encouraging members of a leadership team to ask each other challenging questions. Throwaway phrases such as "let's become digital" or "agility is the priority" are met with scrutiny. This is most effective when one or more leaders challenge the team to surface assumptions and create a shared understanding on the spot. The boss wants "customer centricity" to be a key area of focus next year. What is "customer centricity"? How will we measure it? Who will be held accountable if we don't hit numbers? What will we stop doing to take this on? How will incentives be changed? Our experience suggests simple questions are particularly important with technology initiatives, given that less than one-fifth of leaders understand what "digital" or "agentic AI" means or can mean for their business.[6]

Octopus Organizations create trust and "relational glue" between senior leaders so that they feel comfortable challenging each other. While we expect leaders to be vocally extroverted, the same rules of psychological safety need to be established with boards and executive teams as with employees. David Risher, CEO of ride-share company Lyft, emphasizes the need to check in as a team, taking the time to look at team dynamics and health. "I now start every executive team meeting with the question: 'How are we as a team?' I had to remember that what builds excitement is seeing results. You can't create enthusiasm in a vacuum. Being on a team that feels like it's winning—and starts winning—helps you win more."[7]

Octopus Organizations create shared clarity. At 9 a.m. every Monday, up to thirty leaders come together with Dame Julia Hoggett, CEO of the London Stock Exchange, for one hour and discuss what's on their minds and what's going on in their work. It sends a strong message of unity of purpose for the leadership team. It helps reassure each leader that everyone else is working on the same priorities and can contribute to overcoming hurdles. Dame Julia tries to call on those facing the biggest issues first with new joiners going last so they can observe the culture. In her words, it "makes everything feel joined up."

Octopus Organizations design for interdependence and shared accountability and align incentives. They shape strategic initiatives so they're co-led by executives from different functions. A significant portion of leadership bonuses are tied to overall company performance rather than just siloed metrics. As we've observed in the digital transformation of a UK retail bank, nothing creates more unification of the leadership team than implementing a joint incentive for achieving goals. It drastically changed their openness for collaborating.

Finally, **Octopus Organizations don't treat leadership team alignment as a onetime activity.** It requires constant attention and the ability to call each other out if the team drifts. At Gallo Winery, CIO Robert Barrios talks about "revalidating what winning looks like" within the executive team and all the way to the individual contributors so that everyone sees the leadership team is just that and they are aligned on what needs to get done. Benedikt Böhm, CEO of sports apparel company Dynafit, talks about his personal role in aligning, and aligning again, visiting and revisiting what he calls the "lagebild," which translates to "situation picture" and means just that: a clear picture of the situation and desired future state with his leadership team.

Levers

^ **Test for alignment.** Have leadership team members write down on sticky notes what a goal or strategy means and what constitutes success. For instance, what do "digital transformation," "sustainable growth," or "AI-enabled" mean in your organization? Compare answers to spot dissonance and create common definitions. Alternatively, use new made-up words or phrases for initiatives (for instance, "Operation Kaleidoscope" instead of "customer experience improvement") to force discussions to clarify what the initiative is about.

^ **Read back meetings.** At the end of each leadership meeting, have one leader picked at random share back three key takeaways. It helps ensure an understanding of the key outcomes. Also consider doing a quick round-robin at the end of the next leadership team meeting in which each person shares one thing they appreciated about another team member's contribution that day, and one constructive suggestion for how the team could work even better together next time. Keep it specific.

^ **Link roles to value.** As new leadership roles are created, ensure their titles and remits relate to overall customer or business outcomes where possible, instead of abstract internal or silo-focused skills. In Amazon's structure there is an SVP for "stores" and for "devices and services," and a CEO for "Amazon Web Services." There is no chief data or digital or transformation officer, or even chief information officer.

^ **Join up incentives and metrics.** Agree on common success metrics and connect them to joint incentives for leaders. Propose to your leadership peers that for the upcoming quarter, you collectively track and own one specific, measurable outcome that clearly requires joint effort (for example, "reduce customer onboarding time by X percent" or "increase cross-sell revenue by Y percent between two departments"). Agree to review progress on the shared metric weekly.

^ **Declare your "first team" allegiance.** Explicitly communicate that the senior leadership group is your primary team, prioritizing organizational goals over departmental ones. Frame discussions around how *the leadership team as a whole* can achieve goals, prompting a discussion on what each function needs to do for collective success. Structure agendas around cross-functional organizational outcomes rather than departmental updates.

^ **Cocreate and own key strategic priorities.** Instead of passively receiving strategy, facilitate leadership team sessions to actively debate, refine, and collectively co-own the top three to five strategic priorities. Pull them into a concise document that every leader can clearly articulate and champion. Revisit and stress test it quarterly with questions like, "What environmental changes or internal learnings require us to challenge our assumptions?"

^ **Institute "enterprise impact" decision debriefs.** After any significant cross-functional decision results in a poor outcome, convene the leadership team for a short, blameless debrief. Center the discussion on how different functional perspectives contributed or detracted from an optimal outcome, whether the decision inadvertently favored a particular silo, and what leadership team learning can be applied to future decisions.

^ **Hold "silo-busting" problem-solving sessions.** Once a quarter, dedicate a leadership team meeting to tackling one significant organizational problem that is exacerbated by siloed thinking, lack of cross-functional cooperation, or conflicting departmental objectives. Ensure the problem is framed from an enterprise-wide customer perspective, and consider solutions that necessitate shared effort.

^ **Implement "team effectiveness" peer feedback.** Institute a structured yet straightforward process for leadership team members to provide constructive feedback to one another, focusing specifically on behaviors and contributions that impact *overall leadership team effectiveness* and cross-functional collaboration, not individual functional performance. Use simple prompts like, "What's one thing [Leader X] does that significantly helps this leadership team succeed?" and "What's one thing [Leader X] could consider doing differently to further enhance our collective impact?"

^ **Whiteboard your top three shared battles.** As a team, identify the top three critical "battles" the organization must win in six to twelve months. Define what winning looks like and who needs to be involved. Keep this visual reminder prominent.

DISCOVER MORE

ANTIPATTERNS TO READ NEXT

#2: Whiffing on Purpose Statements

#23: Prizing Individuals over Teams

#31: Avoiding Tough Conversations

DECLARING SUPERFICIAL PRINCIPLES

Values that are useful, lived, and living foster trust and engagement, and independent action.

THE TIN MAN BEHAVIOR

Creating or adopting a list of aspirational leadership principles superficially, missing the hard work of embedding them in behaviors, decisions, and systems

THE RESULTS

- Cynicism spreads as the values are ignored, especially when there is a dissonance between what's said and what's done.
- Missed opportunity to guide key activities like accelerating and bar-raising consistent decision-making or hiring

How Octopus Organizations Behave Instead

- They craft concise and actionable principles to create a shared language of values.
- They focus principles on guiding behaviors rather than abstract ideals.
- They make principles real by ensuring they are the basis for how people are hired, promoted, and celebrated.

The Tin Man Behavior

This antipattern is about adopting the *form* of leadership principles without understanding or committing to their *function*. It often emerges with new leadership that wants to put their stamp on the organization, or at the beginning of a major strategic shift, as an attempt to rally the org, or often just when organizations see a successful competitor whose principles have gained notice.

So, they write up some "Leadership Principles." They include aspirational statements that sound impressive and sometimes run on for a page (we've seen principles that are effectively essays). But these are decorations, beautiful ones, yes, but hardly actionable and often forgettable.

In 2018 Northern Frontier Wealth kicked off a transformation project with CEO Sam's "Values Journey." (It's a real situation with a made-up company and CEO name.) With the help of consultants, a twelve-person task force was given six months to create "The NFW Way." Artificial Intelligence–driven sentiment analysis of thousands of other organizations' principles informed the efforts. The result was a 115-slide deck on the methodology behind the seven selected principles:

- Be profitably ethical.

- Deliver excellence through synergistic teamwork.

- Think like an owner, act like a leader, work like a startup.

- Think outside the box while coloring inside the lines.

- Always be winning.

- Deliver 110 percent effort.

- Practice mindful aggressive growth.

Sam was excited. These principles summed up everything he wanted NFW to be: profitable, flexible, hardworking, innovative, and caring (if it didn't hurt profitability.) The six-month rollout saw managers participate in a principles-themed escape room to drive home their importance, employees sit through a three-hour webinar, and everyone receive a gold leaf–embossed booklet of the principles.

Six months later, 84 percent of employees could not recall a single principle. The only one that stuck with some was "Be profitably ethical" because it had become a cynical catchphrase when discussing questionable decisions. Sam proudly hailed the "cultural transformation," oblivious to its failure. Two years later a new CEO quietly retired the principles.

The creation of organizational leadership principles has become an expectation since Thomas Peters and Robert Waterman's observation in *In Search of Excellence* that exceptional companies had explicit shared values.[1] Can you recall yours? If you can, do you use them to guide your work? Most people don't and can't.

Among our favorite real-world examples of cringeworthy principles are these:

- "We will not harm our employees" [begging the question of what precipitated the need to codify this].

- "We will be number one in our industry" [a worthy aspiration, but hardly a guide for day-to-day behavior].

- "Move fast, break things" [why set out to break anything?].

In the countless examples of decorative principles we encounter, we see three main types:

1. *Cosmetic principles*, introduced to look nice but not woven into underlying behaviors, decision-making processes, incentive structures, or hiring practices. This creates a chasm between the aspirational state described by the principles and the operational reality. Employees receive mixed signals: the principles say one thing, but the way work *actually* gets done, and how leaders behave, says another. As soon as these mixed signals emerge, believability plummets and the principles are doomed.

2. *Generic principles*, written to be aspirational to the point of being unattainable, and offering no clear guidance for navigating real-world dilemmas or making tough decisions.

3. *Self-evident principles* that sound aspirational but refer to ideas and behaviors that should not need to be stated or have no logical opposite, such as "working ethically" or "doing the right thing for customers."

Fundamentally, the dissonance we see repeatedly in companies that are faking principles is the pride leaders take in them versus the use of them in the organization. They've created an *artifact*—a document, a video, a plaque on the wall—and held activities to celebrate that document. Instead, they should have been thinking of principles as habits and routines that allow everyone to *live* them in their everyday work.

What Octopus Organizations Do Instead

Octopus Organizations understand principles as the manifestation of an organization's values. While Tin Man organizations attempt to control behavior through exhaustive policies and procedures, Octopus Organizations use well-crafted principles as a compass, enabling their people to decide and act in line with the values the principles stipulate, especially when the path isn't clear. Principles help make explicit what desired and expected ways of working are. Leaders understand that principles are not a substitute for judgment but a framework for it. In this way, principles enable decentralized decision-making while preserving integrity and coherence, thus reducing the need for heavy-handed, centralized control. While often called "leadership principles," truly effective principles aren't just for those with formal leadership roles; they are a shared operating system for the entire organization, enabling everyone to be a leader.

Octopus Organizations build outward from their principles. Leaders don't just anoint a set of values; they begin by defining the essential values and behaviors they want their organization and people—themselves included—to embody. Then they work relentlessly to establish concrete ways to recognize, reward, and reinforce those behaviors, actively closing the gap between the aspired-to principles and current practices. Uniqueness of the principles isn't a primary goal. Many companies may share a "customer-centric" principle. The distinctness of power comes from the unique combination of principles and their connection with the organization's purpose and strategy, and the activation of all three together.

Octopus Organizations make their principles useful, lived, and living. Let's look at each of these in turn:

Useful principles are more than lofty statements; they offer context and practical descriptions, and they are brought to life through examples and memorable stories.[2] Take Amazon's often misinterpreted principle: "Leaders are right, a lot." It is not about infallibility, as the description explains: "They have strong judgment and good instincts. They seek diverse perspectives and work to disconfirm their beliefs."[3] In practice, this translates to behaviors, enumerated in the principle itself. The *result* of these behaviors is the principle: the leader is right, a lot.

Lived principles are most powerfully demonstrated through consistent leadership behavior. Octopus leaders modeling the principles in their behavior are the most potent communicators of what truly matters. Microsoft CEO Satya Nadella reportedly role models the "learn from others" principle by talking to other CEOs every day.[4] One of Netflix's four core principles is "The Dream Team":

> We believe that what makes a fantastic workplace isn't a great office or free meals and massages—although we have some nice perks. It's the

people. Imagine working alongside stunning colleagues who are great at what they do, and even better at working together. It's why we model ourselves on a professional sports team, not a family. Families are about unconditional love. They can also be dysfunctional, as anyone who's watched *Ozark* or *Wednesday* knows. Professional sports teams, on the other hand, focus on performance and picking the right person for every position, even when that means swapping out someone they love for a better player.[5]

While quirky, this principle is concise and clear about an intolerance for anything other than the best performance. Netflix adds further context through callouts tied to the principles like "Selflessness," detailing the expected behaviors of seeking what's best for Netflix, not oneself or one's team. Examples, stories, and anecdotes help explain the principle and bring it to life. It's a level of detail you won't see in many companies' generic principles, and it's the kind of detail and behavior-driven statements that ensure principles are lived.

Living principles embrace productive tensions and evolve over time. Amazon reinforces this concept by adding "unless you know better" whenever principles are shown or discussed. Organizations periodically revisit, adjust, retire, or add principles as necessary, ensuring they remain relevant tools. Benedikt Böhm, CEO of Dynafit, a sports clothing and equipment company, sends handwritten Christmas cards to his company's leadership team with Dynafit's principles printed on the back. Keeping principles living, he says, "is permanently hard. You have to spar with your leaders about principles—clarity means nothing if you don't find it for the entire team and organization. People can nod along in meetings but dismiss everything at the coffee machine later. Real adoption requires giving people time to reflect and challenge the principles. It's an endless journey that demands the CEO's constant attention."

Octopus Organizations embrace tension between principles. Often, the true power of principles emerges when navigating inherent *tensions* between them. For example, a principle of "bias for action" might sometimes conflict with one about "diving deep" on challenges. Octopus leaders don't try to eliminate the tension by axing a principle; they use these tensions to spark deeper discussion and more nuanced decision-making. People have to decide when to take the time to dive deep into an issue, and when that turns into micromanagement. Wrestling with competing principles, rather than seeking a simplistic answer or blindly following process, builds collective wisdom and ensures that decisions are better and more contextually appropriate.

A result of having widely used principles is that they attract employees who share those values while naturally deterring those who don't. This means

Octopus Organizations can enable their people to work with much greater degrees of freedom because they can trust they will act in alignment with their principles. Such principles also lead to better job satisfaction, engagement, and retention, with at least a third of potential employees using them as an acceptance criterion for jobs and a higher percentage expressing satisfaction resulting in retention for the same reason.[6]

Levers

- **Codify exemplar behaviors into a principle.** Identify a dozen or so employees who already embody desired behaviors. Interview them about their decision-making processes and how they get work done. Shadow them for a day to observe their behaviors. Dissect why they are so admired and effective. Use these insights to craft and test principles. Have your exemplars review them for authenticity and applicability.

- **Connect principles to purpose.** Each principle should directly support your organization's purpose. For each, ask: "How does this help us fulfill our purpose?" If there's no clear answer, discard it. Workshop these connections with cross-functional teams to ensure alignment.

- **Integrate principles into business processes.** Create specific questions and model answers for each principle and weave them into business processes. For instance, structure performance reviews around how employees demonstrated key principles.

- **Bring principles to life.** Have leaders create short monthly videos to dive deep into a principle, what it looks like in action, and what makes it personally relevant. Talk about principles at all-hands and celebrate those employees who role model principles while delivering results.

- **Adopt the language.** Turn principles into everyday language. Thank people in meetings by calling out a specific principle ("Robert, thank you for showing a *bias for action* in gathering customer feedback on our new product launch"). Normalize the language in everyday interactions ("Asia, is this the most *frugal* use of our time?"; "Paula, what's the best way of *earning trust* with our customers?"). Use the language of principles to disagree respectfully with a high degree of psychological safety ("Cal, I want to *disagree and commit.* I believe the analysis of the customer needs is inaccurate, but I know you'll practice *leaders are right, a lot* and look for disconfirming data as you test this hypothesis").[7]

^ **Sample your principles' effectiveness.** Regularly poll employees about their favorite leadership principle and how they use it in their day-to-day work. Focus on understanding usefulness rather than judging compliance.

^ **Practice principle-based decision-making.** When facing important decisions, explicitly structure discussions around relevant principles:

- Which principles apply to this decision?

- How does each option align with our principles?

- What would stakeholders expect if they knew we're guided by these principles?

- How do we interpret these principles in the context of this specific situation?

- Where do these principles create tension or potential conflict? How do we weigh them?

Document and share these principle-based decisions to reinforce their importance and to help others learn.

DISCOVER MORE

ANTIPATTERNS TO READ NEXT

#1: Relying on Jargon

#19: Fetishizing Process

#36: Pretending to Innovate

SPREADING PRIORITIES TOO THINLY

The embrace of a few initiatives that make you say "Hell, yes!" creates focus and impact.

THE TIN MAN BEHAVIOR

Pursuing an overwhelming number of projects, ideas, and initiatives, avoiding difficult choices

THE RESULTS

- Plummeting productivity, resources spread too thinly
- Stressed, confused, demotivated workforce
- Constant firefighting

How Octopus Organizations Behave Instead

- They ruthlessly prioritize a few key initiatives with a "less, but better" mindset.
- They practice *deprioritization* as a data-informed discipline.
- They emphasize impact over effort.
- They foster a culture where saying "no" or "stop" is good.

The Tin Man Behavior

For centuries, the word "priority" was singular, signifying *the* first thing. The plural arrived with industrial era management, and boy, have we pluralized it ever since! We worked with an international fashion retailer whose transformation program had four hundred (!) priorities—alongside other strategic imperatives and business as usual (BAU) activities. When we ask audiences who among them has fewer than five priorities, few hands go up, and usually there are audible chortles.

Organizations add priorities as if they had unlimited resources, but every additional priority subtracts energy and effort from every other. Consider Yahoo! in the early 2000s. Once the dominant search engine company, its priorities sprawled across search, email, news, social networking, advertising, e-commerce, fantasy sports, productivity apps, job recruiting, gaming . . . we could keep going. The relative importance of each priority shifted with leadership changes and new trends, weakly linked to core objectives and lacking clear accountabilities or meaningful outcomes. Yahoo's culture became reactive; internal competition thrived as resources and attention fragmented, all ultimately contributing to a loss of market share to companies like Google, which Yahoo! had *two* opportunities to acquire. Constantly shifting priorities left teams confused, burnt out, and demotivated, not knowing which initiatives mattered most.

The Yahoo story isn't unusual. General Electric, Motorola, and WeWork navigated similar priority proliferation, treating every opportunity as equally urgent, often lacking effective forcing functions, leading to an inability or unwillingness to kill priorities.

Other reasons for such priority proliferation include internal politics where influence, not strategic merit, dictates resource allocation; or susceptibility to the "tyranny of the urgent," where immediate demands overshadow long-term investment.[1] Even business-as-usual work gets marked as urgent—operational issues, regulatory compliance, and much more. Nearly half of tech budgets are consumed by such business-as-usual "priorities" that aren't really priorities.[2]

If everything is a priority, nothing is. As Aaron Dignan suggests in *Brave New Work*, the organization's system itself seems designed for accumulation, not focus.[3] Even when deprioritization is attempted, it falls in a gap. Leaders might *say* they are deprioritizing something, but if resources aren't reallocated, or if people are still informally expected to work on the "deprioritized" ghost item, the decision isn't real.[4]

Unsurprisingly, studies show perhaps only 2 percent of employees can name their company's top priorities.[5] A more optimistic study discovered 25 percent of managers could list three of their firm's top five.[6] Remember, many organizations have hundreds of them. So, at best three-quarters of your organization likely doesn't know what to prioritize, leaving capable individuals to come to work each day without clear direction.

A vicious cycle ensues as productivity sinks from the cognitive tax of constant context-switching across the many priorities. Multitasking isn't a skill; it's a drain. Each switch erodes time, increases mistakes, and damages learning capacity. The impact on individuals is profound. Over 60 percent of employees struggle with time and energy for their core job, stretched thin across too many tasks. These overwhelmed individuals are 3.5 times more likely to struggle with innovation and strategic thinking—activities that require deep focus.[7]

This antipattern behavior flourishes because Tin Man organizations fixate on assigning 100 percent resource allocation to "priority work," which to them equals efficiency. Instead, it blocks opportunities to innovate or automate low-value work (there's no time or people for that). Issues arise that could have been avoided if the organization were not so busy chasing hundreds of other supposed priorities and escalating new priorities, restarting the vicious cycle.

What Octopus Organizations Do Instead

Octopus Organizations champion ruthless prioritization, understanding that focus is a force multiplier. General Sir Patrick Sanders of the British Army framed it as "We will need to suppress our additive culture and guard against the 'tyranny of and'—[this] will mean ruthless prioritisation."[8] They also know that the championing of even a small set of priorities requires constant repetition of those priorities.[9]

Octopus Organizations embrace a "less, but better" philosophy, as championed by Greg McKeown in *Essentialism*.[10] They systematically discern what is essential and eliminate *everything else*. But this isn't random pruning of activities. It's a deliberate choice to focus energy and resources on the (very) few things that matter for maximum contribution. Organizations with fewer, clearer priorities do better. We know that companies focusing on a maximum of three priorities are more likely to achieve above-average growth.[11]

Octopus leaders strengthen their organization "no" muscle. Google's Sundar Pichai is publicly vocal about saying no to good ideas to ensure focus. Warren Buffett said, "The difference between successful people and really successful people is that really successful people say no to almost everything."[12] In *Rework*, Jason Fried and David Heinemeier Hansson advise that "it's so easy to say yes . . . to another feature, yes to an overly optimistic deadline, yes to a mediocre design.[13] Soon, the stack of things you've said yes to grows so tall you can't even see the things you should really be doing. Start getting into the habit of saying no—even to many of your best ideas . . . You rarely regret saying no. But you often wind up regretting saying yes." The fear, of course is that you'll say "yes" and "no" to the wrong things. You can't guarantee you'll get it right. One leader described to us a mental model they use, which is to look for the "Hell, yes" or "Hell, no." What are the investments that get everyone around the table fired up? Those are top candidates to be one of your few top priorities.

Octopus Organizations create an environment where it's acceptable and even encouraged to decline requests. When saying no, people are encouraged to explain why, in terms of existing priorities and strategic goals. This helps maintain transparency and understanding. Lyft CEO David Risher helped by telling his team that any activities beyond ridesharing were up for cutting. "Lyft had become infected with optionality."[14]

Octopus Organizations tap into their people's insight to surface "stop" candidates. Ryan Seaman, CIO of Western Union, asked his teams for two-sentence answers to these two questions:

- What are you working on you should not be?

- What should you be working on and why?

Analyzing the responses helped him halt 60 percent of active projects.

Octopus Organizations write objective kill criteria and use stage-gates. Kill or sunset criteria describe preset conditions or tolerances that, if crossed, trigger a reevaluation. This proactive approach helps counteract cognitive biases like the sunk cost fallacy or commitment bias that keep us from saying no once we start on an initiative. These criteria are reviewed periodically, often quarterly. A software project we followed had kill criteria like "loss of customer need," "work to deliver >60 percent more than expected," and "team attrition >50 percent." Companies like 3M, Corning, and PepsiCo employ stage-gates, embedding go/kill decision points in initiatives. Must-meet and should-meet criteria are checked at each gate; for instance, "Is the proposed project still within our strategic mandate?" "Is this still technically feasible?" "Do we still have the resources to execute?" and crucially, "Is there still customer and financial value here?"

Octopus Organizations cut initiatives, not costs. As companies see initiatives failing, as they inevitably will when they have too many, they mistakenly try to preserve the idea but cut its resources to bring the flagging numbers back in line. But fewer people doing more work doesn't work. Explaining *why* an initiative was stopped gives leaders clarity for future deprioritization decisions. Octopus Organizations make such cutting not just an emergency measure but an *ongoing discipline through deprioritization rituals*, like the above-mentioned stage-gates or other periodic review boards.[15] When McDonald's faced difficulties in 2015, it could have gone the typical route, eliminating staff to bring the numbers up. Instead, McDonald's cut failing and duplicative initiatives, helping free up $500 million, and a lot of talent. Then, it announced just three initiatives: Build an e-commerce system for twenty thousand restaurants. Add home delivery to eight thousand restaurants. Reimagine the service experience through self-order kiosks and table service. Everything changed. Old consensus-driven ways of working simply would not have enabled the company to achieve these goals. Everyone knew these goals—compensation depended on it—whether they worked on the initiatives or not.

Octopus Organizations don't assume that a directive to stop an initiative makes it disappear. In Tin Man organizations, managers know how to hide resources or run stealth projects. Policing this is difficult and only reinforces a compliance mindset. Instead, Octopus Organizations set a few big priorities so obviously important and linked to purpose, strategy, and performance evaluation that the leaders would not be interested in allowing zombie projects to continue or running shadow initiatives.

Finally, **Octopus Organizations and leaders communicate priorities incessantly**: the *what*, the *what not*, and the *why*. Why is this goal critical? How does it support the organization's purpose and strategy? What does success look like? What barriers exist? Alicia Greenwood, CEO of the Johannesburg Stock Exchange's Clear business, prompts leaders to clarify "why X was chosen over Y." Communication drives a deep belief in shared priorities, which in turn drives commitment, honesty, and high performance.

Levers

^ **Create a visible "stop doing" list.** Trust your people to help prioritize, document, and display what you've stopped. Make this list a living document, reviewed regularly, to reinforce the message that deprioritization is an ongoing and valued activity, not just a one-off exercise. Add to the list resources that were freed by stopping.

^ **Establish kill criteria up front.** For each new initiative, define clear, objectively assessable (even if not purely numerical) criteria and time frames for evaluation. These criteria act as triggers, where crossing a tolerance means the default next step is to stop. Create regular review points to assess and be willing to terminate or pivot initiatives that don't meet these benchmarks. Track how many initiatives are scrapped in a quarter and what could be learned from these intelligent failures. Moreover, celebrate stopping them!

^ **Use the "Hell, yes" test.** If a proposed initiative doesn't generate enthusiastic support and clear strategic alignment, don't commit. Create space for robust debate about value and avoid pursuing initiatives out of fear of missing out or political pressure. However, ensure this enthusiasm is then backed by objective evaluation against strategic priorities and customer data to prevent passion alone from driving decisions.

^ **Visualize capacity constraints to generate debate.** Use Kanban boards or similar tools to make work-in-progress visible. Set and enforce strict limits on concurrent initiatives to prevent context switching and resource dilution. Use this visualization to have honest conversations about trade-offs when new requests emerge—if something new comes in, what existing item must be paused or stopped?

^ **Test the waters with smaller-scale versions of initiatives.** Gather data and evidence and evaluate a trial-size initiative's effectiveness before investing in a full initiative. In the absence of promising results, it's easier to terminate or pivot without significant resource investment.

^ **Challenge by default.** Make "Why now?" and "What is the opportunity cost?" the standard response to new initiatives. Focus discussions on opportunity costs, and require clear articulation of why an initiative deserves immediate attention versus later consideration. Frame the deferral positively, emphasizing focus on current key objectives.

DISCOVER MORE

ANTIPATTERNS TO READ NEXT

#3: Making "Everything" the Strategy

#9: Customizing Commodities

#31: Avoiding Tough Conversations

CUSTOMIZING COMMODITIES

Buying wheels instead of reinventing them
frees talent to focus on differentiators.

THE TIN MAN BEHAVIOR

Investing resources into creating products, features, or services that
provide no competitive advantage and customizing them unnecessarily

THE RESULTS

- Diminished ability to adapt and innovate as critical resources are
  wasted on developing commodities
- Maintenance of commodities increases operational complexity and
  technical debt.

How Octopus Organizations Behave Instead

- They ruthlessly identify and maximize investments in what uniquely
  creates customer value.
- They buy or outsource anything that doesn't provide a competitive
  advantage.
- They adapt business processes to standard systems wherever
  possible, not vice versa.
- They refrain from "gold-plating" systems with unneeded features
  and functions.

The Tin Man Behavior

When organizations lose sight of what truly makes them special to their customers and instead pour energy into reinventing wheels or gold-plating standard operations, they waste precious resources, dilute their focus, confuse their identity, and ultimately, cede ground to more discerning competitors.

The British Broadcasting Corporation's Digital Media Initiative was an ambitious project that aimed to create a fully digital production and archiving system. However, it was plagued by delays and spiraling costs, partly because the BBC attempted to build a highly complex, customized solution themselves. They spent months and millions creating tools like digital asset management and workflow automation despite the fact they could have bought those off the shelf, which would have been less expensive, less risky, and simpler. Eventually the plan was scrapped in 2013, after the BBC had spent nearly £100 million.[1]

This isn't an isolated incident. The gravitational pull toward "undifferentiated heavy lifting"—investing precious resources into activities that don't create a distinct competitive advantage—is pervasive. By some estimates, 50 to 85 percent of IT budgets go into non-differentiated investments, a pattern that extends beyond technology.[2] Many companies maintain extensive in-house legal teams to draft relatively standard contracts, or develop customized internal recruitment portals or applicant tracking systems when commercial software offers a superior experience and continuous updates at a fraction of the long-term cost.

The wasted effort on non-differentiated work is compounded by "gold plating," where systems, products, or services are burdened with excessive features and complexity beyond what's required, often driven by a "more is better" mindset, not evidence-based customer needs. Gold plating can manifest as:

- **Hedging.** Adding elements based on hunches they'll be needed rather than evidence. We worked with a software team that developed an internal reporting tool with export options for obscure formats because, they reasoned, *someone, someday* might need those formats, even though current users only used standard Excel reports.

- **Future-proofing.** Creating elements for trendy technologies without understanding their relevance or necessity (for example, unnecessarily implementing blockchain).

- **Legacy baggage.** Mirroring old functionality because people don't want to let go (such as fax machines *still* supported in many modern communication applications).

- **Cherry topping.** Adding impressive-looking elements that offer little functional value such as elaborate animations on a business dashboard.

- **Overengineering.** Showcasing technical prowess rather than solving real problems. The Silicon Valley startup Juicero designed a

Wi-Fi–connected cold-press juicer that used single-serving packets of prechopped produce. The machine exerted an extremely high force similar to the weight of two cars to squeeze the juice packs. It turned out that customers could achieve similar results by squeezing the juice packets with their hands. Operations ceased in 2017 with $120 million of investments lost.[3]

Enterprise Resource Planning (ERP) systems are the poster child for this antipattern. Massive projects try to capture every single existing business process and then tailor the software to them, also piling on features requested by various groups that haven't been vetted for value. Complexity, cost overruns, delays, and poor user adoption are standard outcomes. Around 70 percent of ERP projects fail to meet all their objectives; 25 percent fail catastrophically, with excessive customization being a major contributor.[4]

In general, only 6 percent of product features developed see regular use, and only about a quarter of Software as a Service features, where users access applications over the internet, are used by customers.[5] Everything else is wasted effort that adds complexity and slows releases. These resource drains siphon energy, talent, and capital away from core strategic objectives.

It happened to GE with its digital Predix Platform.[6] GE invested billions to build an industrial internet of things platform that aimed to be the "operating system for industry." While exciting and ambitious, it was a cloudlike platform that would complete poorly with providers such as Microsoft and AWS.

Think about the BBC and GE examples, and you might notice that in both cases, the company was building something that played into their differentiators—video production at the BBC and industrial management at GE. The error, though, came when they made the decision or assumption that to deliver that unique value, they needed unique systems. What you do can be unique even if how you do it isn't.

This antipattern results from a combination of factors. There may be a fixation on "more is better," promoting output (number of features or systems) over outcomes (value). Individual egos, and incentives rewarding building a thing over the impact the thing brings, also contribute. Tin Man orgs struggle to collaborate across silos, and many wasted customization efforts are the result of fragmented ownership, where teams can request features without bearing the cost. Risk aversion manifests as overengineering to try to account for every possibility. And of course there's exceptionalism. Many companies just think they're special and demand special systems, teams, or services to account for their uniqueness.

When organizations lose sight of what truly makes them special to customers, they waste precious resources, create unnecessary costs and complexity, dilute focus, and ultimately, cede ground to more discerning competitors.

What Octopus Organizations Do Instead

Octopus Organizations practice intelligent restraint, prioritizing investments guided by customer value rather than technical sophistication. They achieve clarity and alignment on what constitutes differentiated work, minimizing investments that don't enhance them. That's harder than it sounds. McDonald's spent years debating whether they were primarily a franchise operator, a restaurant company, or a real estate company.[7] Each would have required different investments. Candid discussions between the founder Ray Kroc and the CFO determined it was real estate.[8] Be prepared to have these tough conversations and come to an agreement on your differentiators.

Octopus Organizations immerse themselves in their customers' worlds to identify and hone their differentiated capabilities. They learn what customers want that only their organization gives them. They also observe what customers *need*, often before customers can articulate it themselves. The early Airbnb founders literally lived with their first hosts to understand their core needs and anxieties, which helped them avoid investing seemingly nice features that would turn out to be non-differentiating.

Octopus Organizations deeply consider and amplify their unique superpowers that create value. They observe their teams, skills, culture, and successes to uncover what makes them special. Pixar, for example, has core competencies like animation and production. But its Braintrust—a group that meets periodically to discuss work, solve problems, and surface ideas—isn't just a competency; it's a storytelling and creative problem-solving force that is incredibly hard to imitate and becomes their secret weapon for sustained excellence.

Octopus Organizations carefully choose what not to do, ruthlessly eliminating undifferentiated work. They aggressively seek to commoditize, outsource, or use managed services for anything not directly contributing to unique value. Their mantra is "configure, don't customize." They would rather change a process to use systems out of the box than change the system to match their process. They scrutinize customization requests.

This isn't a onetime conversation. For example, what might have been an innovative capability, such as a differentiated call center platform that you built, may have turned into a commodity that should be bought over time.

Octopus Organizations treat differentiation as an ongoing experiment, testing innovations quickly with customers to prove or disprove hypotheses about what customers value from them. Lyft's pivot toward emphasizing "nice" service and features like Women+ Connect were responses to observed customer needs.[9] Their hypothesis about what customers valued from them was continuously tested and iterated upon.

Octopus Organizations value customer and business impact over complexity, anchoring decisions in evidence of a customer's need being satisfied. Requirements are hypotheses to be tested. Instead of automatically adding advanced filtering to search boxes, they define the problem—"Users struggle to find what they need"—then explore possible solutions rather than immediately adding a feature. A car seat manufacturer's Octopus team might observe parents struggling with car seat installation. They would identify real pain points and focus innovation there rather than on features that exhausted parents don't want or need and that may even add complexity, jeopardizing safety and driving up price.

Octopus Organizations maximize the work that gains the most insights. They focus first on core customer needs than on fancy new features. They accelerate gaining insights using MLPs (minimum lovable products)—bringing back maximum validated learning about customers with least effort.[10] MLPs can be as simple as paper prototypes, costing a tiny fraction of building features that get scrapped anyway.

Most importantly, **Octopus Organizations create environments where teams feel secure enough to challenge requirements.** Rather than being passive recipients of requirements and demands, teams are given ownership for outcomes and problems to solve. Teams accountable for long-term outcomes naturally resist unnecessary complexity and improve resilience. They are skeptical of *any* requirement and demand to know *why* a feature is needed and *how* it supports business outcomes, not just *what* they need and *how* to build it.

When organizations escape investing in undifferentiated heavy lifting and gold-plating behavior, the results speak for themselves: shorter development cycles, higher user adoption rates, and significantly lower maintenance costs. By keeping systems lean and focused, these organizations maintain the agility to respond to genuine market needs rather than being weighed down by unused elements. Their success comes not from building everything possible but from building the right things well.

Levers

^ **Map your competitive advantage.** Pick a critical business function or customer value stream. With a cross-functional team, map all components needed to deliver it. Debate where true differentiation lies and where you might be overinvesting in noncore elements or adding unnecessary complexity.

One tool sometimes used is a Wardley map (table 9-1) on which systems or functions are mapped against four categories and help guide decisions on where and what to invest in.

^ **Champion outcome-based thinking.** Start every initiative with a measurable need (the *why*), not a list of features (the *what*). Set outcome measures for new elements. For example, instead of tracking clicks on a new search filter (output), measure if users found relevant results faster and completed more purchases (outcome).

^ **Demand customer data and validate assumptions.** Require clear data on customer/user needs before committing to any new feature or customization. Challenge assumptions and request evidence. Treat requirements as hypotheses: "We believe that [element/feature] will lead to [measurable outcome] for [user type] because [reason]."

TABLE 9-1

Wardley Maps categories

Category	Definition	Example	Action
Genesis	Novel, uncertain undertakings; usually high risk; might yield future advantage. Think R&D.	AI-driven fraud detection algorithms	R&D
Custom-built	Components or activities tailored to specific needs; potential competitive advantage but require significant investment and expertise.	Proprietary trading platforms; production line control systems	Build
Product	Standard products/approaches available from multiple vendors offering similar solutions.	Document management systems; CRM software	Acquire
Commodity	Widely adopted, often essential; offer little to no competitive advantage.	ATM networks; basic accounting software; email systems	Use cloud

^ **Quantify the cost of undifferentiated work and gold plating.** The burden of maintaining bloated products or systems is often invisible, making it hard to justify simplification. Holistically assess the investments (time, money, resources, opportunity cost) made into noncompetitive ystems or overly complex features. How much do customization, delays to upgrades, work-arounds, and inability to adopt best practices cost for your customized HR system or gold-plated product feature? Encourage teams to track and visualize metrics related to complexity and its cost (for example, proportion of development time spent on old/unused features). Set targets to reduce this spend incrementally.

^ **Audit service and process differentiation.** Examine your customer-facing services and internal processes. Identify where you're maintaining expensive custom approaches that don't create competitive advantage. For example, are you operating your own fleet when logistics partners could handle delivery more efficiently? Creating bespoke training programs when industry-standard certifications would serve employees better? Challenge every "we do it ourselves because we're special" assumption.

^ **Invest in "complexity culls."** Identify two or three "product" or "commodity" internal systems or processes that are bespoke or heavily customized. Have a team evaluate off-the-shelf solutions or outsourcing options, focusing on achieving "good enough" functionality with minimal customization, and present a migration plan. Review ongoing initiatives and internal systems quarterly to see if they're still differentiating. Make concrete decisions to "stop," "sunset," or "simplify." Encourage teams to remove or simplify low-value elements.

^ **Hold a learning day with vendors (and customers!).** Encourage leadership and teams to learn from their vendors about their capabilities. What features aren't being used that could reduce undifferentiated work? Where could business process change eliminate customizations? Spend time with customers to discover where they value you and need you to differentiate.

DISCOVER MORE

ANTIPATTERNS TO READ NEXT

#27: Using Proxies for Customers

#29: Falling in Love with Answers

#34: Segregating Technology

ANTIPATTERN #10

ENTRENCHING SILOS

A focus on the flow of value, from idea to customer, breaks through bottlenecks.

THE TIN MAN BEHAVIOR

They address local inefficiencies in their vertical silos instead of global ones to improve overarching delivery of customer value

THE RESULTS

- Slow time-to-market despite busy individual departments
- Unpredictable delivery timelines that frustrate customers
- Market opportunities missed due to slow organizational responsiveness

How Octopus Organizations Behave Instead

- They create cross-functional teams that focus on overall flow over departmental efficiency.
- They work backward from customer outcomes to determine optimization priorities.
- They build in organizational slack to maintain resilience.

The Tin Man Behavior

We do not like jargon—we even have a whole antipattern devoted to it. But we beg you, reader, to bear with us as we deploy one term that will sound jargony but is essential to understanding this antipattern. That term is "value stream." All we mean by this is the path taken from an idea to the point where customers get value out of it. And the relative pace of traversal for a value stream we call "flow."[1]

Tin Man value streams are hardly free-flowing. Tin Man organizations are typically structured in functional silos, each incentivized to maximize its own output and utilization. Yet most value travels horizontally across these silos. An idea created in Marketing moves to review by operations and finance, and then over to technology to release a feature. While individual departments might appear highly efficient and optimizing their own performance metrics—they might have good flow—the overall journey of value through the organization is an often-tortuous path, riddled with delays, detours, and dead ends. Everyone is trying to keep things flowing, but there's a fundamental misalignment between how work is structured and how value is created that dams it up. It's like a relay race: each runner might be incredibly fast, but they're running on different tracks, the baton being dropped between runners, instead of optimizing for the whole race.

For example, Jana worked at a company that prided itself on its agile delivery approach. Every two weeks the technology teams developed and completed new features. Sounds impressive, but the "two weeks" weren't really two weeks. After that work came eight weeks for system integration, three months for testing, and four weeks waiting for deployment. That's not all. Before all of this could happen, leaders spent four weeks deciding priorities, followed by twelve weeks building proof of concepts. The CFO needed eight weeks for funding approval. The architecture team required four more weeks for technical validation.

This entire value stream from idea to production took twelve to eighteen months across more than thirty-two teams. The greatest bottleneck wasn't development speed; it was everything else.

In siloed organizations, flow efficiency—the actual time work is being done versus time spent waiting—can plummet as low as 10 percent, meaning 90 percent of the time, valuable initiatives are just sitting in a queue.[2] Urgent escalations become the norm for unblocking work that could have flowed smoothly. Valuable outcomes for the customer are agonizingly slow to materialize.

A striking real-world example of poorly flowing value streams can be found in the struggles many large automotive manufacturers faced when responding to Tesla's competitive threat with electric vehicles (EVs). Traditional automakers had immense expertise in individual car components. But their siloed structures and long-established, sequential design-build-test processes optimized for perfecting the internal combustion engines over decades made it incredibly difficult to pivot quickly to electric vehicles and their integrated software platforms. Each department (powertrain, electrical systems, infotainment) operated with its own timelines and process, creating massive friction in the flow of designing and launching a fundamentally different type of vehicle. The "value stream" for a software-defined EV was entirely different, but the organizational structure remained optimized for the gasoline-powered vehicle.

When flow is poor, everyone is working incredibly hard, yet progress feels like wading through molasses. The results are obvious and painful: stubborn bottlenecks (because of a lack of visibility across the value stream), work languishing (because of competing priorities and lack of slack), slower time to market, and an inability to respond to changing customer needs (because of maxed-out teams).

Tin Man organizations are not ignorant of these issues but often revert to one or more types of optimizations:

1. *Optimizing without rethinking,* failing to improve flow because it doesn't get to root causes. A community hospital digitized paper-based patient records but didn't rethink the workflow. The result was slow, inconsistent data entry that delayed patient care. They optimized forms instead of workflow, creating a new bottleneck that was harder to work around than the original paper process.

2. *Optimizing the wrong thing,* addressing symptoms while the cause persists upstream. Improving help desk resolution time is futile when faulty manufacturing creates the complaints.

3. *Overoptimization,* eliminating the elements that help systems adapt to the real world. Highly optimized call handling times to minimize call center costs can force representatives to rush, leading to unresolved problems and frustrated customers who call back repeatedly.

4. *Optimizing what shouldn't exist,* perfecting unnecessary processes. A sales team might spend months developing better sales proposal templates, streamlining review, and training staff that cuts time spent from eight hours to six hours when instead they could use AI-powered proposal generators plus human review to do the same in one hour.

Different thinking is needed to break this antipattern. You don't iterate your way from a candle to a light bulb, particularly in the era of transformative technologies such as AI. Instead you create a new value stream.

What Octopus Organizations Do Instead

Octopus Organizations optimize for the entire value stream, not for departmental performance. They look to optimize those processes or steps that impede flow, including eliminating bottlenecks. They understand that speed of learning and delivery is a critical competitive advantage, and they relentlessly attack the impediments that create friction and delay.

To do this they first make the entire value stream flow visible to and understood by everyone involved in the stream. This often starts with value stream mapping. You don't need anything more than a white wall to get started mapping the existing process with sticky notes, creating a shared understanding of how work gets done at each point in the flow. This generates questions, debates, and brainstorming to find solutions when bottlenecks emerge. Everyone is learning. A perfect map isn't the goal—it's the discovery and debate that matters. Walk stakeholders through the imperfect map to add to it, and field new questions. At Tesco Bank Jana's team put such a map outside the boardroom, creating conversations as executives walked past or waited for meetings to start. Often those intimately involved in elements of the map volunteered their frustrations. Previously unseen bottlenecks became apparent to those who could address them. Walk-throughs of the map brought in others to weigh in, exposing more of the reality of how work really got done, seeing it visualized end to end. After several rounds, these walk-throughs shifted from "How does it work?" to "What can change?" Treat value stream mapping as a continuous practice to identify all the steps, handoffs, queues, and dependencies involved in any stream (for instance, "onboarding a new client" or "resolving critical software bugs").

Octopus Organizations internalize the mantra: "Stop starting, start finishing." By consciously limiting the number of active initiatives or tasks—whether at the individual, team, or portfolio level—they create a "pull system." New work is only started when capacity becomes available. We recognize this feels impractical when stakeholders demand updates on their priorities and everything seems urgent. However, research consistently shows that limiting work in progress accelerates delivery. Less work in progress means less context switching (which one estimate suggests can usurp 20 percent of your time), less waiting, and faster throughput of completed value.[3] When stakeholders see faster completion rates and more predictable delivery, resistance typically dissolves. The teams that feel "too busy" to limit work in progress are often the ones who benefit most from it.

Octopus Organizations work backward from an outcome to understand what to optimize and how. They support this process with appropriate metrics that represent the desired business outcome. In his book *Freedom from Command and Control*, Vanguard's John Seddon highlights how a call center could work from the outcome they want—resolving a customer's issue—and go back upstream to see how to achieve that more effectively.[4] For example, instead of optimizing "calls per hour," they might discover that 60 percent of repeat calls happen because customers receive incomplete information on their first contact. Working backward, they trace this to agents lacking access to all of the customers' data across systems. The solution isn't faster call handling—it's giving agents complete customer context. This reduces total customer effort, improves satisfaction, and ironically makes agents more efficient by handling fewer but more complete interactions.

Octopus Organizations are willing to completely rethink their flows. They start with the question, "What needs to be true?" For instance, what needs to be true to double the drive-thru capacity in a McDonald's? This leads teams away from simplistic answers like "take orders faster" to nuanced ones like "We need to avoid backups that discourage customers." It's a technique that questions whether processes should exist in the first place.

Building internal skills to rethink flow is crucial. Amazon has teams specifically focused on coming into underperforming fulfillment centers to understand the flow and what's blocking it. Octopus Organizations create *cross-functional teams that relentlessly identify and mitigate bottlenecks*, always looking at system-wide performance. They create clear, simple objectives— something like "Reduce the time to market by 30 percent in ninety days." While we aren't fans of absolute metrics over long periods, short-term targets help focus the team on taking action. External facilitators skilled in optimization techniques can help here, too.

Ultimately, armed with an understanding about their flow of value, **Octopus Organizations organize around value streams, rather than in functional silos.** Instead of having separate marketing, product, engineering, and operations teams that hand work off to each other, they form stable, cross-functional "product teams" or "value stream teams." These teams, ideally small enough to maintain high cohesion and minimize communication overhead (often around six to nine people), possess all, or most, of the skills needed to deliver value from idea to customer for their domain. Their primary tribal identity shifts from their functional department to the value stream and the customers they serve, fostering deep collective ownership of the outcomes. This is a radical shift and takes time for aspiring Octopus Organizations, often starting with one or two teams, experimenting and learning what parts of the organization's operating system need to be adjusted to make this work (such as funding models, goal setting, and so forth).

The result can yield incredible results. One oncology team in the 160-year-old Bayer pharmaceutical company followed its value stream to cut through eight hundred internally dictated processes and gates that helped deliver good patient outcomes faster.[5] They accelerated 3D-printing a €6 holder that solved a problem patients had struggled with in using multiple vials for injections. Years-to-value literally turned into days-to-value because they owned the whole value stream.

The path forward requires the courage to surface and address system-wide constraints that cross organizational boundaries, and the humility to accept that sometimes making your part slower might make the whole thing faster. In an era where speed of learning and adaptation determine survival, organizations must choose: optimize for the comfort of familiar silos, or optimize for the uncertainty—and opportunity—of customer impact.

Levers

^ **Map and improve a sliver of value.** Start small. Pick a high-visibility product with improvement potential. Use cross-functional teams to visually map the complete value stream, identifying bottlenecks, handoffs, and wait times. Quantify delays and track metrics like lead time or cycle time to ask "why" rather than blindly optimize. Monitor work in progress. Start narrow, then expand scope as you progress.

^ **Attack root causes, not symptoms.** Regularly ask "What needs to be true?" to achieve breakthrough improvements. Look upstream to identify what creates bottlenecks rather than optimizing how you handle bottlenecks. Try to identify preventable work before improving efficiency of that work. Look for clues like the physical pileups of work or growing digital queues. Spot where people are frequently waiting for inputs. Notice where teams create work-arounds. Pay attention to where the same information is requested multiple times. Note where multiple teams need the same scarce resource. What feedback loops can be built in to help identify these clues more easily in the future?

^ **Identify and challenge one major handoff point.** Looking at your value stream, pick one handoff between two functional silos that causes significant delay or information loss. Bring representatives from both teams together to redesign that specific interaction or even experiment with creating a joint team, aiming to reduce wait time and improve information quality.

^ **Dedicate flow improvement time.** Form a cross-functional pilot team that owns an end-to-end process and have them dedicate a small, regular portion of their time (say, 10 to 20 percent of a sprint, or a half-day every two weeks) specifically to identifying and implementing improvements to their own processes and tools to enhance flow.

^ **Redesign incentives and metrics.** Replace utilization-based metrics with flow metrics like lead time, throughput, and flow efficiency. Create shared objectives requiring cross-functional cooperation. Celebrate teams that identify and eliminate dependencies rather than work around them. Build psychological safety for surfacing hidden constraints.

DISCOVER MORE

ANTIPATTERNS TO READ NEXT

#5: Misusing Metrics

#16: Gatekeeping Approval

#17: Creating Dependencies

ANTIPATTERN #11

GUARDING INFORMATION

Making insights accessible to everyone creates transparency that fosters innovation.

THE TIN MAN BEHAVIOR

Building up bureaucratic restrictions around the knowledge of, access to, and use of strategically important data and information

THE RESULTS

- Poor decisions based on incomplete knowledge
- Loss of competitive advantage, missed opportunities
- Emerging culture of distrust and control leads to the inability to effectively own outcomes and deliverables

How Octopus Organizations Behave Instead

- They cultivate a culture of trust and transparency with information and leaders role modeling the behavior.
- They default to making information widely and easily accessible through "pull-based" systems.
- They establish minimal rules around confidential information.

The Tin Man Behavior

In many traditional Tin Man organizations, the old idea that "information is power" translates into a culture where information is by default closely guarded. Data and insights, especially those that could shift internal power balances, expose underperformance, or contradict established narratives, become sequestered.[1] Access isn't just restricted; it's guarded, with information flowing through only by permission or special dispensation, and even then through narrow, controlled channels, sometimes shaped by gatekeepers acting on their own perception of need.

This isn't always deliberate or malicious; often, it's a by-product of deeply ingrained bureaucratic structures, a perceived need to protect one's domain, or even misguided attempts to prevent information overload or misinterpretation by others. Yet, as *Brave New Work* author Aaron Dignan notes, this tendency, if unchecked, "almost always . . . leads to missed opportunities and sometimes scandal."[2]

Employees operating in such environments acutely sense the presence of these hidden information caches, which makes them feel like they're on the outside of the "inner circle" with no real agency. They're working without a clear understanding of why their tasks truly matter to the (obscure) corporate strategy or why certain decisions are made. They see information used as leverage in internal politics or selectively revealed to specific groups. This lack of access to the real story breeds disengagement and a corrosive sense that people don't feel fully trusted or valued. It cripples their ability to identify with corporate goals, let alone pursue them with passion and initiative.

The resistance to sharing information that was once purposefully hidden, or simply became siloed through years of bureaucratic accretion, often stems from deep-seated fears, beliefs, and systemic pressures:

- **McGregor's "Theory X" mindset.** An implicit assumption that most employees can't be trusted with sensitive information, might misinterpret it, use it irresponsibly, or leak it.

- **Fear of losing control or status.** If knowledge is perceived as power, sharing it can feel like diluting one's personal or departmental influence, especially in environments where resources are scarce and fiercely protected.

- **Fear of scrutiny or judgment, amplified by low psychological safety.** Openly sharing performance data or project statuses (especially if unfavorable) can create vulnerability, particularly where "shooting the messenger" or punishing "failure" is a known risk.

- **Perfectionism and image management.** A desire to share only polished, "safe" information, hiding the messy reality of work-in-progress or uncertain data, often to ensure communications adhere to strict internal approval chains.

- **Historical precedent and structural inertia.** A case of "we've always done it this way." Silos become fortresses, and those within them may lack the incentives, perspective, or even the formal channels to share beyond their immediate confines.

Many organizations invest heavily in analytics tools but keep most of their data away from the tools, only exposing "safe" operational data, while strategically vital, sensitive, or politically charged information remains behind the gatekeepers. Consequently, opportunities are missed: the unvarnished customer feedback that marketing holds on to never reaches product teams; the early warnings from frontline staff on store trends are buried by managers.

The barriers to dismantling these information choke points are rarely technical; they are profoundly cultural and behavioral, often reflecting leadership's own anxieties, priorities, and the very bureaucratic systems they operate within. Sociologist Ron Westrum's work on information flow cultures is insightful here. He described the *pathological* (power-oriented) culture, where information is hoarded and messengers are shot. The infamous instruction to the Chief Actuary of the American Medicare Program by his Bureau Chief, Tom Scully, to keep quiet about budget estimates that disturbed the administration or he would "fire him so fast his head would spin" is a stark example of a pathological culture in action.[3] Ron describes a second type, the *bureaucratic* (rule-oriented) culture, where information flow is constrained by cumbersome, formal channels that incidentally filter critical insights.[4] The reluctance of radiologists to share or act upon early evidence of battered children, due to their limited influence beyond hospital walls, illustrates how even critical information can be stifled in bureaucratic settings.[5]

Leaders, through their symbolic actions (what they ask for, what they punish, what they reward, what they themselves share), create and perpetuate these stifling information climates. Ultimately, these information fortresses, built on distrust and control, do more than just impede progress; they cultivate an environment where the organization becomes blind to its own realities and deaf to the critical signals needed to adapt.

What Octopus Organizations Do Instead

Octopus Organizations believe the greatest risk isn't from sharing too much information, but from sharing too little, too slowly. Trust is not a reward for good behavior, but a prerequisite for it. They foster what Ron defined as the third type of culture in addition to pathological and bureaucratic—a *generative* culture, focused on the mission and overall performance. This culture exhibits good information flow, high levels of cooperation, and trust, with new ideas welcomed and failures treated as learning. Generative organizations make a conscious, courageous choice to cultivate a culture where the default is to share information openly and widely—especially the kind of information that Tin Man organizations keep locked away. This includes strategic plans and performance against them, financial realities, unadulterated customer feedback, lessons from failures, and even individual and team performance data (handled responsibly).

Octopus Organizations work diligently to shift out of a scarcity mindset ("information is a limited resource to be guarded") to a mindset of abundance and symmetry, where all parties have access to the same relevant information.[6] This goes beyond deploying data dashboards; it's about changing hearts and minds regarding what information *should* be shared, by whom, and with whom. Many Tin Man leaders reading this will balk at this, maybe even consider it naive; it's not. It's a calculated strategy based on the belief that:

- **Trust begets responsibility and engagement.** When people are trusted with important information and understand the "why" behind their work, they tend to act more responsibly and feel genuinely included in the organization's mission. Feeling included in the "real story" fosters a sense of ownership and accountability better than control and secrecy.

- **Transparency fuels agility and alignment.** In a complex changing world, speed of decision-making and adaptation is paramount. Open information flow allows for quicker sensing of problems and opportunities, and more rapid, informed responses, as well as getting teams onto the same page.

- **Collective intelligence builds more value than siloed expertise.** Insights emerge when diverse perspectives intersect with rich information. No single leader or department has all the answers, and the next brilliant idea or crucial warning could come from anyone, anywhere in the organization—or unexpected allies *if* they all have access to relevant information.

Octopus Organizations manage the perceived risks of sharing formerly hidden or "sensitive" information. It would be foolish to simply shift from a culture of locked-down data to a completely open one without some management of the transition. To do this, Octopus Organizations:

- **Build robust psychological safety.** This is paramount. They ensure that bringing forward bad news, challenging existing assumptions with data, or sharing imperfect "work-in-progress" information is met with inquiry and support, not blame or punishment.

- **Establish clear, minimal rules for genuinely confidential information.** There will always be some subset of information that cannot be widely shared, such as personal data, legally privileged information, or intellectual property. These exceptions are clearly defined, narrowly scoped, and regularly reviewed, rather than being used as a blanket excuse for broad lockdown of all data and information.

- **Focus on principles, not just policies.** While policies are useful, the culture of transparency is primarily driven by shared principles and leadership behavior. General Stanley McChrystal's provocative "Share information until you're afraid it's illegal" captures this spirit— an encouragement to push the boundaries of traditional secrecy.[6]

- **Design for "pull," not just "push."** Recognizing that overwhelming people with data and information is counterproductive, they make information easily accessible and discoverable through well-organized internal wikis, powerful search tools, and clear dashboards so individuals can pull what they need, when they need it. The emphasis is on *access*, not forced consumption.

Octopus Organizations explicitly reward and recognize information sharing, and cross-functional collaboration based on it. Performance metrics are redesigned to reflect the value of contributing to collective knowledge (for example, number of contributions to internal knowledge bases, or cross-functional projects or initiatives a team member participated in), not just individual or siloed achievements. Accountability for data quality and accessibility is often assigned to business leaders, not just IT.

Breaking down ingrained habits of information hoarding is a profound cultural shift that requires deliberate and sustained effort, and a fair bit of courage. By intentionally prying open the information black boxes and trusting their people to handle the "light," Octopus Organizations don't just unlock insights; they cultivate a dynamic environment of clarity, collective intelligence, and mutual accountability. This is where real strategic alignment happens, where innovation thrives, where employees feel genuinely included and can have the ownership to make a difference, and where curiosity is rewarded.

Levers

- **Be a data sharer.** Leaders can role model the desired behavior by visibly and consistently sharing information they might have previously kept close to their chest: strategic dilemmas, financial performance (warts and all), and their own learnings from failures. This sets the tone more power-fully than any policy.

^ **Challenge the "need to know" culture.** Actively question assumptions about who needs access to what information. Default to "need to share" unless there's a compelling, clearly articulated reason for restriction. Create forums where such reasons can be openly challenged.

^ **Decriminalize "bad news" and mistakes.** When information about problems, failures, or unmet targets is shared, the first reaction must be "Thank you for bringing this to our attention," followed by inquiry and support, not blame.

^ **Cocreate "transparency tenets."** With broad input, develop a set of principles about information sharing. Examples: "We share by default." "We treat information as an organizational asset, not personal property."

^ **Focus on information critical for strategy and performance.** Don't just democratize "safe" data. Prioritize making information that explains strategy, tracks progress against key goals, and reveals customer insights transparent and accessible. Regularly survey or ask employees what information they feel they are missing to do their jobs better, to understand the company's direction, or to feel more engaged. Act on this feedback.

^ **Simplify access to what matters.** While the cultural shift is the primary focus, ensure that once people *want* to share and access information, it's not technically or bureaucratically cumbersome to do so. This is where user-friendly platforms and the intuitive organization of information become enablers.

^ **Encourage storytelling with data—especially the tough data.** Train and encourage leaders and teams to communicate not just successes but also challenges and learnings through clear, honest data-backed narratives. Teach them how to tell compelling stories that bring data to life to enhance understanding.

^ **Rewrite incentives and recognition.** Explicitly build information sharing, collaborative use of data, and transparent reporting into performance expectations and reward systems; for example, "Actively contribute to the team's knowledge base by documenting key learnings from each project sprint in the shared wiki by the end of each project." Define behaviors that demonstrate these principles, like "Proactively share relevant data and insights with team members and stakeholders." Reward data openness through public acknowledgment, bonuses, promotions, or development opportunities.

^ **Conduct "information autopsies" (safely).** When a significant problem or failure occurs due to lack of information flow, conduct blameless postmortems to understand how and why information didn't get to the right people, and what cultural or systemic changes are needed.

DISCOVER MORE

ANTIPATTERNS TO READ NEXT

#6: Working Together but Not as a Team

#13: Gaming Budgets

#25: Granting Artificial Ownership

LEANING ON REORGS

Small, iterative changes and the thoughtful allocation of people to where they are needed keep restructures at bay.

THE TIN MAN BEHAVIOR

Resorting to structural change as a plug-and-play tool for change, in an attempt to improve productivity or shift culture, or mask cost-cutting and layoffs

THE RESULTS

- Destruction of valuable knowledge and networks
- Prolonged drop in productivity
- Attention diverted from delivering customer value to surviving the change
- Change fatigue, anxiety-driven behavior

How Octopus Organizations Behave Instead

- They focus on changing behaviors and how value is created over changing the org chart.
- They learn how work *really* gets done before intervening, favoring small iterative changes.
- Where org changes are genuinely needed, they openly communicate, even when the message is difficult.

The Tin Man Behavior

It's a rare day we don't encounter a company amid a reshuffle. Here's what we hear those leaders communicating [along with what's left unsaid]:

"Team, since joining Acme, I've heard clearly from you that previous reorganizations have been disruptive so [*just like the previous leaders said*] this reorganization will be the last one needed. Our new target operating model is based on a bimodal, agile product model to be implemented in the next 180 days [*arbitrary guess*]. These models are already [*sort of*] adopted by successful organizations. I've personally immersed myself in these [*through PowerPoints I didn't quite understand*]. I am convinced [*or hope to be*] that this approach will make us faster and more innovative, reduce our costs by 15 percent [*the real success metric*], and [*I nearly forgot*] put people at the center of the organization [*check that talking point box*]. On the screen you can see the new structure [*that doesn't reflect how we really get work done*]. Line managers will discuss with you how this operating model will work [*if they understand it*]. New scrum masters and product owners will immediately assume their roles after immersion training [*and will be expected to also juggle existing priorities*]. I know you will rise to the challenge [*as your jobs and mine rely on it*], based on my experience leading such transformations at previous companies [*they weren't this big, but they weren't complete disasters, apart from the turnover and the higher costs due to resistance*]. If your name isn't on the org chart, you will be moving to the new Chief Customer Officer's organization [*who won the turf war for resource and budget*] who will be a trusted partner of ours [*over my dead body*]."

. . .

Reorgs are just a type of transformation aimed at goosing flat or flagging performance by remolding the operating model. Leaders lean on reorgs for many reasons. New leaders see them as visible, decisive leadership even when the change might ultimately be superficial. *I'm doing a big thing.* Some Tin Man organizations think it's a way to make brute-force changes to entrenched bureaucracy and cultural issues. *If we switch to a matrix model, we'll be more efficient.* And of course, reorgs are used by some as a smokescreen for leadership deficiencies. It's a way to recast cost cutting and firing. *What we're really doing is creating synergies and streamlining operations.*

Imitation drives many reorganizations. Companies see industry darlings and think, *It's working for them.* Convinced by articles and consultants of the promises of similar success, they embrace "the Spotify model" and end up photocopying roles, structures, and rituals, the superficial features of the models.[1]

That doesn't work, as Philip Rosenzweig explains in *The Halo Effect.*[2] Success stories oversimplify reality, attributing performance to things that fit a tidy narrative while ignoring underlying behavior and mental model changes. Copying the structure while ignoring these other factors is a recipe for failure. Zappos succeeded with Holacracy, an organizational approach that replaces traditional hierarchies with a radically decentralized structure, not because

FIGURE 12-1

The Target Operating Model

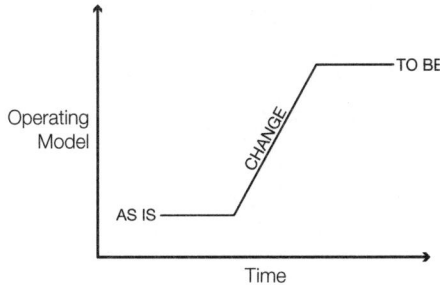

the structure was inherently better than others but because of CEO Tony Hsieh's relentless focus on culture first. When Medium copied the structure without the culture, chaos ensued, and the reorg was abandoned.[3]

The flaw in reorgs often rests on the use of a Target Operating Model (TOM)—a Tin Man concept that suggests there is a blueprint to get you from your current "as is" way of working to some other definitive "to be" model (figure 12-1). These blueprints treat organizations as rational entities: information flows freely, planning conquers uncertainty, employees prioritize company interests, and resources naturally align with strategic goals. It's beautifully simple, nearly linear.

But reality is messier. Reorgs aren't practically linear, and they require much deeper, interconnected thinking to plan for. For example, with Jonathan Allen, former CTO for Capital One, we identified more than *160* changes a company needed to make merely *to set up* cross-functional teams at scale: changes to process, structure, budget ownership, decision-making on priorities and technologies, new career paths and performance evaluation criteria, resource allocation processes, tools, on-call rotations, data ownership, meeting and working rituals, social networks, team development, and hiring processes, to name just a few.

Also, human motivations and behaviors resist formulaic change. As Richard Cyert and James March note in *Behavioral Theory of Firms*, a firm is a coalition without a singular, static goal. It is a living system that must *continuously* adapt—to new technologies, market shifts, talent, customer preferences, and competitive pressures.[4]

You're messing with complex organic connections in ways you are unlikely to fully understand. You can't top-down coarsely rearrange how your company works and expect a good result. Reshuffling severs vital informal networks, and the intuitive "know-how" of collective, undocumented experience is decimated. Intense internal focus pulls attention from customers and emerging trends. As roles become ambiguous and familiar pathways vanish, prolonged productivity dips and disengagement emerges. Hard-won psychological safety within teams is lost, diverting precious energy toward navigating new relationships, deciphering shifting power dynamics, and personal survival.

The result? A staggering three-quarters of reorgs are considered total failures, leading to regime changes that start the cycle over again.[5]

What Octopus Organizations Do Instead

Octopus Organizations resist the bureaucracy and bloat that often necessitate (or at least create the perceived need for) major reorgs. CEO and mountaineer Benedikt Böhm advocates for staying organizationally lean always, not just during a crisis. He asks his team to perpetually challenge adding unnecessary functions and work: "Do we really need these extra boots as we climb Mount Everest?" Do we really need this (new) department? Rather than ask something like "Why can't we close this department?"—a question for which the targeted team will have dozens of answers—he suggests a more direct "gunshot scenario." He asks, "If you had a gun to your head, would you still keep this department?" This hypothetical, initially shocking, became a creative exercise, fostering entrepreneurial ownership-like thinking. One team member even suggested their own departure might be best for paring; others offered to skip bonuses to avoid reorgs for other teams. You can create a common mission and enable ownership. A team's best experience is often overcoming challenges together; that in itself can be a reward and the very opposite outcome of Tin Man reorgs.

Octopus leaders prioritize structural stability while building internal flexibility. Rather than frequent wholesale reorganizations, they create mechanisms that move people and needed skills naturally where needed, forming and dissolving teams around specific customer needs, with high-performing teams preserved and redirected rather than disbanded. The trick is to "change the right bits—the bits that don't work well—and leave the rest alone," as Stephen Heidari-Robinson and Suzanne Heywood say in their book *ReOrg*.[6]

Octopus Organizations nurture complex informal human networks that deliver value—like Charlotte in finance who calls Robbie in IT to unblock issues, or Jack in supplier management who calls Ida in manufacturing because she knows which suppliers really perform. Octopus leaders create opportunities for people to build connections across silos, through communities of practice, internal marketplaces for skills, or cross-functional forums. This requires humility from leaders, to accept that they don't know how all the work gets done.

Octopus Organizations constantly work on smaller-scale change, which holds major reorgs at bay. Marty Cagan of the Silicon Valley Product Group advises, "It is easy to do an experiment, but hard to do a transformation project. Nobody is going to put their company at risk beyond an experiment. Identify a good product team leader, a designer from outside, seriously good engineers. Demonstrate business results. Have a quarter or two to show real results. Be strategic about the pilot team. The important point in the transformation is the first win." Pacing perceived value and progress keeps people engaged, excited, and motivated. Amazon's "two-pizza" team structure—small teams with decentralized decision-making—has evolved over two decades.

Sometimes a coarse reorganization might be seen as necessary such as to jump-start a move to a product-based organization and dissolve silos. In these cases, **Octopus leaders are honest about their objectives,** knowing that employees will see through attempts to hide their intentions. One day, at the bank where Jana worked, a new door with a big lock appeared along a busy hallway. Behind it, everyone knew, were consultants not so secretly redesigning the bank. Staff nervously eyed that door. Fears ran wild. Following a wave of firings, promises of improvements emerged. Those promises were met with educated skepticism; staff knew the reorg was really an effort to meet ambitious numbers. That skepticism made the change they were planning behind locked doors even harder.

Octopus Organizations communicate about reorganization early—even without precise timelines. Many leaders think they are doing employees a favor by keeping quiet for as long as possible during planning. This belies one of the things that will make their restructure difficult—information flows through the organization in ways they don't even understand. They don't control it nearly as much as they think. Leaders get excited about future potential, but employees don't care until they know if they're safe. In our discussion with them, Stephen and Suzanne suggested that leaders needed to flip their script: lay out the planned process first, then communicate benefits once safety is clear.

Effective Octopus Organizations engage their people in reorg processes, seek genuine input, and clearly explain implications. For people who cannot be included directly, Octopus Orgs communicate when things will happen and what they will mean for people. This is potentially slower than bringing in consultants to conjure and then present a massive plan, but it is better to slow this part down and reap the benefits of changes that lead back to productivity much quicker than to be one of the 75 percent of restructures that fail.[7] In doing so, they make it clear that they don't have all the answers and invite employees to help with continuing to fine-tune changes.

When adopting others' methods, Octopus Organizations focus on intent and experimentation. They steal others' ideas, but they make them uniquely theirs. Marty of the Silicon Valley Product Group is adamant that implementing new ways of working, whether in small experiments or full reorgs, requires bringing in people who know what good looks like; practitioners from organizations that have already gone through this transition. Rabobank's HR leader, Kiki van den Berg, invites leaders to take deep dives, visiting organizations that have the desired culture. This helps expose leaders to the complexity and work they have ahead of them—perhaps even dissuading them from doing a reorg.

Successful organizational evolution hinges on balancing stability with adaptability, continuously experimenting and fine-tuning. By fostering ownership, transparency, and genuine engagement, Octopus Organizations transform org change from a disruptive event into an ongoing, collective journey. This approach not only mitigates the risks of costly reorg failures but also builds resilient, motivated teams ready to navigate complexity together.

Levers

˄ **Define outcomes before reorganizing.** Before considering structural change, define the specific problems you are trying to solve. Articulate precise desired outcomes (for instance, reduce features time to market by 20 percent) and brainstorm non-structural alternatives. Conduct a thorough pro-con analysis with trusted advisers and those who will be affected before redrawing the org chart. Have leaders visit organizations that have made similar changes successfully to understand the behavioral and cultural implications and hidden challenges and dependencies.

˄ **Communicate early and honestly ("trust not terror").** Communicate what is and isn't known about planned changes, why a plan is being considered, anticipated timelines, and potential impact on employees before having a full plan. Be honest and empathetic and provide ongoing updates. Repeat key messages consistently through multiple channels. For those you need to let go, don't drag it out, and be thoughtful and respectful—inform them as quickly as possible and look for opportunities to help them find new roles.

^ **Be inclusive and challenging.** Engage the entire leadership team in the change. Avoid the CEO-and-trusted-confidants trap, which breeds resistance and resentment. Have those supporting the reorg argue against it, and vice versa, to uncover challenges, disconnects, and alternatives, as well as building appreciation for the "other side."

^ **Treat implementation as product management.** Treat a reorganization as a product that requires continuous management. Establish ownership for implementation. Use iterative execution, testing assumptions with small experiments and adapting the approach based on feedback and results.

^ **Monitor psychological safety continuously.** Regularly assess team cohesion and psychological safety before, during, and after organizational changes using anonymous surveys and feedback sessions. Create safe spaces for employees to voice concerns. Use this data to adjust the pace and scope of changes to maintain team effectiveness.

^ **Foster communities of practice.** Encourage skills-based or domain-focused groups that share knowledge and build relationships outside their formal reporting lines. Use these groups to share tribal knowledge—the informal expertise of long-term employees.

DISCOVER MORE

ANTIPATTERNS TO READ NEXT

#10: Entrenching Silos

#14: Operating on a Culture of Fear

#19: Fetishizing Process

GAMING BUDGETS

Dynamic forecasting and transparency direct money to where it produces the most value.

THE TIN MAN BEHAVIOR

Engaging in rigid, time-consuming annual budgeting that creates detailed projections about the future that are virtual guesses

THE RESULTS

- Focus is on winning funds, not delivering value.
- Inflated budget requests and year-end scrambles for money
- Inertia tied to fixed budgets allocated months earlier

How Octopus Organizations Behave Instead

- They replace static annual budgeting cycles with dynamic forecasting and flexible budget reallocation.
- They fund outcomes, not departments, and assign resources to stable teams aligned to customer value.
- They tie decisions to enterprise-wide thinking over functions and are transparent about decisions.

The Tin Man Behavior

The annual budget ritual consumes months and, in our experience, is mostly a guessing game disguised as science. This leads to a predictable set of failures—wildly lowballed costs, impossibly rosy revenue targets—and destructive patterns like padding budgets, gaming, and sabotaging other groups. As serial entrepreneur Peter Hinssen comments on the resulting budgets, "More lies have been told in Excel than anywhere else."

The commitment to the ritual creates an illusion of control. Board reporting cycles demand annual commitments. But whatever control is felt bears little relationship to the dynamic market realities or iterative learning that takes place over a year of business. Budgets clash with the need to respond to (inevitable) change. They deepen organizational inertia and cannot compensate for volatile realities, ignoring the significant opportunity costs of ventures not pursued because funds are inflexibly locked up. With market conditions shifting faster than annual budget cycles can accommodate, resources often remain trapped in lower-value activities while higher-impact opportunities languish unfunded. Former Capital One technology Chief Financial Officer Chris Hennesey notes that such budgets are dead on arrival, outdated soon after being locked in. Strategic agility requires a level of financial flexibility that traditional budgeting is not designed to accommodate.

The full extent of this pain is rarely appreciated and extends well beyond the finance department. We know one organization that spent an estimated twenty-five thousand person-hours on its annual budget, only to see 60 percent of its strategic assumptions invalidated by market shifts within six months.

Budgeting as the Tin Man does it suffers from numerous cognitive biases that entrench dysfunction and perpetuate outdated practices. We observe justifications like:

- "We've always done it this way, and it sort of works" [status quo bias].

- "We always meet our year-end number [without a view to the value delivered]" [confirmation bias].

- "If we don't continue to budget for this initiative, it will have been a waste" [sunk cost fallacy].

- "The last two companies I worked for used the same process" [availability bias].

- "A new process will create risks and raise all sorts of unpredictable issues" [loss aversion bias].

- "I needed this money last year, so it's probably reasonable to assume the same this year" [anchoring bias].

These justifications accrue into an overconfidence bias. Leaders are reluctant to rock the budgeting boat, though if they were willing to run a retrospective of past budget cycles, they might be surprised at the answers to common "bias audit" questions. These questions covered the number of projects that were funded primarily due to prior spend (sunk cost), ambitious ideas that were scaled back due to initial low allocations (anchoring), and whether there was a rush to agreement on budgets, potentially silencing potential dissent (bandwagon).

Do not mistake these biases for personal failings. They are a function of misaligned incentives, often creating a *principal-agent problem* where managers (agents) may prioritize personal security (hitting budget numbers) over the organization's (principal's) strategic goals. Finance teams may find themselves in the position of rewarding confident projections they know are wrong over honest acknowledgment of uncertainty.

From this systemic dysfunction, five common destructive patterns emerge:

- **Budgets are allocated to departments, not value streams.** Most value comes from cross-functional work, yet budgets get allocated to functions—a mismatch that reinforces artificial scarcity and internal competition. Each department must include partial funding in their budgets for an important value-creating project, but no single leader *owns* the initiative or, even more important, the outcomes.

- **Annual cycles kill both learning and adaptation.** Rigid budget-planning timelines rarely align with value delivery. Most initiatives require observing, orienting, deciding, and acting (the "OODA loop") based on feedback from customers, external market conditions, and other factors, many of which don't operate on the artificial distinctions of calendar quarters or fiscal years. Teams might delay valuable projects to avoid exceeding budgets, or rush to spend money at year-end in a "use it or lose it" scramble, fostering cynicism and waste.

- **Process perfection overtakes outcome focus.** Organizations obsess over executing flawless budgeting rituals—CapEx versus OpEx classifications, arbitrary spending rules like contractor rate caps, and year-end hiring freezes that disrupt critical projects. The utility of many such rules, if questioned against the outcomes they enable, often reveals itself as purely administrative or historical.

- **Politics crowd out performance.** Political skills can outweigh analytical rigor as complex cost allocation makes understanding true program costs nearly impossible. So leaders optimize for metrics they can control—like budget compliance—rather than outcomes. Status becomes conflated with budget size rather than value delivered. Sandbagging (under-promising results or overestimating needs) and squirreling away slush funds tucked into vague line items ("marketing innovation alignment initiative") become rational survival tactics. We often see risk and compliance functions, for example, secure unchallenged funding through fear-based messaging. While these behaviors can seem political or self-serving, they often reflect a genuine anxiety about being unable to access resources when truly important or unforeseen needs arise.

- **Budget opacity breeds mistrust and missed opportunities.** Organizations guard budgets as confidential information, preventing the broader organization from contributing insights that could improve resource allocation and identify collaboration opportunities.

The system becomes self-perpetuating. Employees learn that mastering the budget games yields better personal returns than demonstrating performance excellence. Talented individuals, frustrated by the opacity of the process and misaligned incentives, either learn to play these games or leave for organizations where value creation is rewarded. Innovation suffers as breakthrough initiatives, inherently uncertain, or transformational opportunities lose funding battles against safer, less impactful improvements.

What Octopus Organizations Do Instead

While we would love to rewrite financial rules and forgo our obsession with EBITDA to more accurately reflect twenty-first-century needs, we understand that would be a quixotic and nearly useless approach. We'll focus instead on practical aspects of budgeting that you can attack.

Octopus Organizations construct financial systems that actively foster adaptability and continuous learning. They understand that finance can go beyond the guardian of accounting rules to be a strategic partner that invests in forecasting, scenario planning, and learning, and works with departments to increase their skills there.

Octopus Organizations move from static budgets to dynamic forecasting. They don't budget in absolute terms for a year. Chris Hennesey notes that such budgets are dead on arrival, outdated soon after being locked in. Instead, they continually assess new inputs and priorities. They start this shift by piloting rolling forecasts (for instance, quarterly, looking five to eight quarters out), focusing initially on three to five key business drivers, like customer acquisition or product usage. They use scenario planning (best/worst/likely) for these drivers. Companies like Equinor and Maersk use such dynamic forecasting as an anticipation tool, not a control mechanism against a fixed number, separating forecasts from fixed targets.

Octopus Organizations establish regular cross-functional gatherings where funding requests are debated on strategic merit learnings and potential ROI, adopting lean portfolio management techniques such as a portfolio review cadence (such as debating budgets quarterly). A growth board, portfolio review board, or value council helps to bring focus to debate, requests, and changes based on these criteria.

Octopus Organizations fund outcomes, not outputs. Where possible, funding is tied to achieving measurable results rather than completing tasks, defined collaboratively with those accountable for the outcome. For example, they shift budgeting from being based on "launch three new features" (output) to funding leading indicators of value, like "increase active new feature usage by new customers by 15 percent within thirty days" (outcome).

Octopus Organizations invest in capacity through accountable, stable teams aligned to value or customer outcomes, rather than temporary projects. "Capacity funding" provides predictable costs but immense flexibility in work undertaken. Octopus Orgs start by identifying a critical value stream (such as "new customer onboarding") and form a cross-functional team with a clear mission and outcome-based targets. Their budget is their operational cost.

For uncertain, innovative ventures, Octopus Organizations use venture capital–style stage-gate funding. Teams unlock contingent budget tranches by proving hypotheses with data and working in increments. This process mirrors how VCs fund startups. They foster psychological safety so teams can report learning from "failed" hypotheses without penalty. Parts of Bosch and 3M have adopted such models.

Octopus Organizations systematically combat cognitive biases through structured decision frameworks and clear guardrails. They use external perspectives, devil's advocate processes, and pre-mortems to surface and challenge biases. For any investment over a certain threshold, they define explicit guardrails (for example, "must align with sustainability goals," "must deliver measurable customer value within six months") that all funding requests must adhere to. But finance teams should continually ask, "What positive outcome does this rule enable?" If the answer is merely administrative or unclear, the rule itself should be challenged.

Octopus Organizations counter budget gaming through radical transparency in funding and performance. Publishing funding rationales, expected outcomes, and even high-level financial performance data makes political maneuvering more obvious and counterproductive. For significant investments, they publish a summary of the rationale and expected impact. Swedish bank Handelsbanken has long exemplified this practice with decentralized P&Ls and open information access. When everyone knows what funding is spent on and why, teams identify collaboration opportunities, avoid duplication, and contribute insights that improve resource allocation decisions.

Octopus Organizations foster collaboration through shared understanding and budget transparency. Making available internally the basis of decisions, the assumptions underpinning them including on other teams and departments, and the expected outcomes creates a healthy dialogue internally on what might be missing or alternative ways of working.

Levers

^ **Create transparency.** Stop the interdepartmental games by moving from chargebacks to "showbacks." Make the consumption of resources publicly visible but not charged back, such as technology investment by individuals, teams, or departments.

^ **Pilot outcome-based funding.** Select one initiative to create an outcome-based team. Have the single-threaded leader define budgets agnostic to departmental boundaries. Use this experiment to better understand and inform organizational changes that would be needed to broadly implement outcome budgeting.

^ **Implement structured bias-breaking.** Establish decision frameworks requiring assumption documentation, external challenge, and regular hypothesis testing. Use red team reviews and devil's advocate processes to counter groupthink and overconfidence in budget projections.

^ **Test stage-gate funding.** Set check-in points for an initiative where further funding will be released based on proving pre-agreed hypotheses validated through data. Take an n+2 approach so that proving the current iteration (n) successfully releases funding for iteration (n+2) so progress is not held up based on a decision. For the first experiment, an entire year's budget might be pre-agreed but not guaranteed to be released unless progress is demonstrated.

^ **Zero-baseline selective budgets.** Choose one function annually to build from scratch without referencing previous investments. Bring in individuals knowledgeable about desired outcomes but not specific initiatives to challenge assumptions. This is resource intensive but used selectively can help find new, better ways of working more cost-effectively.

^ **Create an efficiency mindset.** For every functional and initiative business case, particularly those with a multi-year horizon, make it mandatory for the requestor to define how they will use technology to counter inflationary pressures. Build these commitments automatically into subsequent years and be prepared to fund the initial up-front commitment.

^ **Go step-by-step.** Try combining the levers above, and more, into an incremental framework to slowly roll out changes to budgeting that might look like this:

- Foundation

  - *Build a coalition* educating leadership on traditional budgeting flaws to gain sponsorship.

  - *Create transparency* by replacing chargebacks with "showbacks," making resource consumption visible.

  - *Pilot outcome-based funding* with one or more cross-functional teams to learn about what works in your environment, in a "smoke and mirrors" approach, still working with the standard budgeting processes behind the scenes.

  - *Test stage-gate funding,* releasing funds based on validated hypotheses and delivered value with one entrepreneurial initiative. Success in one stage should release funding for the next so progress is not held up by decision-makers or budget cycles.

- Expanding and refining

  - *Test bias-breaking* by requiring assumptions to be documented, external reviews to be conducted, and hypothesis to be tested.

  - *Try lean portfolio management* with quarterly portfolio reviews, including pivot and kill decisions.

  - *Try rolling forecasts,* testing six-quarter forecasts alongside annual budgets.

  - *Iterate and learn,* conducting retrospectives, documenting and sharing findings.

- Embedding

  - *Refine performance management,* experimenting with ways to reward killing off failing projects, rather than rewarding budget adherence.

  - *Test zero-baseline budgets,* annually rebuilding one or two functions from scratch with fresh perspectives.

- *Replace* annual budgets with rolling forecasts and outcome-based funding.

- *Foster continuous improvement* with regular reviews to refine the funding system.

DISCOVER MORE

ANTIPATTERNS TO READ NEXT

#10: Entrenching Silos

#19: Fetishizing Process

#20: Seeking Perfect Decisions

PART 2

INCREASING OWNERSHIP

One of the biggest challenges for any leader steeped in the Tin Man world is learning to let go. Ceding control feels like a dangerous gamble, a bet against predictability. The paradox, however, is that this obsession with control is what creates the biggest failure of all: a workforce that waits for permission instead of taking initiative. Ownership is the antidote—the space you create for people to bring their full intelligence and commitment to their work.

Leaders love to say things like "People are our greatest asset," and "We put people first." But the antipatterns of Tin Man behavior in this section will show that words and actions aren't usually aligned on this front. Humans are treated in our organizations as *resources* and *capital*—when modern work requires non-routine activity, creative solutions, and dynamic action to address rapidly changing contexts.

Most likely your organization operates in Tin Man models where employees feel like small cogs in large machines. They are shackled into Tin Man structures and processes, forbidden or discouraged from doing much without permission. Risk is eliminated through compliance, often driving managers to micromanage and prod people for productivity. Failures create fear. Even successes that happen outside the prescribed way of doing business can be punished.

There's plenty of research that probably matches your own observations: When people have the perception that they cannot, through any action, control outcomes—when they have no sense of ownership of their work—they fall into a state of *amotivation*. Estimates put the cost of amotivation at $8.9 trillion in lost productivity.[1]

Ownership isn't something you can create by fiat ("everyone take ownership of their work now"), but you can create an environment where people do what needs to be done not through orders but because they self-direct. Two things need to be true for this to come to life: someone needs to be willing to cede a degree of control, and someone else needs to be willing to accept it.

Some leaders might argue that people don't always, or even rarely, want ownership. They want to be told what to do and how to do it. If that's the case, it would be excruciatingly hard to create an organization of owners, thinkers, and boundary-pushers.

But that's not the case. "Let me be a cog" is not our inherent state. A large body of Self-Determination Theory (SDT) research demonstrates that humans evolve from infancy on to be proactively engaging and owning, curious, and with a tremendous ability to assimilate information. It's intuitive. Just think of toddlers, manifesting intrinsic tendencies to take interest in, learn about, and gain mastery of their inner and outer worlds. They explore, manipulate, and understand—to own ("Mine!"). This creates satisfaction: feelings of competence, autonomy, and relatedness, reflecting the deepest sense of human thriving.

Creating ownership restores us to this default setting. Ownership is about acting with choice. Researchers call it "autonomy"—being able to determine what you do, when, how, and with whom. Daniel Pink summarizes it as autonomy over the 4Ts—task, time, technique, and team.[2]

Take autonomy over time. Tin Man organizations value presenteeism. Show up at the prescribed time and remain there for the prescribed time. Octopus Orgs enable workers to shape their time how it works best for them while still driving the outcome wanted.

Two things ownership is not:

One: It's not total *independence*, and we've talked to many leaders who get nervous about this when we start talking about ownership. We're not suggesting a "do whatever you want in the way you want it" approach. Ownership requires carrying personal *accountability* for something: a problem to solve, an initiative, an outcome, the consequences of a decision. In this shift from Tin Man to Octopus we create an environment where people *want* to and *can comfortably* own their roles, and where we change the organization's relationship to what people do, when, how, and with whom.

Two: It's not *empowerment*. Tin Man outfits use this word to convince themselves they're "putting people first." But the term betrays a top-down, control mentality. The prefix *em* literally means *in* or *into*. Thus, empowering is putting your power into an employee or team. It suggests power rests with the organization, and the organization will mete it out in a controlled manner. *Here's a little freedom I will grant you, but please not too much.* Daniel calls this "a slightly more civilized form of control."[3]

Octopus Organizations put so much value on ownership because of its profound effect on performance. The motivation it creates promotes greater connection to the organization, higher effectiveness, higher productivity, less burnout, and greater levels of psychological well-being.[4] High-quality employee motivation and wellness contributes to long-term organizational health, customer satisfaction and loyalty, and financial success.[5]

Conversely, research demonstrates that employees perceiving low autonomy reported heightened stress, reduced job satisfaction, and stronger intentions to leave.[6] As work complexity increases, valuable staff become frustrated by their inability to make progress, and they depart.[7] These factors drive turnover more significantly than limited career advancement opportunities.

Finally, remember that ownership must be paired with clarity, a shared understanding of what our context is. What does "good" look like? What do you own? What are you trying to achieve? How does that fit into the bigger picture? Without this clarity, ownership becomes unproductive and frustrating. At an extreme, it becomes chaotic.

Leaders often intuitively get the value of ownership, but they struggle to truly embrace it beyond token gestures, like launching innovation challenges where the results never see the light of day, or appointing change champions that have no real influence. This section will show you many of the antipatterns that create the resistance to evolving into an Octopus Organization. They will help you shift to treat people as players, not pawns, and set a foundation for organizational practices that encourage and even institutionalize ownership. They will help you shift your leadership, resist the temptation to control people, and instead create the conditions for people to do their best work, and to convert their potential.

OPERATING ON A CULTURE OF FEAR

When honesty is valued and psychological safety is present, ownership blossoms.

THE TIN MAN BEHAVIOR

Creating an environment where individuals hesitate to own tasks, voice concerns, share ideas, or admit mistakes for fear of negative consequences

THE RESULTS

- Decreased employee engagement
- Missed opportunities and threats, from a lack of broad innovation
- People avoid taking calculated risks, stifling organizational agility and growth

How Octopus Organizations Behave Instead

- They create an atmosphere where honesty is valued and individuals take risks and ownership.
- They treat mistakes as learning opportunities.
- They solicit diverse, contrary perspectives and constructive criticism.

The Tin Man Behavior

You can't mandate that people take ownership. It needs to be freely claimed. But nobody will claim ownership if they think they'll be penalized for doing so. That's why this antipattern comes first in the ownership section.

Psychological safety is an individual's belief about whether it is worth taking interpersonal risks without fear of humiliation, rejection, or punishment. It's different than trust, which is built ahead of time between *individuals*.

Psychological safety manifests in *group* settings and happens in the moment as a person assesses whether they should take a risk.[1]

. Such risks could be as simple as sharing an idea or as involved as taking time to use data to disprove conventional wisdom. It could be as high-stakes as questioning a leader on strategy.

Even if you encourage such behavior, this is a difficult antipattern to escape because psychological safety is emotional, rooted deep in our brains, and it will override more nuanced thinking if it senses a threat or has experienced being penalized for the behavior before.

For example, in the late 2000s, Nokia attempted to transform itself to address competitive threats. Despite then-CEO Stephen Elop's efforts to create psychological safety through initiatives like "Nokia Conversations" and open feedback channels, many employees remained hesitant to speak up about growing challenges with smartphone innovation. A post-analysis revealed many employees saw warning signs of Nokia's impending struggles but felt unsafe sharing their concerns, even though leadership explicitly requested such feedback.[2]

Leaders invited them, and the employees refused the invitation. While the specifics of cases like these will never be clear, the reasons they happen (over and over) are consistent and include: historical trauma from when openness led to retribution (whether deliberate or not—speaking up came back to "bite" someone or some team); old processes, formal or informal, that don't support the proclamations of psychological safety (such as metrics that reward supporting the status quo); a lack of clarity on *why* or *how* employees' honest opinions are valued; and a dearth of examples when "speaking up" was a positive event for all involved.

Without getting past all that, no matter how much you *say* you want people to feel okay about owning and speaking up, you have not *created* the psychological safety people need to see that taking a risk is worthwhile. They will revert to following processes, and deferring to others.

We know that some of you reading this are probably skeptical about this idea. When we talk about psychological safety in organizations, heads might nod politely, but privately, some leaders say to us things like:

- "Another touchy-feely HR program. We're running a business, not a therapy session. People need to toughen up."

- "We can't tiptoe around every person's feelings. Sometimes people need to hear hard truths."

- "I didn't have someone holding my hand. My team needs to learn to handle pressure."

- "If people don't feel 'safe' enough to do their job, maybe they're in the wrong company."

The irony is stark: Operational models that dismiss psychological safety as "soft" or unnecessary end up creating the very weakness they fear. They foster an army of cautious bureaucrats who won't rock the boat and avoid responsibility. This weakens resilience and innovation capabilities, as people who don't feel safe don't take risks that are necessary for innovation. Then these leaders wonder why their "tough" culture produces timid results.

What Octopus Organizations Do Instead

Octopus Organizations take the time to understand what psychological safety is and is not. The attitudes in the quotes above represent a flawed understanding of the concept. Psychological safety is *not*:

- Being soft, or inclusion for the sake of inclusion

- Treating every idea and every contribution as equally valid

- Avoiding tough conversations or tolerating repeated mistakes

- Lowering expectations[3]

It is instead a deeply researched concept in the social sciences, biology, and neurology. From the research we know:

- Feeling psychologically safe is *always* an individual's decision. They evaluate the benefit and risk of speaking up constantly and often unconsciously, based on previous experiences.

- *Vulnerability* reinforces psychological safety. The ability to say, "I was wrong," "I don't know," or "I have an idea, but it's different" creates positive reinforcement.

- *Trust* is a precursor. Individuals need to know that the intentions of those they're interacting with come from a place of personal care.

Having a clearer understanding of what the concept really means scotches many of the worst stereotypes around it. If you raise this idea with someone and catch them rolling their eyes, let them know that one organization that prizes psychological safety deeply and whose members score very high on it is the Navy SEALs.

Octopus Organizations don't treat vulnerability as a weakness to armor over. An octopus is vulnerable in a way as it has evolved to not have a shell. But that is neither a mistake nor a weakness. An octopus is *safer* without its shell because it can respond more dynamically to its environment. Similarly, true psychological safety comes from developing the confidence and capabilities to handle vulnerability effectively rather than trying to create a rigid protective structure that deflects contrary information or ideas.

Octopus Organizations recognize the signs of a culture that embraces vulnerability. Some of those signs include:

- *Openness.* People make spontaneous contributions, think aloud, and share partially formed ideas. Individuals speak and debate with each other, not through a boss.

- *Playfulness.* Laughter is prevalent, reducing stress and fear. Rich Hua, founder of Amazon's EQ@Amazon program, tries to get teams laughing in the first five minutes of a meeting.[4]

- *Empathy.* Anger, frustration, and dismissiveness are addressed through efforts to understand an idea from the other person's or group's perspective.

- *Inquisitiveness.* Open-ended questions are asked to elucidate thinking.

- *Reflection.* Individuals are comfortable in silence as they pause to think.

- *Gratitude.* Honesty is rewarded and recognized. Contributions are acknowledged.

Octopus Organizations model vulnerability. Leaders showcase their own learning and mistakes, share their own doubts, and create time for people to get to know each other as people beyond the work. "If you really want people to be unleashed," Alphabet X CEO Astro Teller says, "you need to first put down all your armor, take off all your masks, and then you need to start rewarding people when they do it."[5] Many of these activities will feel awkward at first. It's key to push through the discomfort. For example, one of our colleagues implemented a "raising a light" moment at team meetings, when people would share good news. It felt awkward initially but quickly became normal and now people look forward to it. Another part of modeling vulnerability is assuming others are on board. "Even if someone doesn't have good intentions," Amy Edmondson told us, "you're better off assuming they too are trying to create a better world or product, because then you are going to approach them with a genuine learning orientation, doing your part in creating excellence."

Octopus leaders nurture inclusivity. Former Schneider Electric President and AWS EMEA VP Tanuja Randery CBE observed that "when a junior or diverse talent offers a perspective and finds it dismissed, the immediate loss isn't just that single insight; it's the effect on future innovation across the team. Each unheard voice subtly erodes the organization's capacity to learn and adapt." Invite reticent participants in meetings to contribute without calling them out. "Jack, you have experience in this area. What are we missing?" Express gratitude when people do contribute, especially when you know they may be hesitant. LEGO nurtures psychological safety through its *leadership playground* culture, encouraging employees to be curious, brave, and focused, the same attributes you'd find in children at a playground.[6]

Octopus Organizations eliminate brilliant jerks. Nothing weakens the willingness to speak up more than the person who poisons the environment with arrogance, disrespect, intimidation, or other undesirable reactions to colleagues being vulnerable, no matter how smart or experienced that person may be. They may be correct on every point and they're still creating more damage than value.

Octopus Organizations recognize that breaches in psychological safety will happen. Watch for signs: engaged participants becoming quiet, closed body language, defensive responses, or a lack of eye contact. Acknowledge the situation, validate concerns, apologize if appropriate. Explicitly but constructively, and openly, address what's happening.

Octopus leaders think locally about creating psychological safety. We debated whether it was possible for a large organization to develop a universal culture of psychological safety. We decided it would be difficult. Amy concurred in conversation with us: "There is no such thing as an 'organization,'" she said. "There are groups in the organization. Some have higher psychological safety, some lower. Psychological safety is a *local* phenomenon." So, practices should be deployed locally.

The real challenge breaking this antipattern isn't in understanding what to do; it's in the relentless dedication to doing it, especially when pressure mounts and old habits feel easy.

Levers

^ **Ask, "What am I missing?"** Make this your go-to question in meetings and discussions to role model intellectual humility. Acknowledge that you don't have all the answers and actively seek out different perspectives. Amy suggests using questions such as "What are you worrying about?"

^ **Normalize and learn from issues.** Frame issues and failures as learning opportunities by conducting blameless postmortems. Share your own mistakes openly and discuss what you learned. Celebrate "intelligent failures" that come from ambitious attempts rather than carelessness.

^ **Practice active listening.** Focus on understanding what you're hearing rather than thinking about how you'll respond as someone is still talking. Use clarifying questions, summarize what you've heard, and acknowledge emotions. Avoid interrupting and showing negative body language, which can include aggressive, defensive, or uninterested postures.

^ **"Call in" rather than "call out" people.** When someone makes a mistake or says something insensitive, approach them privately and with curiosity ("Help me understand what you meant by . . ."). This reduces the fear of public shaming, fostering a more forgiving and supportive environment. Ultimately continue to build trust so these conversations can be had openly.

^ **Build inclusive meeting practices.** Implement turn-taking protocols and active facilitation to ensure all voices are heard. Consider rotating meeting roles and deliberately drawing out quieter voices. Watch for and call out dismissive comments and non-inclusive language and body language.

^ **Provide contribution options.** Create multiple channels for contribution beyond just speaking up in meetings for those who may not yet feel comfortable. Actively consider different working and communication styles when structuring team interactions. Ovo Energy's former Chief People Officer Kim Atherton advocates for the use of tools like anonymous voting mechanisms to help introverts feel included.

^ **Assess and discuss psychological safety.** Regularly assess psychological safety through surveys and discussions. Make it an explicit topic of conversation and track progress over time. Use multiple channels (anonymous surveys, one-on-ones, group discussions) to ensure you're getting honest input. Use tools like Amy's psychological safety assessment to measure and monitor perceptions of safety.[7] But also take her advice: "Psychological safety is a means to an end, measuring *performance* is the goal."

^ **Start meetings with check-in questions.** Keep it optional and brief, starting with the meeting leader to model openness. Choose questions that allow both personal connection and professional relevance such as:

- What's one thing that energized you this week?

- What's something you're looking forward to today?

- What is one small win from the past few days that you'd like to share?

- What's one challenge on your mind coming into this meeting?

- On a scale of 1–10, how present can you be today and why?

- What's one thing the group should know about your state of mind?

DISCOVER MORE

ANTIPATTERNS TO READ NEXT

#12: Leaning on Reorgs

#25: Granting Artificial Ownership

#26: Evading Failure

UPHOLDING POOR LEADERSHIP

Empathy, humility, and curiosity transform
leadership from a role to a behavior.

THE TIN MAN BEHAVIOR

Elevating, supporting, and leaving in place leaders who undermine
team potential and sow disengagement, often through power and
dictate

THE RESULTS

- Distrust, fear, disengagement, turnover
- Self-preservation replaces ownership and problem-solving.
- Lost productivity, ethical lapses

How Octopus Organizations Behave Instead

- They treat leadership as a behavior, not just a role.
- They develop leaders who create conditions where people willingly
  claim ownership.
- They promote leaders who model empathy, humility, and curiosity.

The Tin Man Behavior

Poor leadership comes in many forms; not all are deliberate, and many
emerge despite good intentions. The pressure of being expected to be an expert
with all the answers brings the quiet whisper of impostor syndrome. Aggressive demands and command-and-control styles emerge from the ingrained
habit of being seen to be "in charge," when a leader's real job is to "take care
of those in [their] charge."[1] Some leaders plainly lack self-awareness or empathy and the curiosity to develop them, having been rewarded in the past for

driving results in whatever way possible. Some feel comfortable in the rigid structures of hierarchy, never having operated in a collaborative mode. Many turn their focus to the trappings of leadership and focus on their status and control.

It's one of the most common antipatterns of ownership we see, with poor leadership casting long shadows over teams and performance.[2] It creates a culture of permission-seeking. Employees focus on trying to anticipate their leader's needs, not their customers'. They learn to wait for direction instead of taking initiative, to seek approval rather than solve problems, to follow, not own.

We've seen this over and over in the field. Take William (a true story with names changed), CEO of a *Fortune* 100 tech company who, upon entering a meeting room to speak with the team of an acquired business, snapped at one his new employees, "You're in my chair!" The employee never forgot the arrogance that *created immediate distrust*. (The CEO was later fired after a poor run.)

There was also the CHRO of a UK bank who vacationed while her team executed massive personnel cuts, returning tanned and relaxed and, fully *lacking empathy*, asked her traumatized staff how it went.

And there was a person in a large multinational professional services firm who wrote an email inviting senior partners to a key event. Most politely declined. But one senior partner responded with a lecturing screed, copied to a raft of managers, explaining that it was absolutely inappropriate to contact someone with his seniority directly by email, *prioritizing hierarchy over collaboration*.

In ancient Egypt, the shadow was seen as a part of a person's essence that represented a dark reflection of one's true nature. In organizations, this antipattern casts a shadow that similarly represents a part of the Tin Man org's essence. Teams naturally align with their leader's priorities and their underlying assumptions about how things work, and they mirror their behaviors.[3] A leader that acts with impatience, dismissiveness, or avoidance of tough issues fosters teams that do the same. Over time, it becomes an unspoken cultural norm.

In such toxic environments, people focus their energy on self-preservation: looking busy, avoiding risks, managing perceptions, and figuring out how to please (or avoid displeasing) the leader. Their cognitive resources aren't available for problem-solving, collaboration, or customer focus. They wait to be told what to do instead of taking initiative.

Poor and toxic leadership comes in many forms. Table 15-1 illustrates a few archetypes that we've witnessed.

TABLE 15-1

Toxic leaders

Who	Shadow-casting behavior	Result
The Teflon leader	Takes credit for others' work and manages up. Avoids accountability. Doesn't provide resources and direction to teams.	Teams feel unsupported, unsafe, and confused.
The power abuser	Dominates decisions, cultivates an inner circle, and operates opaquely.	Teams feel resentful and excluded.
The micromanaging martyr	Controls every detail, complains about workload, and refuses to delegate.	Creates bottlenecks and stifles teams.
The drama monarch	Uses emotional volatility to control situations.	Teams feel anxious and drained.
The ice monarch	Treats employees as resources, rarely acknowledges individual contributions, and remains emotionally distant, unappreciative, aloof, and overly analytic.	Teams feel low trust and unseen.
[Add your shadow-casting leader type here]		

These archetypes describe some of the most extreme forms of poor leadership, but remember that in many cases, the behaviors are neither malicious nor even desired by the leader. Many leaders have blind spots about how they come off and the results of their behavior. When these blind spots are pointed out constructively, they're happy to fix them.

At its worst, this shadow cast by poor leadership actively corrodes culture and productivity broadly and contributes to the estimated $438 billion annual cost of lost productivity due to disengagement globally.[4] Adam Blitzer, COO of Datadog, calls it the "blast radius" of poor leadership. And the poorer and more toxic the leadership, the wider the blast radius.

But the root problem here isn't bad people or bad leaders; it's the organizational behavior of tolerating and even rewarding the leadership that casts the shadow. Leaders can change, but lasting improvement only comes when the organization changes the conditions that allow poor leadership to thrive in the first place.

What Octopus Organizations Do Instead

Octopus Organizations know the real definition of leadership. Professor Linda Hill of Harvard, who worked with leadership legends like Pixar's former CEO, Ed Catmull, distinguishes the perception of what a leader is from the reality (table 15-2).[5]

This shift from traditional leadership to authentic leadership requires a change in how leaders see themselves and their role. Unlike the command-and-control approach that relies on position and authority, Octopus leaders require continuous self-reflection and the courage to be vulnerable. The path to this transformation begins with honest introspection—recognizing their current impact and consciously choosing behaviors that invite collaboration rather than compliance.

Octopus leaders openly share their style and invite feedback, whether it's effusive, quiet, emotional, analytical, or animated. They adapt their approach based on their values and their understanding of their impact. High-energy leaders don't suppress their energy, for example, but develop the self-awareness to manage its impact and communicate in a way that bridges gaps. The naturally energetic, fast-talking leader doesn't need to become subdued. But they *can* learn the skill of pausing, listening actively, and ensuring that others feel heard in crucial conversations, adapting their *delivery* without changing their core personality.

Octopus Organizations weed out behaviors that create shadows with existing leaders and in recruitment. They understand that effectiveness

TABLE 15-2

Myths and realities of leadership

	Tin Man myth	Octopus reality
Defining characteristic	Authority: I decide what ideas get implemented	Interdependency: I need my people to be successful
Source of power	Formal authority: I decide	Respect: My people see how I can enable them
Desired outcome	Control: People do what they are told	Commitment: People understand what is needed and are committed to it
Key challenge	Keeping the business running	Getting everything out of the way to enable my people to be successful

hinges on self-awareness, active listening, empathetic communication, and the ability to foster collaboration across diverse groups, moving beyond outdated indicators of managerial potential. They screen for empathy and the capacity to hear and understand others. They ask interview questions like "What's the most interesting piece of feedback you've received recently? What made it interesting to you?" "What kind of feedback do you find yourself seeking out?" "What's something you've changed about how you work in the past year? What drove that change?" They revise job descriptions, performance review criteria, and promotion guidelines to explicitly include and weigh social skills, beyond "nice-to-haves." They invest in coaching and development, targeting social skills like active listening, empathetic communication, conflict resolution, and cross-cultural collaboration. They place high-potential leaders in roles that *oblige* them to interact with diverse groups.

Octopus Organizations fundamentally redefine leadership as a set of behaviors, not merely a role. Where traditional models might inadvertently amplify a leader's flaws by concentrating power, this approach recognizes that traits like decision-making prowess and intellect are no longer sufficient to earn genuine support. Instead, leadership now emerges organically from trust, capability, and influence, and transcends formal titles. You'll see this in action when someone without formal authority freely and confidently steps up to guide, solve, or mentor. Team members naturally gravitate toward colleagues who embody qualities like emotional intelligence, empathy, and sense-making—the very antithesis of shadow-casting behaviors of poor leadership. By ensuring that *everyone* practices this type of behavior and that these traits are injected into every role, Octopus Organizations democratize leadership.

Levers

^ **Speak last.** As a leader, hold your opinions until others have shared their views. Create an explicit invitation for others to speak first and use active listening in these situations. This prevents you and other leaders from dominating discussions, allows team members to express their ideas without immediate judgment, and encourages diverse ideas by preventing premature convergence.

^ **Build a shadow cabinet.** Cultivate a group of trusted individuals known for different perspectives and courage, outside leaders' direct report lines. Explicitly ask them to assess leadership styles, challenge assumptions, and point out blind spots. Use prompts to identify potential biases such as "What am I not seeing here?" and "How might my communication style be landing with the broader team?"[6]

^ **Check up.** Periodically revisit these five questions with honest self-assessment.[7] Do you:

- clearly communicate a vision?

- treat people with respect?

- solicit contrary opinions?

- encourage other people's ideas?

- truly listen to other people in meetings?

^ **Connect through shared experience.** Immerse yourself and other leaders occasionally in hands-on work alongside teams *as a learner and contributor*, not a "director." Focus on listening and asking questions with *humble inquiry*: "What's the most rewarding part of this task? What's the most frustrating?" Resist evaluating or directing unless specifically asked for coaching. This approach builds authentic connections, demonstrates humility and empathy, surfaces realities of those close to customers and technology, and strengthens relationships.

^ **Build multiple feedback mechanisms.** Include 360-degree feedback, exit interviews, skip-level meetings, and regular team retrospectives that focus on "how we work together." Where a psychologically safe environment is not yet in place, consider anonymous feedback options. What casual remarks do people make about you or your leaders? Use *feed forward* if you want to, for example, become a better listener.[8] Ask, "If I want to become a better listener, what are the two things I could do?" Instead of asking, "How did I do?" ask, "What's one thing I could do differently next time to make that process smoother?" or "What impact did my comment about X have on you?" Act on the feedback—"I heard the feedback about X. Here's what I'm going to try differently"—to build trust and show you value input.

^ **Stop one thing.** Don't try to become someone you are not. Own your authentic style but communicate it clearly. Focus instead on stopping *one specific behavior* identified through feedback that casts a negative shadow (such as interrupting, dismissive tone, checking phone in meetings, using sarcasm dismissively, sighing loudly when frustrated, rolling your eyes). Track progress on changing the one thing by seeking follow-up feedback.

Focusing on just one behavior makes change manageable and demonstrates commitment to self-improvement, while directly reducing the negative shadow's impact.

^ **Cultivate self-awareness.** Understand your own triggers and patterns. Keep a simple journal over several weeks. Note situations where you felt poor leadership behaviors creep in, when you may have felt frustrated, defensive, or impatient. What was your immediate reaction? What might have been a more constructive response?

^ **Model empathy and vulnerability.** Show up as human, show courage, acknowledging you don't have all the answers. Share relevant struggles or learnings: "I found that last negotiation challenging, and here's what I learned . . ." or "I made a mistake in assuming X, and we need to adjust course."

DISCOVER MORE   **ANTIPATTERNS TO READ NEXT**

#11: Guarding Information

#14: Operating on a Culture of Fear

#25: Granting Artificial Ownership

GATEKEEPING APPROVAL

Tenets and guardrails that remove checkpoints speed up teams.

THE TIN MAN BEHAVIOR

Creating complex, multilayered approval processes that disperse decision-making across multiple siloed functions

THE RESULTS

- Reduced agility, slow time to market
- Increased overhead and costs
- Decreased innovation, morale, and ownership

How Octopus Organizations Behave Instead

- They prioritize speed by letting teams make their own decisions but within guardrails.
- They automate checks and establish clear exception processes.
- They employ tenets that express core values and decision-making criteria to replace gatekeepers.

The Tin Man Behavior

In many Tin Man organizations delivering value requires what former Coca-Cola corporate CIO Miriam McLemore calls "running the gauntlet of everyone who can say no." When your innovative proposal gets dunked, spun, and transformed through layers of bureaucratic obstacles, it is soul-destroying when it emerges, unrecognizable from its original form, if it emerges at all.

Take a case we witnessed: A team developed a breakthrough feature for their company's insurance app that would let customers file claims by simply photographing damage—validation would take "just" twelve weeks. Initial user testing showed it could cut claim processing time by 60 percent. But as the team neared the finish line, their boss dropped the A-bomb: You need senior management "approval."

How ironic: a streamlined customer experience stuck in a bureaucratic maze. Legal wanted to review. Marketing's brand compliance reviewer also needed to cast an eye over the proposal. The user experience team needed to assess accessibility compliance. The "Office of the Chief Information Security Officer" (yes, really) needed to do a security and risk assessment, treating anyone who disagreed with their process as if they were suggesting the company use "password" as a password. Thanks to a legendary app disaster eight years before, even the CEO's team needed to have eyes on it in a governance meeting. Each department wielded veto power, sending the team back to revamp each time. Meanwhile, competitors launched, iterated, and improved the same feature. Frustrated team members started quitting at an alarming rate.

This is what gatekeeping yields: a loss of competitive advantage as the "time value of innovation" is eroded; a drain on resources as teams spend more time navigating the approval process than doing the real work; and a chilling effect on future innovation as teams, anticipating dealing with the approval machinery, just "live with" the problem.

Checks and balances aren't bad—in fact they are vital, particularly in highly regulated industries—but gatekeeping approval in Tin Man organizations tends to have grown arms and legs, and happens highly siloed, evaluating decisions through their narrow lenses—security assesses security risks, procurement assesses contract costs, compliance assesses policy. Each gatekeeper optimizes for their *own* domain's concerns. No one approval decision is wrong in itself, but collectively they make a solution unworkable, too slow, or too expensive in relation to the overall strategic value it's meant to deliver.

Worse still, the more gatekeepers there are, the more points at which anyone can say "no," which they will do for reasons unrelated to the value you're trying to deliver. Usually it's less risky to say "no." If they approve and something goes wrong, they may be held responsible. Since it takes only one "no" to stall, but everyone's "yes" to move ahead, this creates a powerful bias toward inaction.

To deal with gatekeepers, teams pad their timelines to accommodate the hurdles. But they also lose their sense of pride; they literally give up owning the outcomes. The rising complexity and waiting times drive away good innovators, while surviving ideas get diluted to fit approvers' comfort zones.[1] As Netflix's Reed Hastings noted about one challenging time at the company, "What we failed to understand was that by dummy-proofing all of the systems, we would have a system where only dummies would want to work there. Which is exactly what happened. The average intelligence fell and then the market changed and we were unable to adapt because we had a bunch of people who valued the process more than (free) thinking."[2]

What Octopus Organizations Do Instead

Octopus Organizations replace gatekeepers with guardrails. An organizational guardrail is a preestablished rule, principle, standard, or boundary built *into* the flow of the work. It defines a "safe-to-operate" zone, with activities or decisions falling outside the parameters typically triggering a review, consultation, or escalation process. Guardrails are aptly named, tracing back to a railway innovation, the simple flanged wheel—with its built-in guiding rim—which transformed rail transport by embedding guidance into the moving component itself. In Octopus Organizations good guardrails:

- *Speed up decisions* by reducing bottlenecks.

- *Improve quality* through clear criteria and feedback loops.

- *Increase efficiency* through automation and streamlined workflows.

- *Increase ownership and enhance curiosity* through more freedom for experimentation.

Guardrails can still be driven by certain functions, but the key is they enable all teams. They are clear, minimalist, easy to monitor, and periodically reviewed. Table 16-1 illustrates some types of guardrails.

While some actions will require approvals, much can be freed from gatekeeping. W. L. Gore shows how Octopus Organizations distinguish between guardrails and gatekeeping with *the waterline principle*.[3] Decisions above the waterline carry low risk—like putting a hole in a ship above water—and are managed through guardrails. Below-the-waterline decisions could sink the ship and thus require more thorough review.

Octopus Organizations use *tenets* as guardrails to speed up decision-making and guide behavior.[4] Tenets articulate core values, explicit trade-offs, and decision-making criteria. They are concise, practical, and have a defensible opposite. "Security is important" is not a good tenet since you'd never say "Security is unimportant."

Tenets are cocreated in collaboration with gatekeepers. In that way, gatekeepers become advisers rather than approval bottlenecks, and they leave

TABLE 16-1

Examples of guardrails

Guardrail	Example
Financial guardrails define limits on spending, investment criteria, and budget allocations, triggering reviews if limits are passed.	Ritz-Carlton employees can spend up to $2,000 per guest to resolve problems without seeking approval, guided by their "Ladies and Gentlemen serving Ladies and Gentlemen" credo.[a]
Technology and data governance guardrails define technology stacks, security and privacy standards, preferred software platforms, and components that are encouraged or required, triggering reviews when someone wants to implement a new or different tech.	Singapore bank DBS's "P-U-R-E" guardrails pre-approve common data and AI use, with only *new* or *riskier* paths requiring a deeper check.[b]
Ethical and cultural guardrails guide decision-making, especially in ambiguous situations. They often act as principles to consider rather than hard rules.	An HR department can implement a new AI hiring system without review, provided it doesn't introduce bias or flout company values.
Operational and process guardrails lay out standardized steps for critical processes (e.g., safety checks) and risk tolerance levels.	A manufacturing team follows a safety checklist before starting machinery. A customer service team can issue refunds of up to $100 without review, whereas larger refunds require manager approval.
Legal and compliance guardrails proffer in advance the laws, regulations, and internal policies that must be adhered to.	Teams can proceed with ideas that don't run afoul of regulations but must submit to review if there's any ambiguity.

[a.] Chris Richardson, "The Ritz-Carlton Approach to Customer Service: How Can You Apply Those Principles to Your Business?" *Effective Retail Leader*, https://www.effectiveretailleader.com/effective-retail-leader/the-ritz-carlton-approach-to-customer-service-how-can-you-apply-those-principles-to-your-business.
[b.] Fen Zhu et al., "DBS' AI Journey," Case 625-053 (Boston: Harvard Business School, 2025), https://www.hbs.edu/faculty/Pages/item.aspx?num=66332.

the collaboration with the confidence that they and the teams understand the basis for decisions.

An example tenet might be: *We optimize for speed.* Speed enables us to learn quickly, pivot if needed, and scale quickly. And the trade-off might be cost. (Indeed, another firm might have the tenet *We optimize for cost,* which may sacrifice speed.) Another could be: *We build to differentiate.* This might state that "we choose to buy and implement the most vanilla version of systems where they do not differentiate our value by changing business processes first. We are clear on what really differentiates our company." This sets a clear, explicit understanding that there needs to be clarity on the competitive advantage of an organization.[5]

Octopus Organizations make it easy for their teams to adopt guardrails, automating where possible to create what long-term Amazonian and cultural evangelist Stephen Brozovich calls "seductive adoption." One company we worked with took accessibility compliance requirements for websites and coded them into the standard website template, which removed an entire approval process and allowed the team to focus on delivering other value.

Octopus Organizations collaborate to transform gatekeeping into guardrails. The good news with guardrails is they will be *welcome*. Table 16-2 illustrates some transformations of gatekeepers into guardrails.

Miriam recalls when she was at Coca-Cola how shifting from gatekeeper governance to a guardrail mindset energized the teams. A fixed launch date for Coca-Cola's marketing at the Olympics and World Cup helped here, galvanizing everyone around the deadline. "The governance team was asking, 'What can we do to get to the finish line? What can we do to fix the problem?'" By replacing gatekeepers with guardrails, teams move faster, take greater ownership, and deliver better outcomes—all while maintaining the necessary checks and balances that protect the organization. They shift from "Can I?" to "How can I?" creating higher agency and ownership.

Levers

^ **Introduce "If/Then" guardrails for one common scenario.** Pick a recurring situation where teams often seek guidance or approval. Instead

TABLE 16-2

Guardrails turned into gatekeepers

Gatekeeper	Guardrail	Example
Bolting on security through external audits	*Building in* security into the development process	Embedding a security expert into the development team
Manual approval processes	*Automated* controls that embed policies into workflows	Automated expense approval below a set threshold
Service delivery between departments via service provider	*Self-service* of services that teams can use off the shelf with security and governance built in	Installing new software applications without IT intervention
Rules committees that approve ideas and projects	*Guidelines and insights* designed to steer groups to make good decisions and course correct if they err	A brand style guide for new marketing websites

of case-by-case decisions, define a simple "If X condition is met, then you are empowered to do Y; if Z condition is present, then consult [specific person/resource]." Graduating systems can be implemented where teams earn increasing degrees of autonomy based on track record.

- **Transform one gatekeeper pain point into a guardrail.** Connect with the gatekeeper and ask, "What is the absolute worst-case scenario this gate is trying to prevent?" Then ask, "Could a simpler rule, threshold, or checklist (a guardrail) prevent 80 percent of that risk while letting 80 percent of requests flow freely?" This will shift focus from process to actual risk mitigation, opening the door for simpler solutions.

- **Automate routine checks.** Convert manual approval steps into automated guardrails that provide immediate feedback, allowing teams to self-correct. For example, implement an automated procurement system with preferred vendor lists and budget tracking. Allow automatic approval for purchases within these parameters, only requiring manual review for exceptions. Or automate compliance checks that flag issues in real time rather than at review gates. Make these checks visible in dashboards to maintain transparency.

- **Transform gatekeepers into coaches.** Convert one gatekeeper into an early-stage adviser by scheduling regular office hours and proactive guidance sessions. For example, have Legal provide thirty-minute weekly clinics on compliance requirements rather than only engaging with them when they need to review completed work. Measure and reward experts based on how well they enable others' success rather than how many problems they catch after the fact.

- **Institute peer consultation networks.** Create networks of experts that teams can consult for guidance, replacing mandatory approvals with optional expert input. Develop such networks by mapping out and making visible the expertise across the organization so teams know whom to consult for guidance while maintaining decision ownership. Rotate experts periodically to spread knowledge and prevent dependency on individuals.

- **Establish feedback loops and escalation pathways.** Create mechanisms to learn from mistakes and adjust guardrails accordingly. Implement blameless postmortems to refine guardrails rather than adding new gatekeepers. Establish processes for situations that legitimately require exceptions to standard guardrails. Ensure that these processes are low friction so teams do not feel compelled to work around them.

^ **Delegate one small, low-risk decision with clear boundaries.** Identify one routine decision you (or another leader) currently approve that rarely gets rejected. Explicitly delegate it to a capable individual or team. Clearly state the "guardrails" (for instance, "You can decide on X as long as it aligns with Y customer principle and doesn't impact Z system").

^ **Run time-boxed guardrail experiments.** Replace one gatekeeper process with a simple guardrail for two weeks, track outcomes, then refine based on results. For example, "For the next sprint, teams can deploy non-customer-facing changes without QA approval if they meet this five-point checklist. We'll assess results next Friday."

DISCOVER MORE

ANTIPATTERNS TO READ NEXT

#10: Entrenching Silos

#17: Creating Dependencies

#21: Diluting Accountability

CREATING DEPENDENCIES

Self-sufficient teams that reduce reliance on others increase productivity exponentially.

THE TIN MAN BEHAVIOR

Operating with structures and processes that force teams to rely on other teams, resources, or external knowledge to get work done

THE RESULTS

- Fragmented ownership of outcomes
- Bottlenecks and delays hold up value delivery
- Reduced ability to see and react to threats or opportunities

How Octopus Organizations Behave Instead

- They see dependencies as defects that should be minimized or eliminated.
- They detect dependencies and reimagine team boundaries to eliminate them.
- They encourage escalations about dependencies to leadership to clear bottlenecks.

The Tin Man Behavior

Say we write a task on a sticky note for a single team to complete. The team takes it on, and the outcome is beautifully binary: They either complete the task or they don't. Assuming a competent team, there is a high likelihood that they succeed.

Now imagine there's one dependency attached to that task. We rip the sticky note in half and give one half to another team to do their part. Now there are four possible outcomes: Both teams complete it, neither team completes it, the first team completes it but the second team doesn't, or vice versa. Only one of these four is a productive outcome.

Let's add a second dependency. Three teams, A, B, and C, create eight possible outcomes. Each letter represents that group completing its part:

ABC   AB   BC   AC   A   B   C   None

Still only *one* of these, ABC, is a good outcome.

If you're mathematically inclined, you'll see that the likelihood of being successful is $1/2^n$, which means it exponentially decreases as dependencies increase. If we are upbeat and assume a 90 percent chance for completing our task successfully on time with one team, adding just *four* sequential dependencies reduces the success rate of completing the task to 66 percent.[1]

Unfortunately, Tin Man organizations are built on dependencies. They view dependencies as an inevitable consequence of their organizational design that can only be managed or ignored. Dependencies result from operational models built on a foundation of functional specialization, prizing the efficiency of dedicated teams of experts. A team of database administrators is kept 100% busy managing databases; a testing department is fully allocated to testing tasks. This design choice, however, hardwires dependencies into the system. To get any single piece of work done, teams are forced to wait on these specialized groups, each with its own queue and priorities. *The pursuit of resource efficiency (keeping people busy) actively undermines flow efficiency (keeping work moving smoothly toward the customer).* This structure doesn't just create delays; it makes the simple act of collaboration a daily, heroic effort.

Ultimately, dependencies destroy the flow of work by creating delays. Teams spend more time coordinating than problem-solving. A federation of silos trying to connect to get work done weakens ownership by any one team and makes learning and correcting course much more difficult. Classical project management becomes the de facto mechanism to get cross-functional work done, and it makes a meal out of recording, updating, and reporting every dependency as they try to deliver initiatives across silos, though often with little success.

Efficiency and specialization made sense in a twentieth-century manufacturing context. But complex knowledge work typically requires eight to fifteen teams, internal and external. Using our math above, even a small project with eight dependencies means 256 possible outcomes, only one of which is "everyone delivers on time." If you have fifteen teams needed for a project, you have one good outcome out of 32,768.

When bad results inevitably follow from the structural bias of dependencies, old-model organizations double down by creating more coordination, processes, and planning, which inevitably break down. That breakdown results in predictable, yet often counterproductive, coping mechanisms and heroics. Employees either "cheat"—working around processes that are slowing them down, like bypassing approval processes or using unofficial channels—or they use brute force to bust through the dependencies, for example, pulling resources from other teams and pulling "rank." This kind of behavior creates crises and drama as everyone competes for the limited resources to eliminate their own dependencies, resulting in ripple effects on other initiatives and exhausting people.

What Octopus Organizations Do Instead

Octopus Organizations audit and manage their dependencies. First, they sort them into one of three types:

1. *Knowledge dependencies* where expertise from others is required

2. *Task dependencies* that require an activity to be completed to unblock progress

3. *Resource dependencies* where people or things (software, tools, or inventory) are needed to move forward[2]

Next, with their categorized list, they assign one of four actions to each:

1. *Eliminate unnecessary dependencies.* Former Airbus CIO Luc Hennekens cites reducing the number of sign-offs and approvals needed for a task as a classic example of this action. For knowledge dependencies, for example, he advocates aiming for 80 percent of those to be fixed with cross-training, documentation, and education.

2. *Automate dependencies* through software, AI, and intelligent thresholds that eliminate unnecessary approvals. For example, with resource dependencies, many of the customers we work with enable teams to provision their own technology through self-service portals rather than being reliant on technology teams.

3. *Weaken dependencies* that can't be automated. Training or hiring talent with cross-functional skills will eliminate knowledge dependencies. A marketer with a finance background, for example, could reduce a budgeting dependency. Breaking down large systems into smaller ones weakens resource dependencies. Amazon weakens dependencies by relying on service teams, who proffer an API that replaces the need for onerous team communication and coordination to make updates to the website, enabling each team to independently release changes to the software, resulting in the ability to make up to five changes a second to Amazon.com.

4. *Systematically fix residual dependencies.* For example, multiple escalations of contract approvals would point to a systemic task dependency to address. Rather than triaging to just get a set of contracts approved, they would consider building in supplemental legal resources, creating pre-agreed legal templates, or embedding legal resources in teams.

Octopus Organizations set dependency thresholds. Not every team needs their own lawyer to work independently. Do you need a lawyer 90 percent of the time, 80 percent, or 40 percent? What's your threshold? Below X percent you receive a shared service instead of a dedicated lawyer. Some orgs use what's called "systemic swarming," moving specialists into teams *when* they need them such as at the most critical junctures, and then shifting them to swarm another team as work intensifies over there. Bath & Body Works CDTO Thilina Gunasinghe also advocates for setting up "war rooms" when a level of urgency is required to fix issues or accelerate deliverables. This isn't about pulling rank, but the prioritization of work and resources, breaking through the pretense Tin Man hides behind of being able to do everything.

Octopus Organizations foster an environment where beneficial "push dependencies" can naturally develop. The strongest collaborative relationships in organizations arise from voluntary association and mutual benefit, when teams recognize that being dependent on each other's value will create a multiplying effect. These self-initiated partnerships, or "pull dependencies," stand in stark contrast to the artificial and common "push dependencies" we've been addressing to this point. These voluntary networks tend to be more resilient and productive precisely because they arise from genuine need and shared purpose and desire, rather than organizational edict. They're much like effective co-parenting, where partners choose to rely on each other despite being capable of independent action.

Octopus Organizations accept a degree of duplication and build in slack to reduce dependencies. In Tin Man orgs, duplication is heresy: Efficiency is king. But we see duplicative efforts yield faster learnings and more creative solutions as different groups take different approaches to solving problems, then share and consolidate the best ones. Fashion retailer Zara uses *two* supply chains—one that produces trend-sensitive fashion faster, and a more mainstream one.[3] Similarly, Procter & Gamble diversifies its regional manufacturing to reduce dependencies on long-distance logistics.[4]

Octopus Organizations observe communication to detect dependencies and reimagine team boundaries to eliminate them. Awkwardness in interactions and unexpected communication between teams can be a sign of misplaced boundaries. If teams are communicating when they logically shouldn't be, based on structure and scope, it indicates a dependency problem. While collaboration is crucial for discovery and expertise, it becomes unnecessary overhead in areas focused on execution. Silicon Valley Product Group's Chris Jones advises organizations to "look how you divide teams up because there might be some ways that cause more frustrating, pathological dependencies than others." Octopus Organizations take a leaf from Mike Cohn, one of the originators of the Scrum product-development approach, when assessing their own teams' health, asking: "Does the structure minimize the number of communication paths between teams? Does the structure encourage teams to communicate who wouldn't otherwise do so?"[5] Where possible, Octopus Organizations create teams responsible end to end for developing and operating their own service. Each team contains all the necessary skills to operate independently, adhering to the "you build it, you run it" principle, and so minimizing inter-team dependencies to increase speed of delivery.

Levers

^ **Detect and track dependencies.** Visualize dependencies between teams. Doing so creates a common view of dependencies, which helps identify bottlenecks, improve communication, and optimize workflows. We take inspiration here from Dominica DeGrandis's book *Making Work Visible*.[6] She recommends the use of a physical dependency matrix, or "dependency tags," to identify and track dependencies, or a simple spreadsheet, to understand the communication needed to make these dependencies work well:

"Visualizing important cross-team information helps communicate across teams." Once widely visible, the reasons and assumptions for the dependencies can also start to be challenged.

- ^ **Encourage escalations.** Don't wait on dependencies. Encourage fast escalation through standard escalation paths to leadership to prevent delays from impacting multiple teams. Leaders should respond with "How can we help?" When people surface issues early, recognize them. Frame escalations as "raising visibility to unblock progress" rather than "complaining about delays." Focus discussion on the business impact and urgency rather than individual responsibility.

- ^ **Invest in cross-training.** Develop a structured program to train talent with both depth in their primary skill and breadth across related areas. Reduce bottlenecks caused by overreliance on specific individuals or teams for certain skills. Set explicit goals for key people to train others, using techniques like pair programming (two people sharing a screen and program together to cross-train) to force knowledge transfer. Invest in job rotations to enable similar cross-training more broadly across your organization.

- ^ **Establish resource dedication thresholds.** Create clear rules for when a resource (such as legal, design, or data science) should be dedicated to a team rather than shared. For example, if a team needs a specialist more than 80 percent of the time, embed that resource directly in the team. Below that threshold, organize as a shared service with clear service level agreements.

- ^ **Break down responsibilities.** Don't grow work beyond the cognitive capacity of the team responsible for that work. Remove or lessen dependencies on specific teams by breaking down their set of responsibilities and enabling other teams to take some of them on. For example, separate the activities of database development from database administration. Similarly, many publishers now separate content creation (writing articles) from content distribution (marketing), allowing experts to excel in their respective areas.

- ^ **Do a dependency deep dive.** When teams feel overwhelmed with dependencies, bring together subject matter experts and individuals involved in the work in question. Use sticky notes to map out the dependency landscape for teams and deliverables. Look for places where work stops as people wait for handoffs, approvals, or input from others. Question each dependency on the four possible actions: Can we eliminate it? Could it be automated? Could it be weakened? Could it be better managed?

DISCOVER MORE

ANTIPATTERNS TO READ NEXT

#10: Entrenching Silos

#16: Gatekeeping Approval

#18: Centralizing⟵⟶Decentralizing

CENTRALIZING ←→ DECENTRALIZING

A "glocal" approach stops the endless tug-of-war between central control and local freedom.

THE TIN MAN BEHAVIOR

Oscillating between a centralized model of operation and a decentralized one as overreactions to perceived weaknesses of the current model

THE RESULTS

- Periodic massive, costly projects to shift models
- Slow adaptation and lack of innovation when centralized
- Complexity and the inability to scale when decentralized

How Octopus Organizations Behave Instead

- They optimize for speed to value and reserve centralization for truly common needs that enable speed or compliance.
- They think "glocally," combining both global and local perspectives.
- They don't overreact to failures with one model or the other.

The Tin Man Behavior

This antipattern usually starts with noble intent: "What if we centralize decision-making around a single technology across our multinational operations to create efficiencies? After all, our business does the same thing in every country it operates in." So a team sets off to deploy a single payroll system across forty-three countries to replace seventeen existing systems.

A few years later, after discovering a global system is neither efficient nor cost-effective, new leaders promise something better. Something *agile*. Local business units control their own decisions, technology, and processes.

Fast-forward a couple more years: teams are duplicating work (and spend) across similar but different regional systems. Fresh leadership sees an opportunity to centralize it all and cut costs and waste.

The cycle repeats. This endless oscillation achieves neither efficiency nor agility while mortgaging future growth for short-term gains.

McDonald's experienced this cycle firsthand in the early 2000s. It was decentralized, operating in one hundred countries with distributed decision-making and different regional technologies. Scaling innovations like self-order kiosks required country-by-country integration work. So the CEO launched initiatives to standardize *everything* globally, from supply chain to finance to restaurant systems. This plan would enable the company to scale ideas quickly with economies of scale. It didn't go as planned, as social, political, fiscal, and cultural differences had to be accommodated in the new solutions, which created complexity, internal resistance, and declining customer service. By 2004, the initiatives were shut down, nearly $200 million was written off, and the CEO departed.[1] Back to the more local model.

We've heard this story repeatedly from organizations as diverse as the UK government and Coca-Cola, and it usually comes with a lot of tension. As Coca-Cola's former corporate CIO, Miriam McLemore, told us, "There is often a desire from the center for consistency and control [while] local markets are interested in driving unique value for their local business." Organizations treat centralization as the solution to chaos, and decentralization as the solution to rigidity, rather than tools for specific outcomes. The pendulum swings based on the most recent pain point, instead of by strategic design.

Top-down organizations often do not honor this tension, instead mandating a single approach. When we work with organizations, they often think in a binary way about this challenge. We can centralize procurement to achieve efficiency through volume discounts *or* local departments can independently negotiate procurement contracts, better navigating the complex web of local needs and vendor relationships. We can standardize customer relationship management (CRM) platforms to create a single customer view, consistent customer interaction, and the ability to perform company-wide analytics *or* we better use multiple systems to be able to deeply adjust to local customer needs and handle local privacy laws that could never be implemented centrally. We're certain you can add your own examples.

Whichever approach taken, it looks decisive from the leaders' perspective: "This is who we are."

Tin Man organizations all too often centralize with the intent to create more efficiency—that's not necessarily true. Or they decentralize because they think it drives agility—that's not necessarily true either. Often, the conflict is about misaligned incentives. For instance, when procurement organizations focus solely on cost savings without considering total cost of ownership—including service-quality impacts on the departments using those services—they create expensive downstream problems. The issue isn't whether procurement should be centralized or decentralized, but whether the incentives account for the full impact of decisions.

Centralized approaches create traffic jams as business demands overwhelm central offices. Decision-making becomes slow and compromised, satisfying no one and losing sight of the customer. Companies that centralize to outpace competition become disadvantaged against nimbler local competitors. Conversely, decentralization hinders scalability when successful innovations can't be transferred between businesses without significant rework. Complexity through fragmented tools and preferences compounds the issue. A European retailer we worked with allowed each technology team to choose their preferred development language, making code and talent sharing between groups nearly impossible.

The binary approach is self-fulfilling. Organizations often fall into either extreme—centralization or decentralization—but this will create technical debt and complexity that constrains future growth. Over-centralized systems become brittle monoliths that can't adapt to new markets. Over-decentralized systems create integration nightmares that prevent scaling innovations. The decision to go all in on one model or the other helps to create the problems that virtually ensure an overcorrection to the other model.

What Octopus Organizations Do Instead

Octopus Organizations optimize for *speed to value* while building foundations for sustainable growth. Former Qantas and Airbus CIO Luc Hennekens explains, "It's not a pendulum. It's a question of how we can optimize value." Rather than defaulting to either centralization or decentralization, they evaluate each decision through the lens of speed to value, asking what combination of centralized and decentralized elements will optimize for that. Mark Schwartz, former CIO of US Citizenship and Immigration Services, forces deeper thought on the purpose of centralization by assuming decentralization is the default starting point for speed to value. He would only centralize when doing so accelerated value. Centralization carries value with *anything truly common* (processes, digital platforms) *that enables the* *business units to operate faster.* It also tends to be valuable for regulatory, safety, or compliance systems and processes.

Octopus Organizations take a balanced view, embracing "glocalization"—adapting global strategies to local conditions.[2] Luc weighs in here, too: "I would refuse to see centralization and decentralization as opposites in eternal conflict for supremacy. It's more useful to see them as various tactics to manage decision-making and execution, in the same way as vanilla and strawberry ice cream aren't opposites but different flavors that can be combined." You might centralize the base e-commerce platform for consistency, but decentralize tax rules and provide sufficient flexibility for business units to innovate around marketing promotions.

This requires distributed capabilities within business units, guided by central oversight but allowing local flexibility. Former Schneider Electric President and AWS EMEA VP Tanuja Randery CBE emphasizes that "building an effective 'glocal' operation isn't accidental; it's born from a deliberate architecture where global strategic clarity and robust performance frameworks empower local P&L ownership. Autonomy is then earned and exercised within well-understood, shared boundaries."

McDonald's learned from its costly over-centralization by adopting a "glocal" model. The self-order kiosk at McDonald's became a success with this new approach. A global point of sale (POS) solution was created, but it was built with sufficient flexibility to support local fiscal needs and allowed innovative local marketing campaigns. Achieving agreement on what should be centralized and what shouldn't wasn't simple; it required cross-function, cross-business unit trust to be built up over time, and honest discussion about the trade-offs and differing perspectives. But it worked.

Octopus Organizations use an internal customer-obsession mindset, where central teams don't dictate but support the needs of the decentralized units. Think hub-and-spoke: centralized capabilities with decentralized execution.[3] The hub provides core services, platforms, and standards, while business units (spokes) retain autonomy over local operations and customer engagement using the central resources. Imagine "centers of enablement" or "platform teams" rather than "headquarters dictates."

Octopus Organizations adjust performance incentives. Former PepsiCo CEO Indra Nooyi advises rewarding individuals for overall business performance *and* their business units, and also for sharing ideas and adopting others' ideas. This encourages local innovation and experimentation to flourish while scaling good ideas effectively and efficiently. eBay demonstrates how this balance between centralized and decentralized incentives can lead to game-changing success. Under Meg Whitman's leadership, country

managers had significant autonomy and were rewarded for deeply understanding their customers and markets. The German team identified an
unmet local need around the year 2000—a cultural preference for fixed-price
transactions and impatience with auctions.[4] So, they developed a rudimen-
tary alternative to buy something on the site outright without an auction.
Country teams were measured on local success, so the success of this new
way to buy on eBay in Germany carried weight. At the same time, eBay had
structures for country managers to share local successes more centrally.
Eventually, the local innovation became the familiar Buy It Now button,
which revolutionized e-commerce, and the careful balance of incentives
made it happen locally and then scale globally.

Octopus Organizations centralize inclusively, across functional and
geographical boundaries to prevent one faction from deciding what is common among all parts of the business and worth centralizing. They avoid headquarters bias, which is the tendency for the home office to make decisions
based on what they see, missing out on complex in-depth knowledge of the
front lines. Coca-Cola's Miriam says, "You have to be very thoughtful about
what is a global standard and the trade-offs in risk tolerance, and speed of
delivery."

Ultimately, **Octopus Organizations reject the false binary choice
between the two models,** treating centralization and decentralization as
complementary tools rather than competing philosophies. This ensures their
strategies are useful and balanced, and allows them to break free from the
destructive pendulum swing, harnessing the full power of their distributed
intelligence while maintaining the cohesion necessary to execute at scale.
The success of Buy It Now from eBay is a perfect demonstration of this
balance. If eBay teams were only decentralized, the idea never would have
scaled, and if it were only centralized, it never even would have been created.

Levers

^ **Push work to the edges.** Even where centralized approaches or products are required, have business units drive the development or actively
participate. Inject centralized expertise and funding locally and expose
those representing centralization to unit challenges.

^ **Agree on decision-making tenets.** Develop explicit decision-making
tenets that distinguish what should be standardized (safety, security) versus what should be locally determined (market-specific elements). Review

these tenets regularly with diverse stakeholders to ensure continued relevance. Offer financial relief to business units if they are worried that surfacing an innovation will distract from making their goals.

^ **Use capability maps.** Maps show how your organization is assumed to run and the systems that support it. Pull processes and value streams apart to analyze what should be done centrally versus locally, whether for decision-making or execution. It becomes a focal point to debate where centralization may help and where decentralization may be valuable, whether decision-making or execution. Pick one process or system to map with local and global teams working together. Walk through the map, surfacing assumptions about commonality (or lack of) and pain points.

^ **Make your tech "glocal."** Design unified digital platforms that allow central management of core processes while providing tools for local customization. Build in flexibility from the start through APIs and configurable modules, enabling global scale with local relevance.

^ **Use minimum viable centralization (MVC) charters.** For new centralization possibilities, define the absolute minimum scope you could centralize while still realizing value. Explicitly define what remains decentralized. Review annually to prevent over-centralization.

^ **Create transparency; share credit.** Communicate actively, widely, and persistently how you're doing toward becoming a "glocal" company that balances centralization and decentralization. Recognize those who have contributed by name, not function or entity. Phil sent out a one-page update every week for seven years as McDonald's worked to find its balance. It builds confidence and transparency, acts as a vehicle for recognition and successes (or learnings), and gives everyone the ability to ask for more information.

^ **Run local innovation demo days.** Encourage decentralized innovation to gain centralized attention through virtual events where local teams showcase their local innovation. Create informal networks and reduce sharing barriers. Making local successes visible sparks ideas in other business units and creates informal networks, lowering the barrier to sharing.

^ **Offer solution bounties.** Release some centralized resources and/or funds to decentralized teams developing promising grassroots solutions to common problems. Temporarily embed an individual from a central team *into the local team.* Their role is to help the local team build the solution to scale, navigate central processes, and act as a liaison.

DISCOVER MORE

ANTIPATTERNS TO READ NEXT

#10: Entrenching Silos

#16: Gatekeeping Approval

#34: Segregating Technology

ANTIPATTERN #19

FETISHIZING PROCESS

Principles and a focus on outcomes
dismantle bureaucracy and accelerate
innovation.

THE TIN MAN BEHAVIOR

Managing risk through rigid adherence to procedures and responding
to failures with new processes to prevent future failures

THE RESULTS

- Focus shifts from serving customers to following rules.
- Bureaucratic complexity, costs, and time-to-value skyrocket.
- Learned helplessness sets in, paralyzing progress and ownership.

How Octopus Organizations Behave Instead

- They prioritize problem-solving over process adherence.
- They view processes as tools, not end goals or rules to live by.
- They aggressively simplify, automate, or eliminate as many processes as they can.

The Tin Man Behavior

Process devours judgment. What begins as helpful structure calcifies into bureaucracy, where adherence to procedure becomes the focus instead of achievement of outcomes. When process replaces thinking, organizations, like the Tin Man, lose their heart. As processes multiply to address every conceivable edge case and contingency, in a desire to codify behavior for scale, employees become operators kept busy with compliance rather than problem-solvers. Organizations become mechanistic—efficient at following their own rules but unable to adapt or innovate.[1] Educator Steve Blank warns that while process "ensures that you can deliver solutions that scale without breaking other parts of the organization, each layer of process reduces the ability to be agile and lean and—most importantly—be responsive to new opportunities and threats."[2] Rather than enabling an organization's mission, processes become the mission itself, creating an illusion of productivity while stifling and distracting from the very outcomes they were meant to help create.

In the extreme, compliance culture can lead to unfathomable outcomes. In 1999, 440 squirrels arrived in Amsterdam from China on their way to Greece on a KLM flight.[3] The paperwork that was supposed to accompany the cargo wasn't right, and established process dictated a horrifying next step: the disposal of the live animals in an industrial poultry shredder.

Outrage ensued, and KLM admitted "a grave mistake on ethical grounds." Yet the airline maintained it was merely following process and health regulations. Rigid adherence to process overrode good judgment. As one commentator remarked, "When you build a system, you are always building a model of the world, and if something happens which doesn't fit into your model . . . your system might do something awful."[4] We expect process compliance except when we don't.

Take the less existential case of the retail manager for a multimillion-dollar supermarket that made a $200 error on an expense report. The org responded by adding a second approval. Two years on, concerns about lax oversight from second-tier approvers prompted the addition of a third approval. Eventually, in this real case we witnessed, expenses required *ten* approval levels for employees who were otherwise trusted to manage significant P&L accounts. Years of layering on more complexity to originally well-intended processes get to the point where nobody can remember what the process was for, and people are too jaded to question why steps two through twenty of the approval process are needed.

Organizations don't always start this way. Some begin with principles and talented people tackling valuable work, but slouch into process-monsters as overreactions to single incidents and quixotic attempts to manage complexity and uncertainty. Often a deep-seated fear of failure prompts leaders to proliferate processes not because they improve outcomes, but because they provide a sense of control and a place to direct blame when things go wrong: "the process failed." Datadog COO Adam Blitzer describes it as, "One day you wake up and there is a rule of how many items can be on your desk. If you wait long enough you will have a rule for everything."

We use the word *process* in this antipattern as shorthand for many forms of bureaucracy, where rule adherence displaces the critical work of solving complex problems and creating valuable outcomes. It's especially prevalent where predefined paths are absent—which, no surprise, is the majority of today's knowledge work.

Process has its place. Companies like Toyota demonstrated process at its best, using standardized workflows to ensure quality while encouraging continuous improvement from frontline workers. Health care institutions rely on processes to prevent life-threatening errors.

But as processes multiply beyond their original purpose, they create labyrinths of approvals and documentation that distance workers from value creation. This bureaucratic expansion often follows what's called Parkinson's Law, named after a British naval historian who noted that the British Admiralty's staff grew even as its fleet shrank. It suggests that bureaucracy expands by 5 to 7 percent annually regardless of actual workload.[5] The more effort a task demands, the more important it seems to be, regardless of true value. Bureaucracy generates more bureaucracy.

The cost of this bureaucratic drag is staggering. One report suggests workers spend 41 percent of their time daily on work that doesn't contribute to value, the equivalent of more than eighteen working weeks per employee annually.[6] Gary Hamel and Michele Zanini say, "Bureaucracy is like pornography: it's hard to find anyone who'll defend it, but there's a lot of it about."[7] Indeed, 82 percent of organizations recognize the issue, but less than 10 percent are making progress addressing the problem.[8]

The consequences are profound. A culture of excessive process adherence fosters risk aversion and stifles innovation, leading people to develop "learned helplessness." When not following a process is seen as a potential career risk, individuals avoid ownership or exercising judgment. Innovation stalls as rigid rules cannot keep pace with change and complexity. Customer focus is replaced by an inward focus on "proxy" work where the completion of the process is seen as the actual work. Motivation drops as employees become bored and frustrated, expected to robotically comply with process that went from purposeful to bureaucratic over time, their skills and knowledge devalued.

What Octopus Organizations Do Instead

Octopus Organizations understand that fighting unnecessary bureaucracy is a continuous process.[9] They constantly evaluate processes against four questions:

- Can this work be *eliminated*?

- Can it be *simplified*?

- Can it be *automated*?

- Can *principles* replace rules?

So, for the company with the ten approvals for expense reports, an Octopus leader would ask:

- Can the approval process be *eliminated* by providing teams with budgets they own?

- Can it be *simplified* with two approvers, or approval only above a dollar threshold?

- Can approval be *automated* for spending below a dollar threshold, flagging only exceptions?

- Can it be *replaced with a principle* such as "spend money as if it were your own," supported by random audits?

Octopus Organizations embrace a substractive mindset, reflected in principles like Amazon's "Invent and simplify" or Zappos's "Do more with less."[10] Process is eliminated where possible and only applied for ensuring repeatability and predictability where essential.[11]

Octopus Organizations realize that eliminating process overhead often needs a jump start. This jump start might be symbolic to set the tone, like AstraZeneca's "Million Hour Challenge," a global grassroots initiative that challenged employees to collectively save a million hours through simplification across the company's business sites, commercial markets, and functions. It ultimately saved over 2 million hours through hundreds of simplification projects.[12] It involved both top-down changes and bottom-up local "simplification champions."

Pixar, the renowned animation studio known for films like *Toy Story* and *Finding Nemo*, introduced "Notes Day."[13] Just like film teams have days where they get "notes" on their product, Pixar shuts down for a day so employees could give notes on bureaucracy that had begun creeping into its culture, and cocreating possible solutions. Managers were deliberately excluded from certain discussions to encourage candid feedback. Many ideas were implemented, sending a strong signal that meaningful organizational change can come from trusting employees rather than imposing new procedures.

Octopus Organizations use principles, tenets, and guidelines to replace process whenever possible. CEO Reed Hastings uses the principle "Act in Netflix's best interests," which trusts people to make responsible decisions on travel, vacation, and more, obviating the need for voluminous policy.[14]

Southwest Airlines empowers frontline employees to make customer-focused decisions without managerial approval, such as compensating customers, making accommodations, and solving problems on the spot. Instead of handing out scripts, they give their teams permission to care. Founder Herb Kelleher said simply, "If you create an environment where the people truly participate, you don't need control. They know what needs to be done and they do it."[15]

Tenets are a particular, more granular type of principle that turn broader statements about what you value into actionable advice. Amazon uses tenets like "We optimize for speed. Speed enables us to learn quickly, pivot if needed, and scale quickly." Here a trade-off is explicitly being made that speed is being prioritized over, say, cost of functional completeness. Instead of writing "We value innovation," a meaningless, unactionable phrase, a tenet might say, "Bias for action over endless analysis. We test, learn, and iterate rapidly, embracing informed risk for significant customer benefit."

Guidelines tell you in more detail how things are done, but they are still different and preferable to processes that prescribe *how* to do things, thereby removing any opportunity to think or demonstrate ownership. For example, "When designing a new feature, fill out the new feature feedback form, then submit it to the review panel for consideration" is a process. Whereas "When designing a new feature, gain feedback from at least four different customer demographics" is a guideline.

Octopus Organizations accept the occasional risk of poor judgment from using principles, tenets, and guidelines, understanding that preventing a handful of bad decisions isn't worth sacrificing thousands of good ones.

Octopus Organizations think of process in terms of friction. When there's too much process, they remove friction, such as Apple deploying handheld checkout devices in its stores to remove cumbersome point-of-sale processes. When there's not enough friction to prevent processes from emerging, they add it. When Google's interview process ballooned to as many as twenty-five rounds per candidate, Laszlo Bock created productive friction by requiring his approval for any candidate facing more than four interviews.[16] This simple executive barrier eliminated unnecessary interviews without compromising talent quality.

Where bureaucracy is necessary, such as for regulatory compliance or critical safety standards, Octopus Organizations implement *minimum viable policies*.[17] They create the leanest possible set of rules or process steps required, designed with built-in flexibility and iteration.

Finally, **Octopus Organizations encourage employees to challenge existing processes.** They reward the "bureaucracy-buster of the quarter" and create a channel for people to share their ideas on eliminating or simplifying processes, like Amazon's "no bureaucracy" email alias, which allows anyone to flag their idea or frustration to leadership.[18] The more entrenched the bureaucracy, the greater the enthusiasm you'll likely find from individuals eager to participate. But this only works if suggestions are actioned, or else the anti-bureaucracy process becomes just another form of bureaucracy!

Levers

˄ **Develop tenets to replace a process.** Identify one slow, bureaucratic process your team regularly encounters. Have individuals write down four to seven tenets that could guide actions and decisions in place of that process, based on "X is more important than Y." Group similar ideas on a board, discuss emerging patterns, and vote on the top themes. Write simple, clear, actionable statements for each tenet, then pilot these tenets instead of the formal process for two weeks.

˄ **Calculate your BMI and relentlessly reduce it.** Gary and Michele introduced the concept of a Bureaucratic Mass Index, or BMI, as a measure of organizational bloat.[19] Our simplified version looks like this:

$$(NVA + W/T)*100 = BMI\%$$

NVA is non-value-adding time spent on processes like documentation, sign-offs, and so forth. *W* is waiting time spent before value-added activities can continue, like waiting for approval of a budget request. *T* is the total hours in the time you're measuring. The 100 makes the BMI a percentage.

Imagine a developer who spends twenty hours one week on non-value-add activities and another five waiting on others. That developer's BMI would look like this:

$$(20 + 5/40)*100 = 62.5\% \text{ BMI}$$

Have teams keep a simple two-week log of processes they follow along with NVA and W. Calculate the BMI and then target a 10 percent reduction. Reward those who find ways to hit the target and adopt their strategies.

˄ **Deep dive into your workflow.** Assemble a small, diverse, and cross-functional team comprising both newer and tenured employees. Give them a mandate and time frame to "attack" a specific, critical process. Their goal is to design a radically new approach that would demonstrably decrease process and improve speed, customer satisfaction, and/or employee experience by replacing process adherence with ownership. Ask the following questions individually and then in a group to identify opportunities:

- What are we doing that was once useful but is now in the way?

- What is adding needless friction?

- What is impeding teams applying their curiosity?

- If you could change one thing today, what would it be? What is stopping this change?[20]

^ **Implement minimum viable policies and process expiration dates.** Adopt a default stance of minimalism for internal rules. New policies should be the absolute leanest necessary to address a clear, evidence-based, recurring problem. Avoid preemptive, comprehensive rulebooks. Institute process expiration dates for all non-critical internal processes. To continue beyond a set period (say, twelve to twenty-four months), a process must be actively reviewed, re-justified based on current value, and re-approved; otherwise, it automatically lapses.[21]

^ **Automate processes.** Identify automation opportunities using, for example, robotic process automation (RPA) or AI. Focus on reducing friction for necessary tasks.

DISCOVER MORE

ANTIPATTERNS TO READ NEXT

#14: Operating on a Culture of Fear

#16: Gatekeeping Approval

#21: Diluting Accountability

SEEKING PERFECT DECISIONS

Good enough, reversible decisions encourage speed, learning, and growth.

THE TIN MAN BEHAVIOR

Overrelying on data, exhaustive analysis, and many stakeholders to remove as much uncertainty and risk as possible before making the "right" decision

THE RESULTS

- Analysis paralysis
- Slow and mediocre decisions driven by consensus
- Convoluted or diluted ownership of decision-making

How Octopus Organizations Behave Instead

- They embrace good-enough decisions when they are reversible, valuing speed and learning over obsessing to get them right every time.
- They embrace uncertainty by fostering probabilistic thinking and viewing decisions as bets.
- They turn decision-making into a teachable and deliberate practice.

The Tin Man Behavior

What happens when an organization becomes so afraid of making the wrong decision that it forgets how to make any decision at all? Decision paralysis sets in, often from what feels like an overwhelming number of choices, excessive analysis, or a fear our decisions will bring negative consequences. In many organizations, the fear of failure has become so pervasive that making no decision feels safer than making the wrong one—even when inaction itself becomes the failure. This is natural: Losses make us feel twice as bad as wins make us feel good.[1] Our brains evolved to create certainty, finding predictable connections to survive, which is why most of us are deeply uncomfortable with uncertainty and keep looking for connections, especially when careers feel at stake.

But decision paralysis carries its own existential threats. Intel's indecision on entering the mobile and GPU markets, fueled by data gathering and concerns about shareholder reactions, helped Advanced Micro Devices (AMD) gain ground, costing Intel billions in market value.[2] Octopus Organizations are not immune to this either: Netflix's prolonged deliberation over an ad-supported tier saw competitors capture market share, reportedly contributing to a slowdown in subscriber growth.[3]

The fear of a "wrong" decision, especially in intricate hierarchies laden with opinions, unclear decision rights, and dependencies—the organizational equivalent of hidden tripwires—encourages efforts to find an absolute right decision with the least possible risk. Organizations fall into relentless information gathering, as if more data will erase uncertainty, when all it usually does is present more potential options. This is often compounded by cognitive biases like confirmation bias, where individuals seek out and favor information that confirms their beliefs, further slowing the process if new data suggests a different path. While more options seem appealing, they often overwhelm, leading to inaction.

In one notable study, researchers found that if you sold jam at two tables, one with twenty-four options and the other with six, the table with twenty-four options attracted more shoppers (60 percent vs. 40 percent), but resulted in sales just 3 percent of times compared to 30 percent at the simpler table. That's ten times the sales from one-fourth the options. At the table with twenty-four choices, the possibility of making the "wrong" choice increases dramatically. The fear of failure—of choosing poorly and regretting it—becomes paralyzing when multiplied across dozens of options. Choosing one jam might be perceived as "losing out" on the potential enjoyment of the other twenty-three. This potential "loss" sends us to the safest option: *inaction*, also known as *status quo bias*.

Now you, the leader, are the customer in this scenario. Replace "24 jams" with "240 strategy decisions" or "120 revenue ideas" or "24 CFO candidates."

The sheer scale of uncertainty from so much information to consider is, neurologically speaking, unnerving:

- When faced with too many options, decision-makers feel overwhelmed.

- Collecting more data feels good but compounds the issue. Fragmented data, reluctance to share, and differing interpretations add to the issue.

- More people get pulled into the decision process, often for political cover or perceived need for widespread expertise, thereby diluting accountability and slowing down the decision.

- The longer we take to make decisions, the more we become invested in them; cognitive biases like loss aversion and sunk cost fallacy make it harder to change our minds.

After all the deliberation, when decisions do result in a good outcome, people often point to the process as sound, and so this painful prolonged process sets the bar for the organization. But it's a trap explained to us by Annie Duke, former professional poker player and decision-making expert. She calls it "resulting," which means we conflate decision quality with its outcome.[4] But in a complex world, good decisions can lead to bad results (and vice versa with a bit of luck). The failure to distinguish process from outcome creates a vicious cycle of more data collection, analysis, and conferring. Ironically, the eventual decision that's made, no matter how perfect we think we got it, might still lead to a bad outcome. It just happened much more . . . slowly.

What Octopus Organizations Do Instead

Octopus Organizations recognize that exhaustive decision-making processes don't guarantee better outcomes in complex, uncertain environments. They help people get comfortable with uncertainty, and decision-making under uncertainty. Here is how they do this:

Octopus Organizations distinguish between high-stakes and low-stakes decisions. High-stakes decisions are hard to reverse and carry significant negative consequences if wrong, like picking a new CEO or deciding to open a new location. Low-stakes decisions are reversible and create a smaller "blast radius" if they're wrong, like deciding on a temporary product discount in a store or adding a feature to a website. Organizations often treat *all* decisions as irreversible, leading to unnecessary effort and paralysis. For low-stakes decisions, Octopus Orgs encourage fast, imperfect decision-making, even informed intuition. Amazon (which uses the metaphor of one-way doors for high-stakes and two-way doors for low-stakes) encourages people to take these with about 70 percent of the information they wish they had. If it doesn't work, well, you learned and it's reversible. Course correct.

Even for these high-stakes decisions, Octopus Organizations *maintain momentum by setting clear timelines, assigning clear decision owners, and defining decision criteria* to avoid falling into endless analysis loops.

Octopus Organizations fight decision paralysis with estimation. Nobel laureate physicist Enrico Fermi's "Fermi problems" can teach organizations how to break complex decisions into estimable parts based on reasonable assumptions. This method is renowned for creating surprisingly accurate results with limited data. For example, his approach enabled students to make an accurate decision about how many piano tuners there were in Chicago, by connecting a series of estimations. It went like this:

- What is the population of Chicago? [~3 million]

- How many households are there in Chicago? [Assuming an average of about 2.5 people per household, roughly 1.2 million]

- What percentage of households own a piano? [Let's say 1 in 10, so about 120,000.]

- How often does a piano need tuning? [Once a year on average? So, about 120,000 piano tunings per year.]

- How many pianos can a tuner service in a year? [Let's assume a tuner works five days a week, fifty weeks a year, and tunes four pianos daily, giving 250 days * 4 pianos/day = 1,000 pianos per year.]

- So that's about 120 piano tuners.

The Tin Man organization faced with a similar challenge pertinent to their business might default to months of data collection and might even treat estimation as a bad practice. But it's not. This approach helps overcome decision paralysis by:

- Breaking down intimidation—making a large ambiguous problem into smaller, more specific ones.

- Embracing uncertainty—accepting imperfect data and educated guesses, normalizing uncertainty's inevitable presence.

- Revealing hidden knowledge—making explicit what people already know.

- Focusing on critical variables—identifying uncertain or influential assumptions to refine, avoiding irrelevant details.

- Fostering probabilistic thinking—encouraging thinking in ranges.

- Enabling faster action—accepting reasonable approximations, treating decisions as learning opportunities.

Octopus Organizations view decisions as bets and adopt a "probabilistic mindset." "I'm not sure" or "I'm 70 percent certain" is not a sign of weakness, but a vital step to seeing the world more accurately. Making uncertainty explicit allows articulating a "chain of thought" that reveals our understanding of the inherent uncertainties, and examining beliefs and decision biases. A Q1 sales estimate shifts from deciding on a single, paralyzing number we feel like we have to get "right" to exploring a probable range we can manage.

Octopus Organizations accelerate decisions by shifting from "picking" to "sorting," a powerful distinction made by decision expert Annie. "Picking" is the agonizing process of trying to find the single best option among several good ones—like a marketing team spending weeks to determine the perfect campaign from five strong candidates. The effort rarely justifies the marginal gain. "Sorting," in contrast, is the rapid process of categorizing options into "good enough to try" and "not worth pursuing right now" based on clear, simple criteria. An Octopus Organization would quickly sort the campaigns, launch the most promising one to get real market feedback, and iterate. When options are roughly equivalent and the cost of reversal is low, the goal isn't to be perfectly right up front, but to learn as fast as possible.

Octopus Organizations define tenets to speed up decision-making. Tenets are fundamental principles or beliefs that guide choices—simple, memorable statements that help teams quickly evaluate options without lengthy deliberation. They act as decision-making shortcuts, allowing teams to sort through alternatives rapidly by asking whether each option aligns with these core principles.[5]

Octopus Organizations tightly manage the number of voices contributing to a decision. Smaller groups (ideally under five) are effective for high-velocity decisions, and those small groups work best when they bring diverse views, focus on accuracy over confirmation, and reward truth seeking, objectivity, open-mindedness, and outcome accountability.[6]

Octopus Organizations channel disagreement over decisions productively. They use approaches like *disagree and commit*, in which all input is heard and valued, but once a decision is made, everyone is expected to commit to the decision. This requires trust that the decision-maker will listen to countervailing evidence as it emerges and change course if proven wrong.

Finally, **Octopus Organizations make getting better at decisions a practice.** Decisions are documented along with assumptions, process, and other pertinent factors for *fielding*—the disciplined process of analyzing how much of a decision's outcome was due to skill and how much to luck. Usually both play some role. Documenting and regularly examining and revisiting decisions help improve decision-making quality, and help mitigate resulting. This practice also enables people who come new into the organization to study how decisions are made. Ray Dalio's Bridgewater Associates uses a "believability factor," weighing input from those with a documented track record of making good decisions and clearly explaining the cause-effect relationship of their opinion.[7]

Levers

^ **Accelerate decision speed.** For every decision, ask: "How can I make this decision lower-stakes and faster?" Is it a reversible decision? If so, take it with 70 percent of the information you wish you had. Use Fermi estimations to reach a decision more quickly. Push decisions closest to the customer or problem information to improve speed and ownership. When considering a decision, ask:

- What would allow the team to make decisions quickly with incomplete information?

- What would enable the team to get aligned on decisions faster?

- Is the decision reversible? If not, can it be made so?

- What is the cost of delay versus the cost of being wrong?

- What are we really afraid will happen if wrong?

- What would make us revisit this decision later?

^ **Review decisions as you would investments.** To learn and improve, capture the decision process. Record rationale, assumptions, strength of opinions for qualitative aspects, ranges for quantitative estimates, and dissenting views. Review them when results come in to understand flaws and strengths in underlying mental models and to inform future decisions. Focus on process, not just outcome. Ask, "What did we get right? What did we miss? What did we learn?" This systematic review fosters a learning culture and allows for course correction.

^ **Think in bets.** Ask teams to express estimates, forecasts, and recommendations probabilistically. Examine belief accuracy that informed their decision: Why might the belief not be true? What other evidence exists?

What information sources were missed or minimized on the way to reaching the belief? Why might someone else believe something else? What's their support, and why might they be right instead? What other perspectives are there as to why things turn out the way they do?[8]

^ **Practice "disagree and commit."** Embed structured dissent into your decision-making process. Explicitly set expectations for teams to debate rigorously, then commit fully regardless of individual preferences. Assign "devil's advocate" roles to challenge decisions and uncover blind spots.

^ **Check decision commitment.** Post-decision, check in with initial dissenters, who can safely provide feedback based on new data, reinforcing that decision commitment adapts to evidence. Publicly reward employees whose dissenting views improved the final decisions, even when their suggestions weren't adopted.

^ **Define your sort criteria up front.** Before you begin evaluating options for your next initiative, have the team explicitly define and write down three to five simple "sorting criteria." These are the absolute must-haves for an option to even be considered (e.g., "Must be executable within Q3," "Must target our core customer demographic," "Must not require new head count"). Use this list to rapidly sort all incoming ideas into two buckets: "Meets the Bar" and "Doesn't." This forces a focus on what's essential and prevents the team from falling in love with attractive ideas that are ultimately unworkable, turning a long "picking" debate into a fast "sorting" exercise.

^ **Implement a "two good options" rule.** For your next low-stakes, reversible decision, deliberately stop the analysis process as soon as your team has identified two high-quality, viable options. Frame the final choice not as a search for perfection but as a simple pick between two good paths. Ask the team: "If we could only have one of these, would we be happy?" If the answer is yes for both, flip a coin or have the decision owner make a quick call. The goal is to feel the liberation of moving forward and to train your team to recognize when analysis offers diminishing returns.

DISCOVER MORE

ANTIPATTERNS TO READ NEXT

#16: Gatekeeping Approval

#19: Fetishizing Process

#33: Deferring to Data

DILUTING ACCOUNTABILITY

For breakfast, chickens contribute, but pigs *commit*; they foster action and engaged teams.

THE TIN MAN BEHAVIOR

Giving many people a partial say in decisions without any one person having final say or owning outcomes

THE RESULTS

- Painfully slow, inconsistent, punted decision-making
- Stalled and failed initiatives
- Paralysis and a blame culture ensue

How Octopus Organizations Behave Instead

- They empower "single-threaded leaders" who have authority over and accountability for decisions and deliverables.
- They value, coach, and reward people who take ownership of decisions and outcomes.
- They actively fight against indecision masked as consensus building and lack of ownership.

The Tin Man Behavior

A chicken and a pig are walking down the street together. The chicken says,
*   "Hey, shall we open a restaurant together?"*
The pig asks, "Sure, what shall we serve?"
The chicken replies, "Ham and eggs!"
The pig stops and says, "You realize, for you that's a contribution. For me,
*   that's total commitment."*

This joke holds a fundamental truth about ownership in organizations: there's a stark difference between those who *contribute* and those who are *committed* and accountable. We have observed this difference in many companies. There's a "critical transformation initiative" (their words, not ours) with hundreds of millions of dollars thrown at it that makes headlines for its audacity. Meetings about the project are filled with chickens happy to contribute their eggs, in the form of opinions, support for the consensus, and partial approvals.

When it comes to identifying the one person accountable for making tough calls and standing by them, and owning the delivery of the promised value, few want to be the pig. We've seen this create a black hole of accountability, where work is being done but outcomes vanish. We've even seen unclear ownership lead to "zombie projects" that continue to sap resources despite no owners and no real progress, like one Phil experienced, a "smart equipment project" in McDonald's that dragged on for seven years.

Disclaimed accountability comes in many forms. Organizations:

- *delay key decisions* because of an ever-expanding list of stakeholders who need to be "in the loop" but none of whom own the decision.

- *blame other groups and deflect responsibility* when setbacks occur because accountability was never clear.

- *leave support functions to lead what should be owned by functional teams.* We've seen companies allowing the support functions to make key decisions on major revenue-generating projects, rather than the actual P&L owners. That misattribution leads to decisions and solutioning based on support function priorities or their distant understanding of the business and customer needs.

- *create faux ownership* that looks like a single point of accountability but doesn't act like it. The COO of one company we worked with told his team he was the ultimate owner of six strategic initiatives, yet he never turned up to any of the steering groups or took an active ownership role.

Silos are the structural obstacle here. Incentives are the girding. They're typically tied to goals *within* a functional silo, not to the success of cross-functional outcomes. This makes true end-to-end ownership across teams unappealing and fraught with peril. Why would anyone in their sane mind want to volunteer, especially if the organizational culture punishes perceived "failure?" It becomes safer to be *a* voice at the table.

Nowhere is chicken behavior more painfully visible than in an organization's meeting culture. Many spend more time *meeting* about work than *doing* value-creating work. Flocks of chickens migrate from one meeting to another, laying their eggs whether they're needed or not. A significant portion of meetings are unproductive, costing 24 billion hours annually in the United States alone.[1] As Jason Fried and David Heinemeier Hansson note in their book *Rework*, meetings "are usually about words and abstract concepts, not real things . . . and usually convey an abysmally small amount of information."[2] They are a way to be part of the conversation without owning the work. Ten people in a one-hour meeting that could have been a fifteen-minute conversation with three people equates to a massive drain on productivity.

Tin Man organizations built on hierarchy might just turn to their org chart to signal ownership, but that doesn't mean the person at the top of some group with a major project will *take* ownership, even if it's assumed or assigned. After all, no pig wants to become ham.

What Octopus Organizations Do Instead

Octopus Organizations treat clarity of ownership as a fundamental prerequisite for success. They champion the concept of *single-threaded leaders* (STLs), or a similar construct of dedicated outcome ownership (for example, Apple calls it a Directly Responsible Individual, or DRI). Such an individual is accountable for delivering a meaningful outcome and making the necessary decisions to achieve it. They are expected to inject energy and urgency into initiatives, and as former US government CIO and author Mark Schwartz explains, not be passive "champions." They dive deep into issues, maintain and communicate the vision of what success looks like, and keep teams moving forward. They push every day on progress and actively remove impediments. That means *more doing* the work and *less talking about it* in meetings. Their singular focus and ownership and close alignment with execution responsibility makes for much faster decision-making.

Octopus Organizations set up single-threaded leaders for success by:

- *creating clarity* on the scope of ownership, the strategic context, the desired outcome, and how it contributes to the broader strategy (metrics make this tangible).

- *granting genuine authority* to the leader to decide *how* work gets done and *who* to involve (within organizational guardrails, of course).

- *providing coaching and support* to help the owner develop skills and confidence.

- *establishing rapid escalation paths* when roadblocks emerge. Amazon, for instance, encourages fast, early, and "high" escalations.

- *creating a psychologically safe environment* where leaders feel able to make tough decisions, take calculated risks, and even voice concerns or challenge the status quo without fear of retribution.

- *aligning their incentives* to the sustainable success of the outcome, allowing single-threaded leaders to think and act like true long-term owners.

The act of assigning STLs has added benefits. It forces prioritization of initiatives, as there aren't an endless number of leaders to fulfill such a role. If the organization is struggling to appoint a person because they're worried about what they'll be taking them away from, then the initiative may not be that critical.

You might think it's risky giving one individual so much "power"—what if they make wrong decisions, or deliver badly? But the Tin Man system of diffused responsibility is *already* incredibly risky and costly (cost of indecision, resource-intense, slow), just in ways most of us have normalized. The STL model introduces a different type of risk that is more visible and manageable, and comes with a much higher potential for speed, clarity, and actual delivery. An STL is not an unchecked autocrat. They have a clear mandate with clear scope and guardrails in place.

Octopus Organizations treat consensus-seeking as a red flag for indecision. To prevent endless circular debates among chickens, they value input but adopt approaches such as "disagree and commit," by which individuals can ask clarifying questions and debate approaches and solutions, using evidence and anecdotes, but with the expectation that people leave the room fully committed to the decision the STL makes. Trust is key: contributors trust the STL will continue to listen to counterpoints and adapt if new evidence emerges.

In Octopus Organizations action is the default, not discussion. Rather than pre-scheduled status meetings where the chicken flock gathers to be "informed" or "consulted," constantly interrupting work, STLs are trusted to get on with the work. Leaders can join team status sessions or pull automated progress data, but they don't demand their own status updates. Meetings are convened to solve problems together when needed, not scheduled weekly like talk shows about what's been done.

This commitment to clear ownership not only accelerates delivery and improves outcomes but also fosters a more engaged, self-directing, and capable workforce. Taking on single-threaded-leader-like roles becomes a significant career development opportunity, or as Mark calls it, a "good test of leadership."

Levers

^ **Establish your "pig" language.** Whether it's "single-threaded leader," "directly responsible individual," "outcome owner," "driver vs. passenger," or a term unique to your culture, create a shared vocabulary that makes it safe and normal to ask: "Who is the 'pig' for this initiative?" The key is making it safe and normal to ask: "Are you here to advise, or are you here to own?"

^ **Appoint true STLs.** Define a dedicated owner for each critical initiative who has the authority and accountability for outcomes. Provide the time, clarity, and coaching outlined above. In initiative documentation, label decisions with the name of the person responsible.

^ **Spotlight ownership in action.** Create rituals (formal and informal) to recognize individuals who take full ownership. Share stories of their actions and impact: "Lena saw the customer deadline risk and pulled together three teams and owned the problem." Celebrate both the visible wins and the behind-the-scenes heavy lifting. Make it clear: the organization notices and values the courage to take ownership.

^ **Rethink meetings.** Since they are a driver of chicken behavior and disclaiming ownership, find ways to turn meetings into sessions where decisions are owned and made. Meet at the site of the problem instead of a conference room. At the outset of a meeting, explicitly name the single individual accountable for a decision *before* discussion begins. That person should articulate the basis on which the decision will be made. As the owner of an initiative, aggressively cut meetings that have weak agendas or are dedicated solely to status updates. Encourage people not needed at a meeting to leave and get back to work. Demonstrate the value of cutting meetings by calculating the true cost of recurring meetings (hourly salary × number of attendees × meeting duration × frequency). Share this figure with meeting owners and ask them to justify the expense. Set a target for reducing meeting costs by 25 to 50 percent over six months, and track progress visually.

^ **Surface and address "chicken" behavior.** Create non-confrontational prompts to challenge passive participation in decision-making. "For this decision, we need people who can commit resources or approve changes—are you here to own part of this solution?" "Are you contributing expertise, or are you accountable for making this happen?"

^ **Hire and assess for "ownership."** Ask ownership-focused questions to candidates during hiring, such as "What kind of problems do you like to own? What is it about these types of problems? What does ownership mean to you when it comes to initiatives?" Create ownership assignments in onboarding: for example, give new hires an improvement project with unclear boundaries and minimal direction. Pair them with experienced "owners" for mentoring. In performance reviews, specifically evaluate evidence of ownership: "Tell me about an instance where you saw a gap and filled it without being asked."

^ **Implement a "chicken tax."** If someone attends the meeting without taking ownership, they have to contribute to a "chicken tax"—this could be a small donation to a team fund or a fun task. This raises the stakes and makes it clear in a humorous and psychologically safe way that passive participation is not acceptable.

^ **Train on ownership.** Create "ownership incubators"—small, low-risk projects where teams can practice owning decisions. Assign experienced mentors who guide, then step back. Begin weekly ownership circles where teams share real challenges and workshop solutions together—focusing first on problems people actually care about fixing.

DISCOVER MORE

ANTIPATTERNS TO READ NEXT

#16: Gatekeeping Approval

#20: Seeking Perfect Decisions

#26: Evading Failure

HIRING POORLY

A focus on learning agility and values over credentials increases long-term value.

THE TIN MAN BEHAVIOR

Hiring transactionally, driven by skill-laden job descriptions and immediate needs, and treating onboarding as a perfunctory administrative task

THE RESULTS

- Rigid workforce, struggling to adapt to meet evolving customer needs or quickly capitalize on new technologies
- Increased turnover, recruitment, and training waste
- Amplification of existing skills gaps and weaknesses

How Octopus Organizations Behave Instead

- They treat hiring as a critical strategic priority.
- They prioritize values alignment and learning agility over current skill fit of new hires.
- They invest in comprehensive, long-term onboarding programs.
- They only hire when absolutely necessary.

The Tin Man Behavior

If you want to know whether an organization is Tin Man, pay attention to its hiring and onboarding practices. Job descriptions are a good starting point: the bullet-point list of tasks the person will do indicates a focus on activities, not outcomes. The long list of skills required shows a focus on individual aptitude ("must be a team player" is still an individual aptitude unless you enumerate specific collaborative skills). Demands for some set number of years of experience, and a degree of any sort, suggest a box-checking process to filter candidates on reasonably arbitrary measures. Such rigid descriptions attract a rigid, narrow talent.

The same rigidity in the screening process, which is increasingly left to machines, eliminates qualified candidates. ("Lorraine didn't have a keyword mentioned in her résumé!"). For the remaining candidates the interview ~~process~~ trial is conducted by managers untrained in effective interviewing who ask questions and proffer observations inadvertently clouded by personal biases. Candidates similar to them are appealing, whether in education, age, race, or other traits. One study showed that men's ideas were rated more favorably than women's for no discernible reason other than gender![1] This is particularly problematic when staffing innovative roles or practices differing from existing organizational norms, where diversity of thought is critical. Further challenges arise when the hiring managers, fearing hiring people better than themselves, worry these talented individuals might "take their job," reinforcing mediocrity.

Tin Man organizations often resort to rigid competency-based interviews in which questions focus on the individual's résumé. Classic "probing" questions like "Tell me about a time when you had a difficult conversation" get rehearsed answers or AI responses that yield predictable responses and little insight into a candidate's values, aspirations, and personality. Richard Sheridan in *Joy, Inc.* aptly described the process as "lying to each other for two hours."[2]

But eventually someone is hired and arrives on day one to find the job and culture aren't quite what they'd been told. This isn't surprising due to Polanyi's paradox: employees know more than they can articulate about their roles. This, and a lack of understanding of role nuances, means the average manager only knows about 40 percent of what their employees *actually* do.[3] Good luck helping prospective employees know.

Onboarding is often meager and process driven, lacking defined objectives, sufficient support, learning opportunities, and check-ins for new employees. Only 12 percent of employees rate their onboarding process as effective.[4] They're left to figure out how the organization really works, which takes about eighteen months. At the same time, they're expected to immediately take confident ownership and be productive. New executives are especially under pressure to "move the needle" right away.

The result of all of this? Higher turnover, with up to one-third quitting within the first ninety days, many citing "job shock" as the reason.[5] Their day-to-day role was not accurately described, or totally misrepresented, during hiring.[6] Poor performance becomes endemic as new hires are left to fend for themselves and figure out how things *really* work. The unnecessary quantifiable costs associated with this antipattern include rehiring, lost productivity, additional onboarding, and an impact on morale.[7]

What Octopus Organizations Do Instead

Octopus Organizations recognize hiring as perhaps the most crucial responsibility of every leader. They treat hiring not as an inconvenience or a transaction to fill a slot, but as a strategic investment to find another owner—someone who can build, invent, and drive outcomes. This mindset permeates through every aspect of talent acquisition, from shaping jobs and job requirements, to where and how companies seek talent, to the tools they use to assess candidates, to prioritizing interviews in the busy schedules of interviewers, to onboarding. They transform sterile interviews into mutual discovery, where both parties explore values, capabilities, and aspirations. Instead of arranged marriages, these organizations build authentic, lasting, productive partnerships.

First and foremost, **Octopus Organizations validate whether hiring is even necessary.** Following the principle of "hiring to kill pain," they evaluate if existing challenges could be addressed through process improvements, work redistribution, priority adjustment, automation, or reassigning existing employees.[8] They recognize team size as a vanity metric. Hiring should reduce pain where priority work genuinely cannot be done without compromising principles or attributes such as quality. Vigilance here leads to more controlled and strategic head count growth.

Technical skills can be a baseline, but **Octopus Organizations focus first on a fit between the candidate's values and potential over role-specific expertise.**[9] While expertise can be part of an interview, more questions are asked about values, ownership-signalling behaviors, and "soft" skills. Scripted competency questions are replaced with conversations revealing genuine motivations and behaviors. "Tell me about a difficult conversation" allows a person to give you an example, and a rehearsed answer. But the conversational "Give me an example of when you haven't enjoyed an interaction at work. Were you able to address it?" will be more likely to reveal authentic behavior patterns that rehearsed competency answers cannot. In a conversation you may find out a candidate struggles with difficult conversations and would rather avoid them. These sorts of interviewing skills are attainable, though organizations we work with tend not to have considered that possibility. We find it inexplicable that interviewing is so often not treated as a trainable skill when a good interviewer with proven techniques available to them can improve candidate evaluation so much. Structured recruitment processes, including well-structured, skilled interviewing, can double the chances of a good hiring decision.[10]

Octopus Organizations probe for learning agility, humbleness, problem-solving, and curiosity because these are the raw ingredients of ownership.[11] As Eric Schmidt, former CEO of Google, observed, "We run this company on questions, not answers."[12] Bridgewater's Ray Dalio looks for reflective people who can assess their mistakes and learn from them as they "substantially outperform their peers who have the same abilities but bigger ego barriers."[13] An employee who can think through the problems and jobs we don't know about yet provides future adaptability. McDonald's USA CIO Whitney McGinnis listens intently to the questions candidates ask her and whether they show curiosity, flexibility, agility in thinking, and the ability to try and solve any kind of problem. Datadog COO Adam Blitzer looks for attributes such as positivity, self-starting, and modesty. He says that they hire "for your experience, not your playbook," acknowledging that how people think and approach problems is more relevant than pretending how their exact moves in one company will translate into the next.

Octopus Organizations attain a broad view of candidates, by giving individuals outside the hiring team's reporting line voting rights along with hiring managers. The key is getting candidates talking to people for whom the candidate will deliver value and others outside their group. At Nest Labs, former CEO Tony Fadell created a "Three Crowns system." Crown 1 was the hiring manager. Crowns 2 and 3 were managers of the candidate's internal customers who selected one or two team members to do interviews. Feedback was shared and discussed, then the Three Crowns decided who to hire.[14]

Octopus Organizations try to increase the bar with every hire. Amazon expects new hires to be better than 50 percent of the individuals in that job and level. This goal is achieved through "bar raisers." These are skilled interviewers ensuring high standards are maintained, reflecting Jeff Bezos's mantra "I'd rather interview fifty people and not hire anyone than hire the wrong person."[15] Bar raisers challenge hiring decisions, fight bias in hiring, and prevent lowering quality standards for urgent hiring needs, having an equal say in the final decision as the hiring manager.[16] They drastically reduce turnover while increasing talent density.[17]

Octopus Organizations invest heavily in onboarding. Those first days in the new job are one of the most important points for new employees and their future productivity, a slipstream for productivity. Done well, it accelerates recruits' integration into the culture. An end-to-end process addressing social and cultural integration reduces attrition.[18] Good onboarding establishes a unity of purpose rather than a functional loyalty and sets the majority of employees' minds on whether to stay or leave, directly impacting revenue.[19]

Onboarding session(s) explain the organization's genesis, purpose, values, and principles, as well as its strategy, how the organization meets customer needs, makes money, or fulfills its mandate. Simple techniques include:

- creating individualized onboarding plans (at least three months) based on job/level, including key people to meet and time-specific activities like training. Amazon's executive onboarding leader Will Thomas recommends extending this to the full first year as "good onboarding creates a sense of inclusion, and a desire to be part of the team. Simple activities such as a three-month check-in with the hiring manager are invaluable, a demonstration of care."

- Reporting on onboarding progress to ensure it's prioritized, setting an organization-wide expectation that this time will be protected rather than new recruits dropped immediately into fire fights and project work.

- Assigning a leader as a learning buddy, improving performance, retention, commitment, and competence.[20]

Octopus Organizations understand that sometimes things won't work out. At Amazon new hires can move internally one month after onboarding, because they will have been hired for value fit, but they might end up not fitting with the specific team or for the specific role. Where things really are not working, as former Nest's Tony explains, Octopus Orgs should help find a better fit.

Levers

- **Write outcome-based job descriptions.** Connect roles to expected outcomes and organizational purpose. Minimize arbitrary qualifications. Check accuracy with those who do the job today. Replace vague qualities with observable behaviors (such as "meticulously verifies financial data accuracy" instead of "detail-oriented").

- **Try team hiring.** Let existing team members drive interviews, collaborate with candidates, and have strong input into hiring decisions. "Let the team build the team."[21] This could be through interviews, collaborative problem-solving exercises, or team projects.

^ **Embed social elements into the hiring approach.** Enhance interviews to include your work environment and let candidates experience team dynamics. Create opportunities for casual interaction through team lunches, coffee chats, or collaborative work sessions.[22]

^ **Screen for learning drive.** Ask questions that reveal adaptability and learning orientation. Create scenarios that assess how candidates approach new challenges and acquire skills. Look for evidence of self-directed learning. For example, "How do you decide how to hit goals?" (experimental mindset), "What constitutes a bad day for you?" (resilience), "What kinds of people do you work best with?" (adaptability).

^ **Test bar raisers as cultural guardians.** Train experienced employees who embody your values to evaluate candidates independently using behavioral techniques. Give them meaningful input in hiring decisions. As the process matures, bar raisers gain veto power in hiring decisions.

^ **Close the loop.** Perform exit interviews, onboarding assessments, and engagement surveys to assess the efficacy of hiring. Use these tools to improve job descriptions, interviews, and onboarding.

DISCOVER MORE

ANTIPATTERNS TO READ NEXT

#7: Declaring Superficial Principles

#23: Prizing Individuals over Teams

#32: Building Homophilic Teams

PRIZING INDIVIDUALS OVER TEAMS

A high-performing cross-functional team of "average talent" outperforms brilliant jerks, every time.

THE TIN MAN BEHAVIOR

Prioritizing "brilliant jerk" star performers at the cost of cross-functional collaboration

THE RESULTS

- Internal competition and excessive politicking
- People focus on themselves, not customer impact.
- Lack of teamwork, hindered knowledge sharing

How Octopus Organizations Behave Instead

- They recognize and reward collaboration before individual contribution.
- They build cross-discipline teams of experts focused on customers and impact, not function or ego.
- They redefine the meaning of "talent" and what makes a person "talented" in a team context.

The Tin Man Behavior

In a landmark study, evolutionary biologist William Muir split chickens into two groups: average performers that laid an average number of eggs and "super chickens" that were the most productive egg layers.[1] After six generations, the average flock was doing well: egg production had increased steadily.

But in the super chicken flock, all but three chickens had pecked one another to death!

Tin Man organizations historically have focused on hiring as many super chickens as they can, under the assumption that simple math will take over. More super chickens means more eggs. HR focuses on amassing high performers through "talent" recruitment, over-indexing on skills and expertise over social and emotional capabilities.

Going after super chickens or "brilliant jerks" isn't just bad for morale, it's also bad for ownership in teams and it's financially irrational too. One Harvard study found that avoiding hiring a single toxic "super chicken" saves a company more than $12,400 in turnover costs, more than double the gain they get from hiring a top 1 percent performer.[2] And this is conservative, omitting potential litigation, regulatory penalties, and broader impacts such as decreased discretionary effort and increased stress.[3]

The result is easy to grasp if you consider professional sports organizations that try to "buy a championship." Such teams aggressively pursue star free agents at high cost. While some manage to amass astonishing amounts of individual talent, they often fail to build a team. And they lose.

But the super chicken problem runs deeper than just hiring decisions. Tin Man organizations create the perfect habitat for brilliant jerks to thrive: functional silos. When you organize around specialized departments—sales chasing growth targets, operations cutting costs, marketing protecting their turf—you're essentially building separate chicken coops. Instead of one organizational fortress, you end up with *towers of knowledge*. Functional silos and expertise are reinforced by information flows and departmental performance metrics. Functional identity ("I *am* a marketing person," "I *am* a financial controller") weighs stronger than organizational or cross-functional identity ("I *am* a customer champion"). Each silo rewards its own star performers who never have to prove they can actually work with others. The sales superstar can treat Operations like secondary citizens as long as they hit their numbers. These isolated towers become breeding grounds for brilliant jerks—specialists who can dominate their domain without ever having to learn to play well with others.

While Tin Men see the value of teams to bridge these silos, they fundamentally misunderstand what makes teams work. They often treat teams as temporary task forces—collections of their best individual performers handed tasks to complete, not problem-solvers that collectively own challenges and find ways to jointly deliver impact. It seems logical to put all your best people onto a high-profile project. But when you take brilliant jerks from different silos and force them into matrix teams, you get split loyalties, divided focus, and challenges working together due to the lack of collaboration skills. The project manager might have authority over the *what* and the *when*, but the functional manager often controls *how* work is done, along with rewards for individual contributors. These aren't real teams—they're just super chickens from different coops, still pecking at each other but now with the added confusion of competing bosses.

Tin Man organizations fail to grasp that teams aren't just *doing* the work, but that they *are* the work. The cost of that misunderstanding is lost agility, innovation, and genuine human connection—and it means they're optimizing for the wrong kind of talent entirely.

What Octopus Organizations Do Instead

Octopus Organizations recognize that the fundamental unit of value creation is the team, and redefine what makes someone talented in a team setting. Shane Battier was a professional basketball player with mediocre stats. He was a *good* player by the numbers. Yet, every team he joined dramatically improved when he played.[4] *New York Times* journalist Michael Lewis noted that "when he is on the court, his teammates get better, often a lot better, and his opponents get worse—often a lot worse." This insight challenged traditional individual-focused evaluation methods in basketball, highlighting the value of players who elevate team performance—so-called "teammateship"—through subtle contributions—the very opposite of super chicken.

Most corporate hiring and rewards systems overwhelmingly focus on individual performance, actively but unconsciously promoting brilliant jerks. Octopus Organizations hire individuals that score high on three essential characteristics that may seem "ordinary" by traditional HR measures:

- *They're humble.* They can manage ego, recognize others' contributions (ownership), share credit, and define success collectively.

- *They're hungry.* They want to do more, learn more, and own more.

- *They're smart.* They ask good questions, actively listen to what others are saying, and show good judgment in group dynamics.[5]

These qualities replace the blast radius of a super chicken or brilliant jerk with the "halo radius" of a high-performing team member.

Octopus Organizations shift from functional silos to long-lived and cross-functional teams. These teams operate like mini-companies within the larger organization, each taking ownership of a specific customer problem, product, or value stream. The team, not the silo, provides an individual's home and sense of identity. By structuring this way, teams gain several advantages. They make better decisions through accumulated knowledge; they increase innovation because they own outcomes and feel psychologically safe challenging ideas, experimenting, and making mistakes (Google's Project Aristotle identified this as the single most important factor in team effectiveness, enabling open discussion of failures that triggered exponential learning); they work faster and more flexibly with no silos in the way and shared mental models of their purpose and how to get work done; they improve productivity as they're given time to refine their processes, tools, and problem-solving approaches; and they nurture long-term ownership and accountability for outcomes.[6]

Singapore bank DBS's journey exemplifies a path to long-lived teams: First, leaders changed their language from talking about vertical silos to emphasizing horizontal, cross-functional collaboration on shared projects. Then they shifted from separate business and technology silo units to "two-in-a-box" platforms with joint ownership, organizing into thirty-three platforms by 2018, including Risk Platform for credit risk and Consumer Banking Group Customer Management and Analytics Platform. Finally, they introduced "Managing through Journeys" (MtJ), focusing on end-to-end customer outcomes rather than functional deliverables. Cross-functional squads led by "mini-CEOs" oversaw specific projects, creating ownership and shared leadership language across approximately four hundred leaders by 2024. Teams used common dashboards for mutual accountability toward customer delivery. Value-focused language replaced process-driven terms like "raising tickets" and "chargebacks" that had previously reinforced divisions. The Treasury Markets journey exemplified this shift, bringing functions together to transform their foreign exchange business, resulting in 15 percent revenue growth and high customer satisfaction scores.

Octopus Organizations don't disband high-performing. Once they have established highly productive teams, Octopus Orgs avoid the overhead associated with constantly forming and disbanding teams as Tin Man orgs often do for temporary projects, focusing more energy on value-creating work than getting things set up and torn down. As Allan Kelly notes in *Team Topologies*, breaking up such teams is "worse than vandalism: it is corporate psychopathy."[7] While healthy turnover brings fresh perspectives, changes should be thoughtful and minimal. They address underperformance through coaching or removal, and keep successful teams intact when moving to new priorities.

Octopus Organizations align training, performance assessments, incentives, and rewards to teams over individuals. Teams get coaching. Team outcomes are measured as much or more than individual activity. Companies like Nucor demonstrate this by paying bonuses to teams rather than individuals.[8]

When done well, these long-lived teams give Octopus Organizations many advantages over individuals. They serve as:

- *Learning amplifiers,* openly sharing vulnerabilities, weaknesses, and uncertainties, improving candor and problem-solving. Navy SEALs' after-action reviews exemplify this benefit, where open discussion of failures leads to exponential learning.

- *Early signal detectors,* which collectively identify and amplify weak social and technical signals that would be lost in individual work, allowing teams to respond long before formal systems would catch them.

- *Pattern-breaking forces,* challenging and redefining existing mental patterns in ways individuals cannot, the way Google's AdWords team completely reimagined the advertising model, breaking free of individual cognitive biases.[9]

It might surprise you to know that the octopus, often thought of as one of the ocean's most notoriously independent creatures, is a team player. It will prowl coral reefs with a group of fish to find a meal. The orchestration between them is uncanny. They form cooperative hunting teams where the fish act as an extended sensory system for the octopus by exploring and identifying prey locations, while the octopus serves as their coordinator and also traps prey beneath rocks, creating a mutually beneficial relationship that appears to save energy for the octopus.[10] But this isn't just a fascinating David Attenborough moment; it's nature's master class in the power of collaboration. Forward-thinking organizations are discovering what our eight-armed friend already knows: true excellence requires collaboration, not a bunch of chickens pecking each other to death.

Levers

^ **Assess your focus on individuals.** Frankly ask, "Who are the brilliant jerks?" and "Do people get ahead here by doing great work and helping others, or by ignoring and even undermining colleagues, and blowing their own trumpet?"[11] What signals can you send that the brilliant jerks won't get ahead? Create explicit hiring criteria that evaluate candidates not just on technical skills but on trust-building capabilities. Adopt Datadog's and Atlassian's approach by screening for qualities like humility and team orientation. Develop specific interview questions that assess how candidates handle conflict, give feedback, and contribute to team dynamics.

^ **Stop hiring jerks.** Make it clear during hiring that jerks aren't welcome in your organization. Phil experienced one interview that started by assessing how he treated his driver and the reception staff. Serial entrepreneur Sir Richard Branson was known to have experimented with picking up senior leadership interview candidates for one of his US-based companies disguised as their taxi driver. In doing so he assessed how the candidates treated people. "Some of them were very rude about being in the back of the taxi."[12] Add questions to the interview process that help form an opinion on the individual's jerkiness such as:

- "When you last disagreed with a colleague, how did you feel? What did you actually do?"

- "Describe a manager you struggled with. What made it hard?"

- "What's a mistake you made that you're still thinking about? What happened?"

- "If I called your last three teammates right now, what would they say about you—really?"

- "You're the new person on a team. Day one, what do you do?"

^ **Implement team formation protocols.** Develop a team formation protocol that includes using tools to understand each other's communication styles. Create individual "letters of understanding" where team members explicitly document their working preferences, strengths, and areas for development. Schedule dedicated team formation sessions when new teams are created.

^ **Develop team-focused leadership training.** Create a leadership development program specifically focused on team skills, including how to help teams go through the process of "storming-forming-norming-performing." This widely recognized model describes the natural stages teams experience: forming (coming together), storming (working through conflicts and establishing roles), norming (developing shared ways of working), and performing (achieving high effectiveness as a unit). Understanding these stages helps leaders guide teams through inevitable challenges toward peak performance. Train leaders to facilitate team dynamics, remove barriers, and create psychological safety. Include learning on how to balance individual recognition with team cohesion.

^ **Create team performance measures and tune-ups.** Develop metrics that measure team effectiveness beyond individual contributions. Include measures of team health such as psychological safety scores, collaboration levels, and knowledge-sharing effectiveness. Implement regular team health checks that assess both performance and relational aspects of team functioning, asking the questions "How well are we working together?" and "How might we get better at it?"[13] Periodically ask everyone on the team for one word that describes how people are feeling about the team, and what it should do more or less of.

^ **Run a team strengths spotlight in team meetings.** Dedicate five to ten minutes in regular team meetings to spotlight individual strengths. Each week, rotate through team members and have them briefly share a strength they bring to the team, such as a technical skill or interpersonal skill, or a problem-solving approach, and give a quick example of how they've used it recently. This builds team awareness of collective strengths and diverse capabilities, increasing the appreciation for individual contributions and fostering a more supportive and collaborative team environment. It also subtly counters the "superstar" mentality by highlighting the value of diverse strengths within the team.

DISCOVER MORE

ANTIPATTERNS TO READ NEXT

#6: Working Together but Not as a Team

#24: Mismanaging Incentives

#32: Building Homophilic Teams

MISMANAGING INCENTIVES

Opportunities for ownership and mastery drive the most powerful incentive: intrinsic motivation.

THE TIN MAN BEHAVIOR

Trying to drive behavior primarily through incentives focused on financial rewards

THE RESULTS

- Reduced ownership, collaboration, curiosity
- Important work that is not incentivized gets neglected.
- Development stifled

How Octopus Organizations Behave Instead

- They create intrinsic motivation by connecting work to purpose and opportunities for ownership and mastery.
- They invest in sustainable rewards beyond pay, including growth opportunities and learning.
- They provide equitable base pay and separate compensation from gameable performance metrics.

The Tin Man Behavior

Tin Man organizations *love* incentives but don't really understand them. In the operational playbook of many old-model organizations, "rewards" equal "incentives." "The reward I offer you," a manager might think, "is the incentive to do the work."

Alas, the reality is they are not one and the same.

Let's clarify their distinct roles. *Incentives are forward-looking propositions*: the carrot: "If you do X, then you get Y" is designed to guide future action. These are typically extrinsic and transactional, aiming to steer behavior toward predefined goals. A sales team is promised a bonus for smashing quarterly targets, or developers get an extra day off for vanquishing a specific list of bugs.

In contrast, *rewards are retrospective*: the trophy. They're bestowed *after* desired behaviors have already occurred. They are designed to reinforce positive actions and build loyalty. While rewards can be transactional (like a spot bonus), they also hold immense relational and intrinsic power, fostering feelings of appreciation, value, and belonging. This can be as simple as a leader publicly recognizing an engineer's dedication in a team meeting, or a team receiving unexpected kudos for exceptional ownership.

Trouble brews when Tin Man operations conflate the two, thinking they are providing rewards when really they're driven entirely by incentives. Incentive structures still echo Douglas McGregor's somewhat dated Theory X—the assumption that individuals are primarily cogs, nudged into action only by external inducements. This perspective, perhaps suited to repetitive assembly lines, can backfire spectacularly for work requiring creativity, deep thinking, and collaboration. Such approaches can:

- **Feel coercive,** with the "If you don't do X, you won't get Y" undertone implying a threat, which breeds fear and compliance over genuine engagement.

- **Spark destructive competition,** pitting colleagues against one another to grab limited carrots.

- **Narrow focus unduly,** as people take incentivized paths, deprioritizing crucial un-incentivized activities like taking broader ownership, deep learning, or collaboration.

- **Hijack true ownership,** when metric-chasing overshadows outcomes and the intrinsic motivation gained from the sheer joy of solving a problem or mastering a skill.

- **Promote short-termism,** eclipsing vital long-term organizational needs by rewarding quarterly metrics over sustainable practices, immediate wins over capability building, and individual heroics over systemic improvements that benefit the organization over years rather than months.

- **Trigger unethical behavior** to gain incentives.[1]

Perhaps the most significant oversight of this approach lies in the fundamental assumption about what constitutes a "good" reward. Frederick Herzberg's seminal two-factor theory offers critical insight on this: money, while essential, is primarily a "hygiene factor." Its absence breeds demotivation, but its mere presence doesn't automatically ignite motivation. For many Tin Man organizations, pay raises become the default recognition, morphing into an expectation rather than a motivator. Once people feel fairly compensated, more money yields diminishing returns on drive and satisfaction.[2]

What Octopus Organizations Do Instead

Octopus Organizations harness purpose and intrinsic motivation by providing meaningful work, supportive leadership, and genuine ownership. This approach taps into Douglas McGregor's Theory Y and Daniel Pink's metaphor of solar energy in *Drive*: intrinsic motivation is sustainable, nurturing, and naturally renewing.[3] When employees clearly see how their work creates value, motivation becomes self-sustaining. While targeted incentives have their place, a thoughtful combination, typically weighed more toward rewards, is ideal.

Luc Hennekens, former CIO at Qantas and Airbus, saw engineers motivated by effusive customer feedback, which fostered pride and allowed them to showcase their knowledge and quality of work. Former UK government CDO Craig Suckling describes teams finding deep motivation by creating data systems that help vulnerable citizens. In both cases, purpose and ownership drives performance more effectively than financial incentives alone.[4]

Octopus Organizations value rewards over incentives. Knowing the self-sustaining power of rewards, they actively inject them into the organization, sometimes swapping out incentives in the process. A bonus (forgive the pun) from this is inspiring others to adopt the desired behaviors as they seek similar rewards. All these actions reinforce a culture of ownership and highlight what "good" looks like. Examples include:

- Zappos's "WoW Awards" (extraordinary customer service or demonstration of values)

- Southwest Airlines' "Heroes of the Heart" (exemplification of customer experience by behind-the-scenes departments)

- McDonald's Circle of Excellence (cross-functional teams delivering business-wide impacts)

- Nike's VP of Product Michael Newton used company-wide recognition for people creating new customer value or simplifying processes, which were more impactful than monetary rewards.

- Ferrari CEO Benedetto Vigna notes recognition that patents create a sense of gratification and ownership in those who file them.

Well-designed rewards are perceived as equitable, distributed fairly, and accessible; connect with direct achievements, not abstract organizational targets (like company-wide profits); recognize ownership; value deep thinking, problem-solving, learning, and experimental curiosity over productivity or "busyness;" and are clearly communicated so everyone understands them.

Octopus Organizations look at rewards across multiple dimensions, including results, skills, behaviors, and both individual and team contributions. Product development teams often benefit from group rewards focused on learning and iteration rather than hitting specific metrics.[5] For small, highly interdependent teams (typically fewer than ten members) requiring close collaboration (like restaurant staff), team-based or hybrid rewards outperform individual incentives.

Octopus Organizations build both formal structures and informal opportunities for rewards that drive intrinsic motivation. If companies value cross-functional collaboration, they must create formal opportunities for that behavior to be rewarded. Leaders need both responsibility for their people's success and resources to support them. Effective formal team rewards might include shared equity or profit-sharing based on collective performance, team retreat budgets that increase with achievement. An informal reward might be the collective ownership of new initiatives that successful teams can claim. The key is ensuring that team rewards genuinely require collaboration—not just individual contributions that happen to occur on the same team. Other informal opportunities that may not even feel like rewards to the HR department but to the employees feel very rewarding, like access to networking events, learning opportunities, and the chance to take ownership of something at work.

Octopus Organizations consider the personality of the people they're rewarding. If they don't, extroverts may be rewarded more because many rewards that drive intrinsic motivation are appealing to extroverts in their focus on public recognition and celebration. Effective rewards for introverts include private recognition (thank-you notes) or self-directed professional development opportunities that allow for growth through reflection in lieu of group activities.

Rather than primarily using variable compensation as motivational lever, **Octopus Organizations establish *equitable and consistent base pay,*** separated from gameable performance metrics. We regularly observe organizations that attract and retain exceptional talent despite average market compensation because their employees feel valued and connect with a deeper sense of purpose.

When employees perceive equity in base pay and benefits, they engage in autotelic experiences—finding inherent satisfaction in their work, driving achievement toward objectives that transcend traditional incentives. This shifts motivation from mechanical compliance to intrinsic satisfaction, putting the "human" back into "human resources."

The Lego Group, for example, focuses on family-friendly policies that align with their core purpose and account for employees' different life stages. This reflects their brand values and mission, creating meaning for employees beyond just compensation.[6] Netflix offers high degrees of freedom and ownership to employees, unlimited vacation days, and no formal expense policies.[7] Airbnb's "Live and Work Anywhere" policy allows most employees to work from anywhere for up to ninety days a year and provides an allowance to travel.[8] This flexibility has become a key reward for work-life balance. There is no broad-brush solution, though. Some employees will still prioritize financial compensation, while others might value autonomy or purpose more highly. A manager's understanding of their team is critical.

Octopus Organizations consistently align their rewards with their leadership principles, such as customer centricity, ownership, and speed of learning. They regularly audit who gets promoted, who receives public recognition, and who gets the best opportunities to ensure these align with stated values rather than just traditional metrics. This includes specifically recognizing and rewarding single-threaded leaders who take complete ownership of outcomes through highly visible promotions for those who shepherd complex initiatives from conception to delivery, or recognition that celebrates leaders who take personal accountability for difficult challenges others avoid. If an organization claims to value customer focus but only promotes based on internal political skills, the disconnect creates cynicism. Effective orgs track whether their highest performers and most rewarded individuals actually embody the behaviors they want to see replicated throughout the organization.

Effective Octopus Organizations recognize that reward systems must evolve as rapidly as work itself changes. Regular assessment of reward alignment with strategic priorities, team structures, and employee demographics ensures continued effectiveness. Balancing financial compensation with purpose, autonomy, mastery opportunities, and recognition creates an environment that truly nurtures potential and improves organizational performance. These intrinsic motivators are harder for competitors to match than pay raises.

Levers

^ **Broaden recognition methods.** Create multiple ways for people to receive acknowledgment—company-wide platforms, storytelling (on blogs, video series, social media channels) dedicated to showcasing stories of teams making a remarkable impact to inspire and reinforce desired behaviors. Discover which recognition matters to your people. Do they want to be onstage presenting about their successes, or do they want be recognized for patents registered, or do they want creative customer interactions?

^ **Institute "peer-to-peer recognition budgets."** Set up small, decentralized budgets (karma tokens, gift cards, team lunch funds) to spot reward one another's contributions *immediately* and directly. Emphasize social recognition over monetary rewards. Amazon uses recognition points that can be converted into gift cards or tangible items.

^ **Design context-specific rewards.** Tailor reward systems to team types, expanding beyond individual rewards—such as team-based rewards for collaborative product development, mixing result and behavior-based rewards. For product teams, weight rewards toward customer impact over delivery speed; for sales, balance revenue targets with customer success. Include at least one team-based objective in every reward or incentive structure. Include potential recipients (individuals and teams) in defining and giving out rewards.

^ **Make purpose visible.** Use dashboards to help people see how their work contributes to the broader purpose. Ensure rewards align. Include regular customer contact opportunities for people to directly experience how their work affects users.

^ **Broadcast rewards.** Make individual and team contributions visible across organizational boundaries. Develop attribution tracking for successful initiatives, with leaders explicitly acknowledging diverse contributions. Celebrate both successful outcomes *and* valuable learning from initiatives that didn't achieve expected results.

DISCOVER MORE

ANTIPATTERNS TO READ NEXT

#2: Whiffing on Purpose Statements

#5: Misusing Metrics

#35: Downplaying People Development

GRANTING ARTIFICIAL OWNERSHIP

Creating organization-wide conditions for trust and agency to solve problems ignites innovation.

THE TIN MAN BEHAVIOR

Giving responsibility to people without providing the conditions for them to execute on these effectively and safely

THE RESULTS

- Cynicism and disengagement, a feeling of powerlessness that reduces the inclination to take initiative
- Slowed decision-making, reduced agility and innovation
- Resources wasted on oversight rather than value delivery

How Octopus Organizations Behave Instead

- They recognize the signs of "fake ownership culture" and work to remove them.
- They develop leaders to shift from commanding employees to coaching owners.
- They experiment with ownership boundaries, pushing for more autonomy, providing principles to guide owners, and rewarding ownership.

The Tin Man Behavior

We've carefully considered including this as our last antipattern in the ownership section: organizations often believe that they've distributed ownership when they've not. Ownership has two sides: someone needs to give it, and someone else needs to take it. Much can go wrong between these two sides.

When it comes to *giving* ownership, do you find yourself:

- Demanding frequent detailed updates?

- Asking for input, but stopping short of transferring decision-making authority?

- Giving ownership, but inadvertently withholding critical information or resources so the "owner" needs to consult you?

- Defining how work should be done or redoing work that doesn't match your vision?

- Overruling decisions others should be making?[1]

- Maintaining oversight powers that mean the new "owner" cannot take an entirely meaningful decision or create a deliverable?

When it comes to *taking* ownership, do you find yourself:

- Deferring decisions to leadership?

- Building excessive consensus on what a product should do rather than making clear choices?

- Incorporating all input into new products or services rather than making trade-offs?

- Avoiding decisions, hoping they will go away or someone else will make them?

- Deflecting responsibility when deliverables are missed?

- Thinking "what would leadership want?"

It's a cruel joke to those on the receiving end of faux ownership that often results in deep-seated cynicism. We've heard many employees say it's worse than not giving hope of sharing ownership in the first place. Shonda Rhimes talks about "if you hired people to do a job, you should let them do that job. Like, it's not my job to micromanage you. And if I've hired you and I don't have faith in you enough to do that job, then why have I hired you? When people are sitting around waiting for you to tell them what to do, it's painful for them and for you."[2] Unfortunately, we observe artificial ownership regularly (all true stories!):

- The COO and sponsor of a major technology platform told us that his product teams are empowered, but then we saw him screaming at them and threatening to fire individuals if he wasn't happy with decisions or deliverables.

- A leader being angry at a new owner for making a bad decision, only to realize later that she had failed to enable that person to own that decision by not giving enough strategic context.

- Another COO, keen to make a difference, shrugged his shoulders in resignation when asked about what he thought about the commitments the company had made. "The CEO told me to do it," he said wryly. "You might as well get entry-level staff into our roles if you're going to get told what to do by the CEO."

First attempts of aspiring Octopus Orgs often don't quite go to plan. One example we witnessed gives you an idea of the types of challenges you might recognize: A manager gave autonomy to a product team. When the first major decision of the team didn't work out as planned, the manager faltered—perhaps because of fear that he would be blamed by his own manager, or because he simply didn't know how to coach instead of direct. Weeks of the "empowered" team thoughtfully prioritizing what they'd deliver and how got wiped away as the manager single-handedly prioritized something different along with directions on how to deliver. The manager's poor reaction and control saw the new owner step back and defer to the manager again. The manager saw this as validation that they did indeed knew better and had—phew—saved the day. Goodbye ownership!

We've observed various reasons for leaders struggling to relinquish ownership, most innocent and unaware, including:

- **Perfectionism** and the feeling that everything needs to be done exactly as they envision it

- **Habit** of being conditioned to direct and decide rather than coach

- **Fear** that team failures will reflect poorly on them

- **Envy** that a team's success might threaten the leader's value

- **Loss of importance** and hence becoming "unnecessary" if teams can function independently

- **Lack of skills** in areas such as coaching through problems and decisions by asking good, thought-provoking questions

Similarly with those shunning taking ownership, reasons include:

- **Habit and experience,** having never learned how to exercise ownership effectively

- **Lack of clarity** of boundaries about when and where they can take the initiative

- **Risk/reward imbalance,** with a perception of more downside than upside in taking ownership

- **Resource limitations** such as lacking the information, authority, or resources needed to execute effectively

- **Organizational complexity** with so many dependencies and approval layers to make meaningful decisions that it's hard to be an owner

We've deliberately left this antipattern for last in the ownership section. That's because relinquishing ownership is dependent on so many factors: attitude to "failure," the difference between opinions and ownership, the behavior of leaders, and too many dependencies, to name just a few. We did this so that you could pass through and evaluate the previous ownership antipatterns that might prevent you from creating the kind of ownership that Octopus Organizations create. We're willing to bet that your organization, like so many that we work with, professes a message of ownership, but perhaps you now realize that your leaders, or you yourself, engage in at least a few of these behaviors and despite your intentions, chances are you're stuck in this antipattern and haven't truly created an ownership culture . . . yet.

What Octopus Organizations Do Instead

First, **Octopus Organizations acknowledge artificial ownership exists in their organization.** Observing this problem could be as simple as identifying how many of the antipatterns in this part of the book exist within your own organization using the questions in the Tin Man section. Octopus Organizations examine these behaviors for what's driving them. For instance, "Progress reports seem to be used to relieve anxiety around relinquishing control." Or "We didn't have a good definition of ownership, which led to the assumption that input alone is ownership."

When you notice the symptoms we describe in the antipatterns, follow them like a bad smell. When you notice that you fall into prescriptively telling someone what to do, remind yourself that your influence cannot scale this way. Ask yourself whether that level of perfection is really needed. Can they get it 80 percent right and be good enough? Will their approach, at worst, create a hole above the waterline of your organizational ship or below? If the former, is the minor "damage" worth the trade-off that they feel ownership, curiosity, and enthusiasm? If you start feeling envious about the success of those you coached to have ownership instead of pride, ask yourself where that's coming from and what must be true to feel differently. For leaders, ownership means building a system where trust is the default, not the exception.

Getting real about your own actions and feelings helps well-intentioned leaders to acknowledge the shortcomings of their attempts at ownership and removes cynicism from employees who see their leaders calling out the fact they're not "walking the talk."

Octopus Organizations clearly understand what ownership means to avoid unintentionally promising it and then not delivering. For employees, true ownership isn't about some vague feeling of being "heard." It's about the authority to make decisions and solve problems toward a clear purpose and outcome, with clear roles, responsibilities, and boundaries, and the confidence that acting in this context won't be career limiting (on the contrary!). Ways to foster ownership include:

- Making information accessible and transparent to enable decisions and problem-solving

- Increasing the freedom over resources: who to work with, what tools to use, and how to use funding

- Giving latitude to teams to decide how to operate, solve problems, and deliver outcomes

- Being clear about what decision-making is in scope

Octopus Organizations use principles and guardrails to enable more ownership. Instead of detailed procedures, they establish principles and guardrails—like customer-first values, financial boundaries, or quality standards—that serve as a compass rather than a map. This allows owners to make contextual decisions while staying aligned with organizational objectives, striking the balance between preventing costly mistakes and enabling innovation.

Octopus Organizations experiment with ownership models. For organizations in the process of moving away from artificial ownership, it can be helpful to try different approaches, and then measure and iterate. For example, use decision mapping to understand how many and which types of decisions are made where, and at what speed. Allocate a small "bets budget" to teams or individuals, allowing them to experiment with new ideas or solutions without needing extensive approvals, accepting that some of those bets will fail.

Octopus Organizations know that true ownership doesn't equal less leadership; it means different leadership. In ownership organizations, leaders switch from command to coach. Leaders become enablers, actively understanding through dialogue with teams where external dependencies or a lack of resources are barriers, and then addressing them. They stop doling out tasks and instead provide what the military call the "commander's intent," a broad definition of what a successful mission or outcome will look like in its end state. Former McDonald's senior director Sue Pittacora highlighted how in major initiatives, leaders consciously checked their desire to take control and give answers, instead sending positive messages of trust in their team and positioning themselves as barrier removers and resolvers for escalations. When someone comes to you with a problem, resist giving the answer immediately. Ask questions like "What outcomes are you hoping for?" "What options have you already thought about?" or "What support do you need to tackle this?" "And what else?" (These are inspired by coaching experts like Michael Bungay Stanier.[3]) Focus praise on effort, strategy, and learning ("I really admire how you persisted through that tough analysis and the clear strategy you developed"), rather than just innate talent ("You're a natural!"). Recognize publicly and reward when people take ownership, make sound decisions, and contribute to customer impact.

Octopus leaders serve as clarifiers, because that enables owners with the context they need to take responsibility and make decisions. Instead of telling teams how to solve a problem, they share the organizational context so the team can solve the problem. As London Stock Exchange CEO Dame Julia Hoggett puts it, being clear about the exam question to be answered is critical. Acknowledging your own distance from the details and their closeness to the details puts the team in a better position to make decisions and builds their confidence. This requires more than RACI matrices, team charters, and job descriptions, which are rarely detailed and nuanced enough to accommodate every situation that arises. An ongoing dialogue between team and people leader helps surface potential conflicts, a lack of understanding of roles, or gaps in understanding of the desired outcomes, allowing these to be addressed and clarity brought to roles.

Werner Swanepoel, SVP for Digital Transformation at Sibanye-Stillwater, says:

We communicate that we do not wish to own things at the center, but drive ownership at the edge. We identify activated people in the business, make them pioneers that explore the unknown, and lead. We put them on a pedestal and shine a light on them and showcase what they have done, encouraging others that they can do it too. That recognition activates people, and we use that platform to see how to build more ownership capability around individuals. When people get recognition for their efforts, they see a whole new world open up, opportunities for people to see a different career gets them excited, hopefully they will become ownership champions scattered through the business.

Octopus Organizations recognize the fragility of ownership. As Johannesburg Stock Exchange Clear CEO Alicia Greenwood notes, "It takes a lot to build a culture of ownership but very little to destroy it." Leaders must consistently behave in a way that doesn't contradict the culture of ownership and drive cynicism and disengagement. The minute employees see command and control that contradicts what they've been promised or what they've experienced, there will be problems.

Walmart founder Sam Walton noted, "When employees think, act, and feel like owners, they make better decisions—decisions that are in the long-term interest of the company." So go forth and avoid pretending. Either you trust your people, or you don't. If you don't, be honest about it. If you do, get out of their way and let them own it.

Time to advance to real ownership.

Levers

^ **How long can you go without making a decision?** See how long you can resist your command-and-control urges. "I pride myself on making fewer and fewer decisions," said Netflix's Reed Hastings to a TED Talk audience. "Sometimes I can go a whole quarter without making a decision."[4]

^ **Use the power of language.** Frame requests as open-ended questions, inviting owners to contribute their expertise ("What's the best way to . . ."). Acknowledge and appreciate when employees take initiative and make decisions ("Thank you for owning that"). Discuss desired outcomes and goals but give people the autonomy to decide how to achieve them ("What do we need to do . . . ," not "How do we . . ."). Reinforce your role as an enabler, rather than a dictator ("What support do you need?").

^ **Frame the intent.** Start initiatives or teams with documenting and communicating the "commander's intent"—what success looks like and why it matters—then let teams determine how to achieve it. For instance, retailer Patagonia states the intent to "Build the best product, cause no unnecessary harm, and use business to inspire and implement solutions to the environmental crisis." It's not prescriptive but means something to every department: design focuses on durability, supply chain on sustainable materials, marketing on activism.

^ **Invest in coaching.** Train leaders to use coaching questions to help teams accept and use ownership. Respond with questions rather than solutions when you see challenges or when teams ask for help. Establish coaching relationships where leaders help owners develop their own problem-solving capabilities. Bring in professional coaches for leaders.

^ **Reward smart risk-taking.** Publicly call out learning from failure and decision-making. Create visible celebrations of teams that take ownership, regardless of outcome.

^ **Conduct ownership reviews.** Regularly assess the effectiveness of ownership structures through focused discussions about decision-making patterns, identifying opportunities to push authority closer to the customer. Work with teams to identify and mitigate unnecessary dependencies and gatekeepers, and other potential blockers to ownership.[5] Reflect on your own default responses to situations to understand your own behavior and potential blockers to enabling true ownership. Seek feedback from others on this.

^ **Create metrics to track ownership.** For example, track the number of decisions made that were reviewed by "higher" management. If this number consistently exceeds 20 percent per quarter, ownership is weak. Or, conduct a simple anonymous survey asking team members: "On a scale of 1 to 5, how clear are you on the decisions you can make independently?" If the average score is below 4, autonomy is muddy.

DISCOVER MORE

ANTIPATTERNS TO READ NEXT

#14: Operating on a Culture of Fear

#15: Upholding Poor Leadership

#21: Diluting Accountability

PART 3

INCITING
CURIOSITY

Which animal has three hearts and blue blood?

Notice what happens as you read this question. There is a knowledge gap that you feel a desire to close, a tension between what you know and what you want to know. And yet, learning the answer provides no obvious extrinsic reward. That's curiosity: gaining pleasure through the voluntary pursuit of new information and knowledge.

It's an octopus, by the way, with three hearts and blue blood. These lovely creatures survive and thrive by learning about their environment. They detect challenges and threats by constantly scanning with their eyes, their skin, and their tentacles. They navigate these challenges—predators nearby, complex spaces to get through—by running constant rounds of testing and learning and moving forward with each small success. They have the most abundant ability to use RNA editing to adapt their chemical makeup to new problems and challenges. Their distributed brain allows independent exploration within different parts of the body. More "arms" running more experiments faster, independently of the other arms, maximizes the collective intelligence and contribution of all the arms to the overall goal. This intelligence has helped them learn to, for example, build walls and unlock cages.

Building your organizational curiosity will allow you to do much more than that. Curiosity is the desire to learn, and it's the same feeling and drive that organizations need to develop to escape their rigid operating system. Tin Man organizations' need for compliance and predictability actively dissuades curiosity. Octopus Organizations move from a collection of individuals acting as passive receivers of information to curious teams on quests to *learn*.

Former PepsiCo CEO Indra Nooyi, from whom you'll hear more in this section, provides a forthright observation about curiosity that serves as a warning for organizations that don't develop it: "Shame on the board who picks a leader who isn't curious. The game has only just begun."[1] Her words highlight a fundamental truth overlooked in many organizations: in an era of unprecedented change, the absence of curiosity is a competitive weakness. Ignoring this inherent human need for exploration and understanding will hinder learning, cooperation, analytical thinking, creativity, and plain old problem-solving. That is, overall performance.

At the same time, it's going to feel risky and uncomfortable embracing curiosity. Asking questions can challenge norms, and venturing into the unknown carries the possibility of failure. You may already be resisting the idea, thinking, *We're doing pretty well. I deliver consistent results. That's the best approach.* In stable times, perhaps. But we no longer operate in that context. Under uncertain conditions, curiosity enables problem-solving and better decisions informed by broader perspectives. It unearths unexpected opportunities and expands options.

For most of us, it's not a lack of ability that prevents us from being curious; we're just out of practice. But, if you think about it, you'll realize you were wildly, uninhibitedly curious as a child. The average young child fires off between 27 and 107 questions per hour—more than one every minute![2] Every day is full of "Why? Why? Why?"—about the color of the sky, how gravity works, and where the sun goes at night.

But then the rate of questioning plummets to three questions per hour at school. Educational models can be Tin Man, too, prioritizing and praising correct answers over asking insightful questions, dampening this natural curiosity. It's a system that subtly teaches us that knowing the answer is more valuable than seeking it.

Our diminishing curiosity has a tangible impact on our ability to learn. Fewer than 20 percent of adults are engaged in lifelong learning, right at a time when what we know becomes obsolete faster than ever before.[3] The useful lifespan of skills has plummeted to as little as eighteen months. Continuous learning, adult curiosity, is paramount.

Organizations love to say they're seeking "curious" and "creative" thinkers, but they, like schools, are often structured to prevent those traits from emerging. One study found that twice as many organizations preach a culture of curiosity as those that practice one.[4] Another, more scathing report showed that across countries only 9 percent of workers felt they were extremely encouraged to be curious, take risks, and explore new ideas.[5]

This gap between what organizations seem to desire and what they do is only going to become more pronounced as artificial intelligence proliferates in organizations, removing routine tasks and demanding more nuanced, creative problem-solving from humans.

The good news is that even the least curious among us can learn this skill and foster it in our organizations, if we work at it. You'll need to overcome negative stereotypes you may harbor about the people who feel comfortable rocking the boat, asking hard questions, and failing. You'll need to get comfortable with not knowing answers, and with the idea that when your carefully crafted hypothesis is proven wrong, that's a good thing. You'll need to devote resources that won't directly translate to productivity or efficiency, that will *feel* like a waste (it's not).[6]

Octopus Organizations overcome the discomfort. They understand its potential to eliminate low-value work, accelerate learning, learn to ride the waves of emerging trends, and even spark the next industry revolution.

To do that, you first must understand the behaviors that are diminishing, even blocking, curiosity from taking hold in your organization. Let's look at the Tin Man behaviors holding organizations back and how to replace them with Octopus-like curiosity.

EVADING FAILURE

Productive setbacks provide quick
and valuable learning and reduce risk.

THE TIN MAN BEHAVIOR

Treating all failures as equal, as inefficient, a threat to short-term goals (such as stock price), and therefore an outcome to be avoided or to be penalized if it happens

THE RESULTS

- A risk-averse culture
- Suppression of experimentation, creative problem-solving, and learning
- Bigger failures from avoiding small, controlled experiments

How Octopus Organizations Behave Instead

- They treat intelligent failure as valuable data, a necessary and expected by-product of innovation.
- They systematically lower the cost of failure by running many small, fast, and inexpensive experiments.
- They believe the best way to avoid catastrophic failure is to embrace small, controlled, and intelligent failures.

The Tin Man Behavior

While leadership teams frequently espouse the value of learning from failure—with 91 percent of C-level executives claiming they encourage experimentation—only 35 percent of ground-level teams report this encouragement translating into reality.[1] In fact, most organizations are terrified of failure. It's treated as expensive, embarrassing, and competitively disadvantageous, as competitors, leaders suspect, race ahead while they clean up messes.

The leaders we speak to also worry that if they tolerate (never mind encourage) failure, they invite people to give less than their best.

Because of Tin Man orgs' focus on predictable processes to scale work, they thrive on knowing the "right" answer and making safe choices. Failing is an impediment to efficiency. The relentless Tin Man pressure to deliver predictable, positive results every quarter discounts following curiosity, which is not "safe." Nobody wants to be the leader who explains a dip in performance because they dared to try something new. The CIO of a *Fortune* 500 science and technology company told us he cannot fail with the introduction of new technology, as the culture and power politics would exploit the failure detrimentally. Yet his R&D unit is expected to experiment and fail daily.

Hierarchy plays a role, too, where the Tin Man's middle management becomes a crucial bottleneck. They're caught between executive demands for innovation and the reality of incentives focused on hitting numbers.

Tin Man leaders fall into this avoidance behavior because for one, failure feels painful and shameful on a personal level, and secondly, it also often leads to negative career repercussions. This one-two punch of personal fear and professional risk makes it understandable that people instinctively avoid and/or hide failures. There are cognitive traps at play as well that make it difficult to rethink failure as anything other than what we've been taught it is our whole lives: bad. Prospect theory (losing feels worse than winning feels good), confirmation bias (we like ideas we agree with), and fundamental attribution error (our failures aren't our fault, others' failures are their fault—simplified), all contribute to these feelings.[2]

Organizations have found many creative ways to manage the fear of failure, sometimes without realizing what they're doing. One classic approach is to engineer failure out of experiments, or what we call "non-experiments," that are run by teams that have become either emotionally attached to an idea, or deaf to negative signals from data and customers.[3] One company we worked with tested a new fried chicken sandwich designed for a national launch in a region known for its love of fried chicken sandwiches. The test was a smashing success. The national launch flopped.

Evading failure also amplifies sunk costs. Doomed initiatives are propped up despite negative outcomes that are downplayed or hidden, when in fact the company should be following the *first rule of holes*: when you're in one, stop digging.

Ultimately, evading failure leads to organizations becoming either paralyzed by the need to get everything right or so risk-averse that inaction leads to future crises.

It squelches experimentation, learning, innovation, and responsiveness to opportunities and threats, and demotivates talent as the most creative employees learn to give up on ideas or just leave the company.

We've talked in the "Clarity" section about the increasing amounts of "newness" thrown at organizations from all corners, from legislation to technology, and how handling the resulting uncertainty is a competitive differentiator. To manage these conditions necessitates trial and inevitably plenty of error.

What Octopus Organizations Do Instead

Octopus Organizations view failure as necessary learning. They remove the fear that our culture has associated with failing—but don't conflate this with the "fail fast, break things" credo, which almost sets failing as a goal. They view failure as an inevitable consequence of being curious of learning. As Ray Dalio puts it, "Fail *well* and love your failures and see them as opportunity to improve."[4]

This understanding of learning's true value becomes clear when considering what Astro Teller, CEO of Alphabet X's Moonshot Factory, brings to life when he asks people how much time it would take them to recreate what they have built if they had lost all their intellectual property, hardware, code, and so forth. On average that's 10 percent of the original time. So what took the other 90 percent of effort the first time?[5] That's the critical learning that had to happen. He calls these learnings and those from failed projects "moonshot compost" on which new projects can "grow."

Octopus Organizations understand that not all failures are created equally. They distinguish between "good failure" (learning through intelligent experimentation) and two problematic types that must be actively prevented: "complex failures," which occur when familiar systems break down due to unexpected combinations of events, and "preventable failures," which result from deviations from known processes due to skill gaps or behavioral issues.[6]

Octopus Organizations analyze problematic failures beyond superficial first-order answers such as *"the process was not followed"* or *"it was the employee's fault."* Instead, they use what Amy Edmonson calls "thoughtful reflection" and cross-functional analysis, bringing together different disciplines to look at root causes without assigning blame for these types of complex or preventable failures. They identify contributing factors across interconnected systems for system improvement and risk mitigation, to arrive at better learning: *The employee did not follow the process because they were overworked and tired and were given an unreasonable deadline. It was the system's fault.* Garry Ridge, CEO and Chairman of WD-40, reframes these as learning moments with a "positive or negative outcome of any situation that needs to be openly and freely shared to benefit all."[7]

Octopus leaders normalize failure to remove fear. They explicitly emphasize the context of uncertainty and what's at stake. For good, intelligent failure, they position potential failure as a source of valuable data that, while not fun, must be considered good news because of the insight it brings. By creating this clarity up front, the true objective becomes to avoid the *real* failure: trying something, learning it doesn't work, and continuing anyway.

This normalization often requires dramatic gestures to break through ingrained fear. An executive at a failing insurance company put a large jar of glass marbles on the table during an executive meeting. The marbles represented the number of customers they were losing every single day. The organization was already *epically* failing (complex failure), she noted to us. The jar worked magic because it took away the pressure to avoid the good experimentation failures, creating a freer mindset. Ferrari CEO Benedetto Vigna publicly talks about failures in investor relations calls and with the press to send a signal that failure is natural and expected with innovation.

Octopus Organizations work to reduce the pain and fear that comes with failing. Octopus leaders mitigate the fear of good failure by deliberately changing the language from one of execution to one of discovery. To reduce the fear that paralyzes teams, Octopus leaders use a powerful tool borrowed from the scientific method: they depersonalize failure ("I *am* wrong") by framing work as hypotheses to be tested.[8] This creates psychological distance between an individual and their idea. The focus shifts from the immense pressure of *being right* to the collaborative process of *finding out what is true*. If the hypothesis is disproven, the experiment is still a success because it generated valuable knowledge. The individual isn't wrong; the team has simply learned. It's the difference between the anxious pronouncement, "We *are building* this," and the intellectually honest exploration, "We *are testing if* this should be built."

Octopus Organizations systematically lower the cost of failure while maximizing learning. They run many, inexpensive small experiments. By keeping failure costs low, they remove the fear that paralyzes decision-making and create space for rapid iteration that drives innovation.

Ironically, Tin Men think avoiding failure reduces risk. But this risk-averse mindset creates a dangerous trap: by avoiding small, controlled experiments and the inevitable small intelligent failures that come with them, exposure to catastrophic failures down the line is amplified. Leaders become trapped in a cycle of safe choices. You don't explore with a perfect map. You need to send out scouts. If you punish the scouts for bringing back bad news, you'll fail in the same places, but more catastrophically with the whole organization.

Octopus Organizations fail in the future to learn in the present with tools like "pre-mortems." Here, teams imagine their project has failed spectacularly and spend time brainstorming what went wrong. This surfaces concerns that people might otherwise keep to themselves due to optimism bias or team pressure. In conversation with Astro, he shared with us what he said to his Wing team:

> It's three months from now. We had our launch one month ago, and it was so bad, we feel physically sick, we can't even make eye contact. We're so embarrassed. You have two minutes. This is a test. Write down why we're gonna screw up so badly. This got the team into the mentality of the sixteen-year-old, wanting to get an A on the test. It put them into this new mental state. They wanted to prove to themselves and everybody else that they knew the whole time so they scribbled furiously all the things that could go wrong. At the end of it, we collated all their ideas and we worked our butts off for two months and the launch went flawlessly.

Octopus Organizations embrace intelligent failure and let go gracefully. They learn in a "passionately dispassionate" way, being passionate advocates for innovation and customers while remaining disciplined and dispassionate critics of their own work, ready to pivot or abandon an initiative based on evidence.[9] They care about their projects, but they are not wed to them. They work hard and continuously to overcome biases and their deep-seated fears of failure. Many organizations create "quit criteria" that tell them when to stop and move on.[10] Annie Duke, drawing from her experience as a professional poker player, says every bet you make should include clear criteria for when to fold, given that most decisions are probabilistic. By documenting the decision-making process and regularly assessing progress against predetermined criteria, Octopus Organizations create a culture where stopping an unsuccessful project is seen as good stewardship.

They encourage this by **rewarding intelligent failure to foster a culture where people don't feel afraid to swing and miss.** The systems at Octopus Organizations are designed to counteract the natural inclination to hide failures to protect reputations, bonuses, or promotions. They actively encourage intellectual honesty by celebrating when an initiative is shut down, for its learning, including through public recognition and bonuses. Datadog's COO, Adam Blitzer, points out that there is a "tendency when people do a lot of work on a project, and it does not get implemented, not to celebrate. It could be many months of someone's life. Debrief, celebrate it, why was it valuable, how will it shape the next two things we will do?" Astro encourages public sharing of failures to be met with a standing ovation, a simple yet powerful gesture.

Some best practices are hard to sum up in a single sentence, but this one isn't. To be curious and innovative requires the courage to learn by casting aside the need to always be right. If we had to boil all this down, we'd just say: Octopus Organizations don't fail fast; they learn quickly and efficiently.

Levers

^ **Prioritize learning over features.** Here's a tactic borrowed from Astro: Get your teams to create an Important List that includes ten features for your experiment. Then ask them to make a Learning List of the things you could learn, ordered from most to least learning. Let them implement the first two Learning List items. Then ask them to make the Important List again. Invariably it would have already changed based on what happened with the first two learnings.

^ **Start with hypotheses.** Frame new initiatives with "We believe that X change will lead to Y improvement for Z reason" statements. This reframes potential failures as data points rather than personal shortcomings.

^ **Create a failure résumé.** Astro talks about creating a "failure résumé." This is a public list of an individual's worst failures, a "fun and cathartic" exercise that challenges others to think about whether they are taking enough risks in innovating and getting comfortable thinking and talking about failure.

^ **Celebrate the courage to fail.** Make sure those people who are "passionately dispassionate" and have proven something has *not* worked get standing ovations, bonuses, and prime spots in new high-value initiatives.

^ **Practice blameless postmortems.** After each project (success or failure), conduct a formal review focusing on what went well, what didn't, and what can be learned. Focus on systemic patterns, not blame. Use the "5 Whys" technique (see Antipattern #29, "Falling in Love with Answers") to move past surface-level explanations and uncover deeper second- and third-order reasons for failures.

^ **Reframe success metrics.** Shift from measuring outcomes to tracking learning velocity. Follow Amazon's example by measuring how quickly hypotheses are proven or disproven with the fewest resources.

^ **Make current failures visible.** When facing complex or preventable failures that are already happening, place a visible reminder in a prominent place showing the real cost of the current situation. This removes the pressure of avoiding experimental failure by making existing problems tangible and creating urgency for trying new approaches. When teams see the cost of not trying new approaches, they become more willing to test intelligent solutions.

DISCOVER MORE

ANTIPATTERNS TO READ NEXT

#14: Operating on a Culture of Fear

#20: Seeking Perfect Decisions

#30: Avoiding Hard Problems

USING PROXIES FOR CUSTOMERS

Deep obsession with getting close to and understanding real customers ensures long-term impact.

THE TIN MAN BEHAVIOR

Relying on inadequate proxies like internal voices, assumptions, past experiences, and easy-to-implement metrics to avoid the messy work of engaging directly with actual customers

THE RESULTS

- Missed opportunities to meet unidentified customer needs
- Increased irrelevance to evolving existing customers
- Wasted resources on mismatched products/services

How Octopus Organizations Behave Instead

- They directly engage with real customers and invest in deep quantitative and qualitative understanding.
- They are obsessed with and positively paranoid about customers' changing needs.
- They anticipate needs beyond what customers tell them.

The Tin Man Behavior

Between 2012 and 2017 McDonald's lost roughly 500 million customer transactions, a year-on-year average drop of 1.7 percent.[1] While many hypotheses existed for what happened, one thing was clear to many, including Phil, who was international CIO at McDonald's at the time: McDonald's had forgotten who the customer was.

Like most companies, Phil's team and the business in general talked a good game on customers—but decisions, Phil eventually realized, were being made instinctively with a question in mind (or even said out loud): "What would the franchisees think?" All-day breakfast? Too operationally complex for the franchisee. Home delivery? Expensive for the franchisee. We had taken our eye off the real customer. In our work today we see such once-removed or complete inward focus across every industry. We hear insurance companies, for example, talk up policyholder satisfaction but focus on their brokers.

Misunderstanding customers starts with losing curiosity and customer focus, which happens in a few ways. First, success breeds complacency. Teams stop listening, especially to those who "quietly send us their money without complaint. We take them for granted, forgetting how to excite them and turn them into our greatest fans and strongest sales team," entrepreneur, adviser, and author Barry O'Reilly observes.[2] There's arrogance, too. We believe we know what customers want because we've succeeded with them before. One COO we worked with said to us, shockingly, that his successful firm had a "divine right to exist," and we knew right then he wasn't curious about customer needs. Others mistake their technical expertise for customer understanding. We listened to one distinguished engineer with a PhD and thirty years at a company tell us the reason his product flopped was because the customers were stupid and didn't understand how good his solution was!

Second, proxies create false images of customers. Proxy measures such as Net Promoter Score (NPS), a golden metric to chase that will ensure customer focus, miss signals. They're used because, well, they're easier than engaging with customers (you get what you pay for), and also because customers are complex. These measures simplify the complexity, but they don't capture mildly happy customers who will jump to a competitor for an even slightly better price or product, or even just more attention from their vendor. Even poorer proxy measures send signals that are the opposite of what they intend. A call center's call volume going down is treated as a sign of customer satisfaction, but maybe it just means you have more customers giving up. Proxy voices like Chief Customer Officers are valuable, but they are often overrelied on to become the one Voice of the Customer *instead* of actual customer engagement.

Third, weak, subtle signals of customer changes are ignored or explained away, often with data. For example, limited opt-in surveys that report overall customer satisfaction give a false sense of security when those who see the customers every day notice changes in customers that need to be addressed.

Once focus is lost, you stop gaining insights you need, and you misunderstand customers' problems and needs. At that point, it becomes simply impossible to be clear on how to deliver value to them. And if you're a big company, you likely move too slowly to adjust to do what smaller, nimbler companies are doing—listening to what customers want—and delivering at speed. The examples are legion. Netflix and Blockbuster; Uber and taxis; Spotify and iTunes. This is disruptive innovation, and it starts with someone understanding a customer need better than you.

Fail to serve, satisfy, and continue to be hungry for your customers' business and they will reward you by leaving. Conservatively the cost of this poor service and lack of customer-centricity is $1.9 trillion in the United States alone.[3]

The 2016 Amazon shareholder letter coined a term related to this: "Day 2."[4] It's the bad brother of the "Day 1" culture that drives continuous reflection and improvement at the company, even when customers profess to be happy. Jeff Bezos defined Day 2 as "Stasis. Followed by irrelevance. Followed by excruciating, painful decline. Followed by death." Melodramatic, maybe, but that's how Amazon sees the cost of ignoring customers.

What Octopus Organizations Do Instead

Octopus Organizations are customer-obsessed, designed, like our real octopus, from its neural clusters to its tentacles, to be constantly sensing and responding to the customer environment. Customer value is the purpose of the organization, the driving force behind every decision, every innovation, and every interaction, and they never let teams forget it. At Amazon an empty chair is often present in a meeting room as a reminder of the customer. At Tesco supermarkets' headquarters, public spaces are covered with photos of customers. Meeting room interiors were designed like the interiors of typical customer homes.

Octopus leaders and teams directly engage with customers. Digital design teams of a US hardware retailer went into their own stores to buy custom paint, and chatted with customers also buying paint, before building an online version of that process. Lego develops fans' ideas for sets into official products. The Salesforce Ventures Innovation Advisory Board is composed of prominent Salesforce customers, who offer feedback on new features and products. We're also advocates of examining how value is delivered by walking in the steps of those experiencing your product or service. Phil spent at least a few days a year working in McDonald's restaurants, and more days eating in them. At Tesco Bank Jana listened to calls from insurance customers, used her own company's banking products, and stacked shelves in the retail business during Christmas, interacting with customers.

Octopus leaders seek raw unfiltered customer feedback. They gather unfiltered, accurate, and as close to real-time as possible information from customers and the front line of the organization, avoiding filtering and sanitization of the information. In his book *Unlearn*, Barry reminds us of a story about unfiltered communication: When T-Mobile CEO John Legere joined the company in 2012 he didn't just commission reports on the business: he had a phone line installed in his office to listen directly to customer service calls for three hours a day, an unfiltered firehose of customer feedback. It requires vulnerability and curiosity for leaders to speak to customers. John replies personally when customers send him messages. His unfiltered approach led directly to the company's first prepaid product.[5] Similarly, former PepsiCo CEO Indra Nooyi sought out direct frontline feedback by visiting her own restaurants and riding with delivery drivers.[6]

Octopus Organizations start with the customer and work backward to the solution. Amazon approaches solving for customers this way using the Working Backwards mechanism, otherwise known as the Press Release–Frequently Asked Questions (PR-FAQ) mechanism. It requires teams to write a PR-FAQ document as if their product had already launched, forcing customer-centric thinking. The press release portion describes the customer need and how the product solves for it in language a customer would understand, while the FAQ section anticipates tough questions about feasibility, competition, and cost.

This isn't a superficial exercise—it's rigorous, iterative work that demands deep immersion in customer needs. Teams often go through multiple drafts, conducting extensive customer research, analyzing pain points, and validating assumptions before the narrative becomes compelling. The process forces uncomfortable questions: Are we solving a real problem customers will care about and pay for? Can we articulate the value in terms customers actually care about?

Teams maintain autonomy in deciding how they solve problems such as the technical approach, features, and timeline for their product. The only requirement is demonstrating clear customer value through a compelling narrative and addressing foundational questions such as:

- Who is the customer?

- What is the customer problem or opportunity?

- What is the most important customer benefit?

- How do you know what customers want or need?

- What does the customer experience look like?

This approach simply says, "Show us you're solving real customer problems" while leaving the solution path mainly up to the team. The review process is neither prescriptive nor hierarchical, but it does include soft rules such as ensuring there is enough feedback from those closest to the problem plus two levels of leadership above them to enrich the idea.

Octopus Organizations cultivate productive paranoia about their customers—assuming that customers are changing and that they will always want new and different things. They presume switching costs are low enough that any customer will bail for an even slightly better situation. They use technology and analytics to monitor these assumptions. As part of their Voice of the Customer program, Amazon's own heartbeat tool aggregates near-real-time data from more than a dozen sources, giving customer service teams unfiltered insights.

Octopus Organizations pay attention to anecdotes that differ from research and data. Customer anecdotes—a tweet, a comment on a survey, or a call center conversation—are documented, studied, and used to inform strategy. These anecdotes are often discarded as outliers but might instead indicate a significant emerging issue missed in the statistics.

Octopus Organizations invest in minimum lovable products (MLPs) to create customer excitement. Traditionally organizations create minimum *viable* products (MVPs), intended to maximize learning with the least effort.[7] Jeff Wilkie, Amazon's former CEO Worldwide Consumer, found that MVPs prioritized speed over customer delight. They become what developer teams thought would be achievable in the time available, not necessarily what a customer needs. Customers might be OK with an MVP, but they don't *want* an MVP. Jeff started to describe a new type of experiment in which you create something with just enough features for early customers to *love* the experience, which tends to make those products climb up the adoption curve rapidly.

The good news is that reconnecting with your customers isn't about mastering a complex new art. It's reawakening an innate curiosity and making direct engagement a tangible, daily practice—one that often brings a fresh sense of purpose to your teams and helps your organization stay truly meaningful to those it serves.

Levers

^ **Reduce distance between customers and leadership.** Leaders, not just people at the edge of your organization, should regularly engage directly with customers to gain firsthand insights into their needs, expectations, and perceptions of the company. Require senior leaders to actively engage with customers through dedicated time on service lines, feedback review sessions, and industry events. Microsoft's Satya Nadella is said to find the time to take two calls a day from other companies' CEOs.[8]

^ **Keep customers visible.** Create visual prompts to remind people of the centricity of your customers. It could be an empty chair in the meeting room, public displays of valuable customer data, or visuals of customers in office spaces.

^ **Create customer opportunity statements.** Before starting any initiative, ground your approach in customer understanding. Your opportunity statement can follow a structure like this: "[Customer type] currently faces [specific problem/challenge] when [situation occurs]." Support this statement with both qualitative and quantitative data about customer benefits, avoiding assumptions based on internal experience. For example, "Small-business owners struggle to manage inventory effectively when dealing with seasonal demand fluctuations."

These statements become the North Star for design decisions, to evaluate features, prioritize efforts, and test whether proposed solutions actually address the customer problem. When teams debate competing ideas or get pulled toward technically interesting but customer-irrelevant features, the opportunity statement helps them to refocus.

^ **Explicitly define your customer** using detailed personas. For instance, "Meet Lorraine, the Busy, On-the-Go Consumer. Lorraine values convenience, speed, and efficiency. She is a working professional who is always on the move and has limited time for meal preparation." Make these personas tangible by giving them names, stories, and specific scenarios. Use these clearly defined personas in every decision-making process ("What would Lorraine want?")

^ **Dive deep into research early.** Incorporating user research and empathy mapping will make products more connected to customer needs rather than assumptions about customer needs. In Amazon these might include understanding what customers are searching for, the path they take in clicking through the website to get it, when customers drop out of the buying process ("funnel analysis"), customer reviews and feedback, and social media mentions.

^ **Change the language.** Talk about your products from the customer perspective. Instead of "We're implementing a new claims processing system," say, "We're helping families get back on their feet faster after disasters by building this system." Instead of "we sell mortgages," say, "We are putting people into homes."

^ **Incentivize customer adoption.** Tweak rewards, whether financial or recognition, for achieving customer results rather than completing projects or building the product. McDonald's developers were incentivized with compensation for building systems that customers adopted. You will get pushback ("It's not in my control") for trying this, but it works.

^ **Live with your customers.** Procter & Gamble famously sends product teams to live with customers for days, observing how they use household products, which isn't always how you might assume they do. Microsoft transformed their Xbox strategy after discovering through home visits that gaming consoles were becoming family entertainment hubs.

DISCOVER MORE

ANTIPATTERNS TO READ NEXT

#3: Making "Everything" the Strategy

#9: Customizing Commodities

#29: Falling in Love with Answers

MORTGAGING THE FUTURE

Ambitious exploration helps companies forge new futures for customers and reshape markets.

THE TIN MAN BEHAVIOR

Believing that optimizing today is safer than inventing for an uncertain tomorrow, so focuses on short-term gains and incremental improvements as risk-reducing strategies

THE RESULTS

- Increased risk of disruption and erosion of market position
- Mediocre performance
- Missed opportunities to redefine markets

How Octopus Organizations Behave Instead

- They embrace ambitious thinking about the future.
- They learn to balance exploitation and exploration.
- They cultivate a culture of curiosity and data-driven risk-taking to discover transformative innovations.

The Tin Man Behavior

During the rise of mobile computing in the early 2000s, Intel focused intensely on *sustaining* innovations—making faster, more powerful chips for its most profitable customers. This focus led to spectacular results at the time, but it blinded the company to the disruptive potential of low-power, low-cost processors needed for smartphones and tablets.[1] Competitors moved in and eventually captured the vast majority of that exploding market while Intel struggled to adapt its power-hungry chipsets.

Inside Intel's halls, the rationalizations probably sounded like ones we've heard from companies in similar positions. They all talk about and explain the world as it is, not as it's becoming. *Mobile chips aren't profitable enough* or *Our enterprise customers demand maximum performance.*

Organizations like Intel—or Blockbuster, or Toys "R" Us, or Sears, or even, ironically, Xerox PARC—couldn't see the future. The tragedy is that they saw it, even *invented it*, but still chose to focus on the now, not the next. Like a frog in slowly heating water, they mistook current stability for long-term safety, until things boiled.

The frog may not have had a choice, but companies do. Still, they sit in the warming water because Tin Man models abhor uncertainty, and breakthrough innovations require betting on unknowable outcomes.

Biases come into play here, too: availability bias, familiarity bias, and *present* bias—five dollars now feels better, safer, than *maybe* ten dollars, but also maybe *no* dollars, a week from now. Astro Teller, of Alphabet X's Moonshot Factory, poses it more starkly:

> Choice A: You can give a million dollars of value to your business this year guaranteed, or

> Choice B: you can give a billion dollars of value to your business this year, but it is not guaranteed. It's one chance in one hundred.

Most people he asks select choice B with a confident smile. When he then asks if in their wildest dreams and best days their managers would support choice B, they inevitably answer "no." Astro says to them: "You don't need a lecture on innovation. You need a new manager." We all ask for breakthrough innovation, but in practice Tin Men are not actually prepared to support it because innovation is mostly about "making a mess" and betting on potential future value, and the business is neither tolerant of the mess (not efficient) nor comfortable with the uncertainty (added risk).

Several issues prevent Tin Men from thinking bigger:

- **Cost.** Markets and investors put pressure on hitting short-term earnings targets and meeting rigid ROI requirements.

- **Leadership.** Risk-averse executives protect their tenure and compensation, often tied to quarterly results. Jeff Bezos observed that "we tend to overestimate risk and underestimate opportunity so that thinking small becomes a self-fulfilling prophecy."[2]

- **Inertia.** Success breeds complacency; futures that threaten existing success (such as product cannibalization) are frowned upon.

- **Cognition.** Many leaders struggle to imagine radical change because it feels so uncomfortable.

- **Structure.** Siloed departments, legacy systems, technical debt, and bureaucratic decision-making processes limit the agility needed for curious exploration of potential futures.

Even if there is some desire deep down in the Tin Man to consider the future, so many executives are overworked and exhausted, aching to get to a weekend (if they're afforded one). There is no energy left for the future. Given the decreasing average tenure of C-level executives, there's also simply no incentive to make ambitious, long-term plans.

What Octopus Organizations Do Instead

Octopus Organizations focus on what's to gain, not what's at risk. Instead of spending an inordinate amount of time calculating downside risks and protecting existing assets, Octopus Orgs become energized by upside potential, future opportunities, and possibilities of new technologies. This shift from loss aversion to gain orientation changes everything—decision-making becomes faster, bolder, and more innovative. When you're focused on what you might gain rather than what you might lose, experimentation feels exciting rather than threatening, and the future becomes a source of energy rather than anxiety.

Octopus Organizations think big. Waymo, Alphabet's self-driving car, has completed more than 33 million miles on public roads and aims to revolutionize transportation safety and efficiency.[3] Alphabet X's Project Loon used high-altitude balloons to provide internet connectivity to remote areas in Kenya and Peru, helping bridge the digital divide.[4] Big thinking isn't restricted to high-tech companies. Think of Lego's expansion beyond physical bricks into films, video games, and theme parks, or Disney's MagicBand technology.[5] Any organization can learn to think beyond its perceived boundaries.

Big ideas share several key characteristics:

- *Ambitious vision* that may seem impossible or far-fetched at first glance

- *Contrarian challenges* to the status quo, thinking beyond conventional limitations

- *Radical solutions* to significant problems, often leveraging new technologies

- *Transformative, exponential impact* for individuals, organizations, or society as a whole

- *Risk* and accepting the possibility of failure as part of the innovation process

- *Patience* and understanding that iteration and payoff will take time

You might be thinking, *Why are they wasting my time talking about big ideas when my organization cannot even fathom a big, future-focused project?* We argue it can, and that achieving something ten times bigger is counterintuitively easier than making something just 10 percent bigger. An incremental-improvement mindset keeps us tethered to existing tools and limitations. Big 10x goals, though, free us from that mindset precisely because we know we can't get there with what we have now. This freedom inspires ownership, curiosity, and hard work. Which do you want to work on—creating a shopping experience without checkout or increasing returns on invested capital from 12.1 percent to 12.6?

Octopus Organizations understand that disruption isn't a future threat—it's woven into the fabric of today's operations. It thinks both expansively and practically, connecting ambitious, imaginative big goals with the concrete steps needed now to start to get there. One example that illustrates this kind of thinking is Amazon's "Just Walk Out," which lets customers check-in to a retail store, pick up their goods, and literally just leave, bypassing both lines and paying, a time-consuming annoyance to many customers.[6] If Amazon were short-term obsessed, this kind of project would never get off the ground with all its not-yet-invented tech and processes and the relative uncertainty of whether it would work. But the company approached the challenge by working backward from the ideal customer experience: a friction-free shopping journey, then taking practical steps to incrementally develop the technology to make that happen. Working backward from the opportunity or problem is preferred over limiting a vision to what's currently possible.[7]

Octopus Organizations think of strategy as an infinite game.[8] Finite games, like a tennis match, end with clear winners and losers. Infinite games, like Lego, can go on forever, and the goal isn't to win, but to *keep playing*. This simple distinction creates radically different questions and actions. The finite player, trapped in the quarterly cycle, asks, "How can we maximize this quarter's profit?" The infinite player asks, "What investments must we make now to ensure we're still delighting customers a decade from now?" This infinite orientation makes curiosity and ambitious exploration not just options but mandatory practices for long-term relevance.

Octopus Organizations play the movie backward, as Moderna CEO Stéphane Bancel describes it.[9] Project three, five, or ten years into the future, envision the destination, then rewind, playing the movie backward and mapping out the necessary milestones to get to that envisioned future. In Octopus Organizations, as Jeff has said, "Friends congratulate me after a quarterly-earnings announcement and say, 'Good job, great quarter. . . .' And I'll say, 'Thank you, but that quarter was baked three years ago. I'm working on a quarter that'll happen in [three years' time] right now.'"[10]

The Octopus doesn't make reckless bets, as Astro, Alphabet X's CEO, notes. Future-focus is counting cards, not gambling.[11] It's about iterative learning: trying, evaluating, learning from reality, and de-risking through evidence. Principles from the Lean Startup methodology help here, building minimum viable products to test assumptions rapidly, conducting rapid experiments to accelerate the build-measure-learn feedback loop, and maintaining willingness to pivot when validated learning reveals better strategic directions.[12] Instead of walking in with a fixed mindset, there is openness to what projects could be. Projects with slow learning loops are deprioritized in favor of those that yield rapid insights. Success is measured not just by immediate progress but by the "learning per dollar."[13] The faster you're learning, the more likely you are to be successful, no matter how big the future goal is.

Octopus Organizations show ambidexterity in embracing the future by pursuing simultaneously incremental and discontinuous innovation. You don't necessarily need massive up-front investment to start thinking big or long-term. Organizations can efficiently exploit existing business to fund long-term explorations. They can dream big but start small. Crucially, you need to establish processes for data-driven evaluation—"card counting"—to guide long-term investments.

Octopus Organizations are willing to be misunderstood for long periods of time, as Amazon puts it, underscoring the company's commitment to long-term, audacious goals that often challenge conventional wisdom, like seemingly cannibalizing the company's book business with an e-reader.[14] Octopus leaders need to be audacious because most people around them do not want to be. They need to love the idea of a 1 percent shot at $1 billion more than the $1 million guaranteed.

Levers

^ **Visualize future scenarios vividly.** Hold sessions where teams collaboratively imagine and detail potential future states of their industry, customer needs, technological possibilities, and organization in three, five, or ten years, confronting the implications of current decisions and potential disruptions. Use techniques such as "pretotypes," storytelling, day-in-the-life, and visuals to make the future more visceral.

^ **Think 10x, not 10 percent.** When presented with a proposal, ask, "What would it take to make the outcome 10x bigger?" Ask teams to make assumptions and constraints explicit and challenge them. Ask them what experiments need to be run to prove out new thinking. Rather than aiming for what is immediately achievable, ask questions such as, "If we succeeded beyond our wildest dreams with this, how big could that be?" and "If we had no limits, what would this look like?"

^ **Decouple thinking big from feasibility.** Develop ideas first; figure out feasibility quickly after and at low cost. Don't let feasibility and assumptions about current constraints stand in the way of embracing the future.

^ **Encourage future-casting communities of practice.** Former NASA/JPL CTO Tom Soderstrom created a team of futurists interested in solving today's problems with tomorrow's tech. Have such a team actively monitor industry trends, technological advancements, and competitor activities, providing updates that highlight potential threats and opportunities that demand long-term consideration.

^ **Align incentives, metrics, and resource allocation.** Tackle internal drivers of short-termism. Revise executive compensation and performance management to include an element of longer time horizons (three to five years) and metrics tied to strategic milestones and innovation outcomes, not just quarterly financials. Protect exploration budgets and use stage-gated funding based on validated learning milestones.

DISCOVER MORE

ANTIPATTERNS TO READ NEXT

#3: Making "Everything" the Strategy

#30: Avoiding Hard Problems

#36: Pretending to Innovate

FALLING IN LOVE WITH ANSWERS

Love of problems and deep investment
in learning the *why* behind them produces
superior solutions.

THE TIN MAN BEHAVIOR

Rushing to solve challenges with urgency to show progress before
deeply understanding the problem to be solved or validating the
solution, rewarding action over understanding

THE RESULTS

- Poor solutions based on the incomplete understanding of root causes
- Ineffective products and services
- Missed opportunities to create impact and solve problems

How Octopus Organizations Behave Instead

- They focus on why they're doing something before deciding what
  they're doing.
- They spend as much or more time on problem definition as on
  solution generation.
- They systematically test assumptions and reward impact over
  project completion.

The Tin Man Behavior

The 1990s Silicon Valley company General Magic, packed with former Apple
geniuses like Bill Atkinson and Andy Hertzfeld, isn't a company many talk
about today.[1] Its mission was to create the Magic Link, a device that would
include a phone, touchscreen, email, games, downloadable apps, and animated

emojis. This was years before the first iPhone. The press described it as "absolutely, flat-out, ahead-of-its-time amazing."[2]

Magic Link sold only about three thousand devices, mostly to family and friends of the company. The product and the company failed, leading to tens of millions of dollars of losses.

And the signs of failure were there from the start. It wasn't engineering failure—the Magic Link was indeed a technical marvel. It was a failure to be curious about what customers wanted and what problems they could solve for customers.[3]

Instead, the company was deeply focused on making Magic Link the most advanced personal computing device in the world, which was not something customers needed or a problem customers were looking to solve. The company skipped user research and only started testing once engineering was done. When testing went poorly, they didn't adapt.

Not long after, Palm emerged with a successful personal digital assistant that was not an engineering marvel, really, but it *did* solve a customer problem: How can I bring my Rolodex with me on the go?[4]

Even the brightest people can succumb to Tin Man tendencies. The Magic Link team wasn't stupid. They were just in love, which is what happens with solutions. We are seduced by them. Spending time on solutions *feels* more productive than time spent trying to understand causes. But as organizational psychologist David Hofmann describes, this seduction leads to many problems: rushed decision-making focused on "What should we do?" and reinforced by cultures that favor action over questions.[5] It creates over-reliance on past experiences, which is where the brain first goes to solve problems, and competitive advocacy that emerges as various teams try to get their solution to win rather than to collaborate on defining the problem better.

Once we fall in love with solutions, our biases try to prevent contrary information from interfering. Confirmation bias makes us crowd out or explain away contradictory data. The availability heuristic makes us favor ideas that come to mind easily, and, related to that, the anchoring bias makes us favor ideas we hear first, even when we have evidence of better options. The "neighborhood of symptom" rule means we tend to try to solve problems where we see symptoms when we should be asking why this symptom is present.[6] A missed sales target prompts investigation of the sales department, then perhaps pricing and product quality, but less often extends to questioning fundamental assumptions about the market or customer needs.

There are some easy ways to spot this antipattern in your organization. Does your org tend to fall in love with tech trends and try to create solutions from these? Does your organization tend to jump to familiar solutions, especially ones that worked in different circumstances in the past, so-called habituation? Does it reward teams that often provide solutions and promise fast change? Have you struggled with colleagues who purport to want to find good solutions but just seem wedded to their own idea?

These are all telltale signs of Tin Man organizations wedded to a "bring me solutions" mentality that doesn't ask the right questions or seek root causes. That's because Tin Man organizations' focus on productivity and their propensity to value busyness means solutions become hard currency, a way to show activity. And it results in products, or change efforts, that miss the mark. Without a clear understanding of problems and root causes, organizations waste time, money, and energy on features and products their customers or business don't need or want. Seeking understanding, which is slower at first, is more open-ended and can look downright inefficient. Impatience, arrogance, misapplied experience, and just a desire to get going are some of the traits of organizations that regularly fall in love with bad solutions and then struggle to escape.

What Octopus Organizations Do Instead

Octopus Organizations fall in love with the problem. The Octopus leader makes sure that the *why* drives the *what*, not vice versa. Classically this is described as "people don't buy drills, they buy holes."

Octopus Organizations deliberately slow down problem-solving. They don't rush this understanding step. There are multiple forms of this slowdown. Amazon uses the "Working Backwards" process, which requires teams to write a press release and frequently asked questions (PR-FAQs) for their proposed solution before building anything to create a deeper understanding of who solutions are for, what needs they meet.[7] Toyota uses the "Five Whys" method.[8] "Problem-solution pairing" is another approach: presenting solutions only with clear, specific customer stories. This prevents teams from wasting weeks designing for the wrong customer group, forcing early validation of whether the problem affects customers who are actually a good fit for the product.[9]

Disney slowed down to deal with declining performance by asking "How else could we fix this?" Rather than go straight to cutting costs or raising prices, they instead focused on reducing the time guests spent standing in line. They learned from a pharmacy in Tokyo that used radio-frequency identification technology to reduce lines, turning that into Disney's MagicBand. The product gave guests more time to play—and spend. It increased quarterly results by 3 percent without raising gate prices. This solution was one of the biggest single revenue-generating hits in Disney park history.[10]

When Spotify noticed declining user engagement, instead of rushing to add features, they spent six weeks mapping user journeys, which revealed a root cause: their recommendation algorithm was creating echo chambers, a systemic issue that quick-fix feature additions would have missed. When Netflix faced video buffering complaints, rather than immediately investing in faster servers, their systematic analysis revealed that partnering with internet service providers to install local content caches would be far more effective.

Octopus leaders encourage a quick path to "no." Alphabet Moonshot Lab's Astro Teller observed that if a team says to him, "We know what the right thing to do is," red flags go up. "We will definitely stop it as soon as they turn out to be wrong, which they inevitably will. A team that says from the first moment 'We're probably wrong' has a better chance of turning the loop faster, so we're going to bet on them longer."[11] Successful teams take the approach that "if our attitude is 'how quickly are we gonna get to yes,' then we are in for the wrong thing."[12] Instead, if we are going to start many experiments, ask, "How efficiently can we get to 'no'?"

Progressive Octopus leaders also move *away* from the mantra "Don't bring me problems; bring me solutions." When Anita Krohn Traaseth took over Norway's government innovation efforts, she specifically *solicited problems* through "speed dates" with employees across fourteen offices, gathering insights about bottlenecks before considering solutions.[13] As former president of Starbucks International, Howard Behar, told us, "Leaders sometimes think they need all the right answers. It's the opposite of this—they need to ask the right questions. That's what they get paid for."

Levers

^ **Mandate clear problem or opportunity statements.** For example, "The current process for X results in Y inefficiency/error/problem, costing Z. We need to find a way to achieve W outcome." Amazon uses the following rubric to describe the customer opportunity statement: **Today** <customer type> **have to** <describe problem/opportunity> **when** <situation/scenario> occurs. Make these agreed-upon statements *highly visible*, such as on team boards and in meetings, and use them as a constant reference point for decisions about solutions.

^ **Ask better questions.** Good questions lead with "How might we?" "How could I?" or "What would happen if?" "*What core assumptions are we* *making about the situation?"* *"What evidence contradicts our hypothesis?"* *"What would need to be true for the proposed solution to fail spectacularly?"* *"If we were starting from scratch with no constraints, what would the ideal solution look like?"* Use such questions to prevent existing knowledge (and solutions) and biases from limiting your ability to imagine new possibilities.

^ **Practice delayed intuition.** Before excitedly committing to an idea, take the time to research, prototype, and gather information. The more exciting an idea seems, the longer to wait before committing to it. This process involves researching the idea, developing business and product plans, and seeing if the excitement remains. Delay commitment, not exploration.

^ **Practice problem-solution pairing.** Request concrete customer stories that show why a proposed solution is the right one and that it solves a genuine issue. This enables crucial discussions about customer demand: does this problem affect customers who are actually a good fit for the product, or are we designing for the wrong customer group?

^ **Employ specific discovery techniques.** Don't just "do design thinking." Use concrete methods: create detailed customer personas and empathy maps based on real interviews; meticulously map customer journey diagrams and service blueprints to pinpoint friction; conduct jobs-to-be-done interviews to understand underlying motivations; use prototypes to test ideas and gather feedback.[14] Adopt Eric von Hippel "extreme" or "lead" user approach, which involves identifying and studying users with the most advanced needs or those who have already developed innovative solutions to their specific problems, as a way to drive breakthrough innovations.[15] This approach can help accelerate insights into future market trends and develop products that meet the needs of a wider audience.

^ **Demand multiple possible solutions.** Set an expectation that nothing will move forward before multiple solutions are explored. Support this expectation through structured divergent thinking exercises such as "Crazy 8s" sketching sessions, where teams rapidly generate multiple solution concepts; brainstorming techniques such as SCAMPER, designed to stimulate creative thinking and problem-solving; or brainwriting sessions, where ideas are recorded silently in writing rather than verbalized to create safety in sharing ideas, as well as inclusivity and idea diversity and quantity.[16] There are many techniques available; explore them, and find the ones that work for you.

^ **Avoid habituation.** Challenge the status quo by noticing and questioning the issues that others have accepted. Use techniques such as Gemba walks to see what *really* happens on the front lines, "fresh eyes" reviews that invite perspectives from people outside the immediate team and domain, immersive "Day in the Life" studies with customers or employees, and "negative brainstorming" in which you invite people to suggest ideas for making a product or experience worse to reveal hidden assumptions.

^ **Prototype the whole experience** across the entire customer journey, prioritizing speed and learning through low-fidelity paper or storyboard prototypes before investing heavily in mock-ups and minimum *lovable* products. Use generative AI to create working prototypes. Have a customer experience specialist sit with the engineers and rapidly prototype something that can be tested with customers.

^ **Say what you're doing.** Meetings can be clearly delineated problem-seeking, problem-solving, or advocacy for a potential solution. Use different facilitation techniques, ground rules, time allocations, and expected outputs appropriate for each type of meeting. For problem-seeking, prioritize active listening, inquiry, and data gathering; for solution advocacy, focus on evidence, assumptions, potential risks, and quit criteria.

^ **Implement continuous discovery habits.**[17] Introduce the practice of teams engaging in frequent, small-scale research activities such as weekly short customer interviews and rapid usability tests as part of regular workflow.

DISCOVER MORE

ANTIPATTERNS TO READ NEXT

#24: Mismanaging Incentives

#32: Building Homophilic Teams

#36: Pretending to Innovate

AVOIDING HARD PROBLEMS

To put a talking monkey on a pedestal, start with the monkey problem, not the pedestal.

THE TIN MAN BEHAVIOR

Choosing to tackle the more achievable parts of challenges first and focusing on visible progress rather than validating that the hardest parts are achievable

THE RESULTS

- Costly delays discovering critical roadblocks
- False signs of progress
- Missed opportunities to learn and pivot strategy

How Octopus Organizations Behave Instead

- They tackle the hardest, riskiest part of a project first to learn and validate.
- They get to "no" quickly when the hardest parts prove insurmountable.
- They reward intellectual honesty and learning from failure.

The Tin Man Behavior

If you wanted to get a monkey sitting on top of a ten-foot pedestal to recite Shakespeare, where would you begin? According to Astro Teller, who uses this image to explain a fundamental principle of the approach his Alphabet X's Moonshot Factory takes, the right answer is to train the monkey first. Astro's moonshot lab uses #MonkeyFirst to describe how it starts with the hardest parts of a project.[1] "A lot of work, weirdly, goes into the pedestal early on at a lot of companies—sometimes even at X—because there's so much pressure to get rewarded for having done a good job. 'Hey, nice pedestal!' [A]t some point the boss is going to pop by and ask for a status update—and you want to be able to show off something other than a long list of reasons why teaching a monkey to talk is really, really hard."[2]

The temptation to start with the pedestal and solve easy problems first is natural and understandable. The pedestal:

- **provides immediate gratification** from visible "wins" that boost morale in the short term.

- **provides the ability to showcase** to leaders who often prefer presentations that highlight concrete achievements.

- **helps with resource constraints** that put teams off tackling complex problems that require significant time, research, and effort to understand and solve.

- **keeps teams in a comfort zone** of what they know; solving familiar problems feels safer than venturing into uncharted territory where risk of blame and repercussions for failure await.

These temptations are not moral failings of leaders or teams, rather just the by-product of the Tin Man's need to *see* progress. Early wins look good on quarterly results reports and can be used to justify budgets and performance. Incentive structures, additionally, reward productivity over curiosity and learning. We even laud this focus on making progress in corporate speak, talking about going after the "low-hanging fruit" first.

Conversely, tackling the hard problems often involves working through ambiguity, uncertainty, and the high potential for failure. This can be daunting, especially in risk-averse corporate cultures that drive toward the security of achievable outcomes and reward progress. Tin Man companies' limited bandwidth, budgets, and talent create pressure to focus on issues that can be "solved" quickly.

What Octopus Organizations Do Instead

Octopus Organizations apply curiosity to the hardest things first. That's where understanding of risks and learning comes from. You've noticed we've been amassing animal metaphors in this book, and here's another colorful one from Mark Twain: "Eat a live frog first thing in the morning and nothing worse will happen to you the rest of the day." The same is true in tackling the hardest task first.

Octopus Organizations get to "no" faster. The faster you figure out your monkey can't learn Shakespeare, the less time, money, and effort you have sunk into the initiative, making it easier to quit. Building pedestals means you're spending time, money, and other resources on things that get you no closer to figuring out whether you can achieve what it is you are striving for.

Nothing else matters if you don't solve the hard thing first. But also, beware of false progress. The Foghorn team at Astro's lab, for example, developed a way to turn seawater into carbon-neutral liquid fuel. Their "pedestal" was building the technology to generate the fuel. Their "monkey" was figuring out how to make their fuel cost competitive. When they realized their monkey was unlikely to come to fruition, Foghorn called it quits to free up X's resources for ideas more likely to succeed.[3] Though the decision was rational, letting go of something the team had poured their hearts into was undeniably difficult.

Astro articulated another, simple example to communicate the challenge.[4] Imagine that you set yourself one year to establish a massively successful podcast. You can spend that year building up your followership, work hard to create lots of compelling episodes, do lots of marketing, and so forth. That's your pedestal. Or you could spend the first month brainstorming unusual, unexpected, and smart ideas to make it successful. Then you take three months to test these ideas as quickly and inexpensively as possible. You then take another two months to invest and test more deeply in the top ideas. That leaves you with six months to deliver and scale your podcast. You won't get as much early satisfaction from the latter approach, but you're more likely to succeed.

Octopus Organizations strive to be intellectually honest, which is difficult because when you take ownership of a project and commit to personal investment, when you really want it to work, it can feel strange to spend the first few months doing that hard thing that might tell you to let go of the idea. Octopuses understand that most value comes from first proving viability. Paradoxically, this early investment in tackling the hardest things is *less* risky than grabbing the low-hanging fruit, particularly as you try to do this with minimal investment and the greatest honesty.

For people to be open about this, you need to reward them—emotionally and financially. Share their contribution and learning, however it goes, to share insights that will help other teams and spare others from duplicating failures. Too often, the operational model will incentivize the opposite. If a team knows that being honest about challenges won't get recognition or promotions and will damage future efforts, they will end up working secretly on lots of things that are still likely to fail, just more slowly. So instead, teams work on lots of things they secretly know are not going to make it.

In return for embracing this way of operating, Octopus Organizations:

- Develop solutions with broader and unexpected applications. Project Loon, Alphabet X's attempt to use lasers held aloft by balloons to provide global connectivity, ended up becoming an earth-based communication system.[5]

- Develop unique capabilities and offerings, setting them apart from competitors.

- Are more able to attract and retain top talent with meaningful and challenging work, providing opportunities for intellectual stimulation and growth.

Levers

^ **Set ambitious goals to get your team to focus on the monkey first.** Get your project in contact with the physical world ASAP. Getting ready for real-world application naturally requires your team to face monkeys. For the autonomous car company Waymo, Larry Page set the team the "Larry 1000 test," asking them to get a car to one thousand miles self-driven without any intervention. If your teams achieve it, they will have made a leap, and if not, they will have learned a lot about the monkey problems.

^ **Cultivate intellectual honesty.** Celebrate stopping projects when the hard problems prove too challenging, through public recognition, bonuses, or similar. Intentionally give verbal praise at least twice a week to team members who demonstrate intellectual honesty, vulnerability, or "monkey spotting" skills. Consider a lighthearted, symbolic recognition like a "Golden Monkey Award" (or something similar, tailored to your team's culture) that would be well received and genuinely reinforce the desired behavior. Doing so helps prevent procrastinating on the pedestals for fear of facing the monkeys.

^ **Change your project review and demo culture.** For the first several check-ins on new, risky projects, forbid teams from showing polished slides or discussing "pedestal" progress. Instead, require them to demonstrate their messiest, most incomplete progress on the single hardest part of the problem. If they're trying to teach the monkey to talk, you want to see a video of them attempting to get the monkey to make a sound, not a presentation on pedestal acoustics. This shifts incentives from looking good to making real progress on what truly matters.

- ^ **Engage teams' natural desire for being recognized for creativity and forward thinking.** Frame this as an opportunity for people to demonstrate their curiosity and creativity. Ask, "What are the things that could derail us here? What are we *not* seeing?" Thank contributors and highlight how their insights improved the project. When someone points out a flaw, respond with genuine curiosity: "That's an angle I hadn't considered—can you walk us through your thinking?" to allow them to showcase their expertise safely.

- ^ **Reframe monkeys as learning.** Avoid always talking about the challenge, the hard part. Ask: "What are the biggest *learning opportunities* we anticipate?" or "What are the *key unknowns* that will help us learn the most?" Consistently ask "What if?" questions. "What if our key assumption about [market condition] is wrong?" "What if [technical challenge] proves harder than we anticipate?" "What if [competitor] takes a different approach?" This reframing encourages exploration of different possibilities, including negative ones, in a less threatening way than direct risk assessments. Scenario planning makes exploring potential problems a structured, analytical process, rather than an emotional admission of weakness.

DISCOVER MORE

ANTIPATTERNS TO READ NEXT

#24: Mismanaging Incentives

#26: Evading Failure

#31: Avoiding Tough Conversations

AVOIDING TOUGH CONVERSATIONS

Honest dialogue and constructive
conflict dissolve surface-level harmony
and boost performance.

THE TIN MAN BEHAVIOR

Discouraging disagreement and difficult conversation for fear of a loss
of progress and social cohesion

THE RESULTS

- Suppression of crucial information
- Increased vulnerability to failure
- Erosion of trust

How Octopus Organizations Behave Instead

- They embrace constructive conflict and open dialogue.
- They encourage and model vulnerability and intellectual honesty.
- They create structured methods for surfacing and navigating
  conflict and difficult conversations.

The Tin Man Behavior

You've probably experienced this common scene: you're in a meeting where concerns hang heavy in the air but remain unspoken. Some participants know the flaws in what's been proposed, others struggle to grasp unexplained concepts, while many bristle silently at decisions handed down without discussion. The atmosphere is thick with unaddressed tensions, where subtle cues—averted gazes, stiff body language—telegraph disagreement that never finds voice. There are awkward silences. No one speaks up, some for fear of rocking the boat, while others just don't want to look foolish.[1] It's a kind of faux harmony. Yet afterward, everyone nods in agreement when asked if they're all good, and then they exit the room to privately express their reservations in whispered conversations with trusted colleagues. This parallel communication system of "meeting after the meeting" creates shadow organizations where the real work of sense-making happens, disconnected from formal decision processes.

Surface-level harmony masks deeper organizational dysfunction. When conversations about strategic misalignments, operational inefficiencies, or cultural concerns go unspoken, consequences compound. Unchallenged assumptions cascade into failed initiatives, and uncontested toxic behaviors seep into organizational culture. A retailer facing declining sales we worked with suffered from this antipattern. Driven by the CEO's and VP's operational- and merchandising-centric viewpoint, rooted in their long and successful careers in traditional retail, the company initially focused its strategy on efficiency and "revitalization" in stores through stricter merchandising, cost-cutting measures, and transactional training. The strategy neglected e-commerce integration or experiential concepts that junior analysts saw emerging in their data—customers looking for new in-store experiences and personalized shopping journeys. But the retailer missed the opportunity, and performance suffered, as the vocal few and their limited perspective blocked others' ideas and with it the chance to adapt to changing customer expectations.

Many organizations love to talk up a culture of open-door policies and ask-me-anything sessions. But subtle cultural norms and leadership behaviors that compound over time create a reinforcing cycle in which such culture doesn't materialize. By one report, a staggering 85 percent of individuals in organizations are afraid to raise concerns.[2]

An overemphasis on social cohesion is in part a psychological phenomenon. Solomon Asch's 1951 (core Tin Man era) experiments showed that people are likely to conform to group opinions even when they know those opinions are wrong.[3] But conformity also happens through leadership dictates ("We all need to get on board!") or a desire not to upset others.[4] Former life sciences CIO Tom Godden notes that excessive politeness can become its own form of suppression, as legitimate concerns get buried under layers of social niceties. Creative breakthroughs require what Frans Johansson calls "the Medici Effect," where intersections of different disciplines and cultures create an explosion of extraordinary ideas.[5] But these collisions can feel uncomfortable, even contentious. Prioritizing harmony and niceness effectively censors revolutionary ideas before they can be voiced.

We've seen the CHRO of a major telecommunications company jump at the opportunity to introduce agile to her new organization. She laid out plans to train hundreds of people in superficial rituals like daily stand-ups, and she publicly shut down well-meaning people who raised concerns, leaning on her successful implementation at other organizations as evidence for not questioning the plan. The implementation, you might have guessed, didn't go well.

Difficult conversations and raising a voice of opposition, or even concern, are all *really* hard. Our opinions and ideas are fused with our sense of self. We feel anxiety that the conversation might go badly, that the others on the team might dislike us, and that we might even be wrong.

But it's not just personal. When someone raises concerns, the concerns require discussion. They suggest possible futures that require new and different work. They cut into productivity and efficiency. Old-model orgs are built to avoid that.

Hierarchy plays a role here, too. Old operational models are based on deference to authority. Don't criticize anything the boss might have created; don't speak without data; avoid raising issues when higher-ups are present. Understand what gets you promoted or flagged as difficult. These rules, learned through observation and experience, create a complex web of constraints against speaking out.

Social psychologist Robert Kegan attributes the failure to speak up to "the organizational immune system"—defensive routines that protect the status quo.[6] It manifests as requests for excessive documentation before alternative ideas are considered (the "prove it" defense), dilution of bold ideas through bureaucracy (the "process" defense), or rejection by invoking organizational constraints (the "that's not how we do things here" defense).

This suppression of dialogue extracts a far steeper price than momentary discomfort. The cost of this antipattern is devastating, and not just measured in failed projects or missed opportunities—it manifests in the slow erosion of trust, the gradual disengagement of talented people, many of whom will leave, and the eventual calcification of organizational learning, or, in some cases, crises.

What Octopus Organizations Do Instead

Octopus leaders are open to surfacing conflict and emotions, ensuring curiosity leads to better outcomes. Did you know that the octopus literally changes color when it's agitated? For leaders, saying "I don't know" is changing a color. Encouraging meeting members to express concerns is changing your color. Good leaders also understand and respond to body language, tones of voice, and all emotional signals of uncomfortable surface-level harmony. The real measure of an Octopus Organization isn't the *presence* of different ideas and opinions, but rather if and how they are surfaced, explored, and channeled into better decisions.

Octopus Organizations distinguish between relationship conflict and task conflict. The former is destructive, but the latter is generative. They implement structures to be, as negotiation experts Roger Fisher and William Ury put it, "hard on the problem, soft on the people."[7] This distinction allows teams to debate ideas without damaging relationships. Amazon's version is "disagree and commit"—acknowledging that people can examine the same evidence and reach different conclusions, yet still move forward together once a decision is made.

Octopus leaders use humor to make speaking up less fraught. Our octopus friend is funny. It will squirt water at researchers or mates, or even steal objects to play with. In the workplace, authentic humor can be used to build rapport, reduce tension, facilitate open conversations, and manage conflict.[8]

The Octopus Organization creates spaces and symbols to signal it's OK to disagree. They frame debates not as win-lose, but as creative explorations.[9] Symbols are a powerful way to signal it's time to get curious and debate ideas. It can be as simple as the specific meeting room that we saw one organization turn into the "candor cauldron" or Alphabet X CEO Astro Teller's use of the "Fool" tarot card analogy, reminding everyone of the need to embrace uncertainty and the willingness to appear naive when exploring new possibilities.

Octopus leaders are careful and productive with their language when engaged in debate. They:

- use phrases like "I sense that a few of us here feel uneasy, so I'd appreciate it if we can debate this as a team."

- surface their assumptions and mental models as a starting point for debate, framed as "Here's where my head is at currently."

- say "I don't know" when they don't know. It's an invitation for collective discovery.

The Octopus Organization values accuracy over surface-level agreement, intellectual honesty over false consensus, and productive debate over social cohesion.[10] The goal in debates is not winning but truth-seeking, acknowledging that few issues are binary and conflicting ideas can collectively birth better ones.[11] To achieve that, **Octopus Organizations practice**

inquiry as a main form of engagement. Inquiry just means asking questions that aren't centered on advocacy. It's particularly powerful for navigating power dynamics, as inquiry allows people to challenge ideas respectfully through questions rather than direct opposition. Inquiries can be simple to frame:

- When someone presents a strong view.

  - Could you help me understand what experiences led you to this perspective?

  - What do you see as the key factors that shaped your thinking on this?

- When facing resistance to an idea.

  - What aspects of this proposal give you pause?

  - What would need to be true for this to work in your view?

- When trying to bridge disagreement.

  - Where do you think we might have common ground on this issue?

  - Could you walk me through your reasoning on this?

- To explore assumptions.

  - What information or evidence would change your mind on this?

  - How have you seen similar situations play out in the past?

Allowing the team time to explore an inquiry to resolution (*Is this the right answer?*) is key. The team needs time to dive deep into issues rather than gloss over complexity.[12]

Organizations that actively bring in productive debate discover benefits beyond innovation: They surface operational inefficiencies before they become crises, hold each other accountable to stated values, and create space for authentic personal development conversations. They transform conflict from a source of tension into a catalyst for organizational health and innovation, using it to sharpen thinking and foster genuine ownership.

Embracing productive conflict and difficult conversations ultimately becomes like a controlled burn in forest management. While the process may *appear* destructive, it creates the conditions essential for renewal and resilience.

Levers

^ **Audit your meeting practices.** Track speaking time, participation rates, and decision outcomes across demographic groups and organizational levels. Use this data to redesign meetings with structured turn-taking, anonymized idea submission, or designated devil's advocates. Rotate meeting leadership and facilitation roles to disrupt power dynamics. After implementing changes, measure again to track improvement.

^ **Use "I," not "you."** When expressing concerns, start with "I" statements ("I'm concerned that . . .," "I'm wondering if . . .," "I feel . . ."). Avoid "you" statements that can feel accusatory. When facing a "you" statement, immediately reframe it as an "I" statement (for example, "I can understand why you might feel X, and this makes me think . . .").

^ **Identify your "avoidance triggers."** Reflect on past situations where you avoided a tough conversation. What were you feeling? What were you worried about? Write down your reflections. The next time you notice that feeling rising, pause and recognize it. After a difficult conversation, write down what went well, what you could have done differently, and what you learned about yourself. Share your lessons with a trusted colleague and ask for their perspectives.

^ **Reframe conflict as curiosity.** Instead of focusing on who is "right" in a disagreement, ask, "What could we have learned from each other?" Ask to understand a contrary or dissenting position instead of immediately defending your own position. Train employees on the use of curiosity-based language (such as "What if," "Help me understand," and "I'm curious why").

^ **Use humor intentionally.** It diffuses tension by triggering positive emotions and creating a sense of shared experience. It levels power dynamics and softens critical feedback. Avoid sarcasm and in-group humor.

^ **Practice the "listening triangle."** Implement a structured communication method where participants must ask about others' views, listen carefully without preparing counterarguments, and restate what they heard in their own words before responding.

^ **Create structured dissent processes.** Implement formal mechanisms that normalize disagreement as part of the decision-making process. These might include designated "challenge sessions" where proposals must withstand structured critique before moving forward, rotating dissenter roles where team members take turns playing the skeptic, or scheduled perspective rotations where people argue against their own position. The key is making dissent procedural rather than personal, removing the social stigma from disagreeing.

DISCOVER MORE

ANTIPATTERNS TO READ NEXT

#24: Mismanaging Incentives

#26: Evading Failure

#31: Avoiding Tough Conversations

BUILDING HOMOPHILIC TEAMS

Cognitive and intellectual diversity in teams amplifies problem-solving acumen.

THE TIN MAN BEHAVIOR

Forming teams made up of people with similar mindsets and backgrounds to create cohesion and harmony, and for perceived progress, within the group

THE RESULTS

- Poor decision-making due to blind spots
- Reduced team adaptability and resilience
- Stifled innovation and curiosity

How Octopus Organizations Behave Instead

- They build teams with cognitive and intellectual diversity.
- They amplify constructive conflict.
- They reimagine talent strategies to avoid biases and focus on culture-add, not just culture-fit.

The Tin Man Behavior

In 2013, Google's ambitious new wearable technology division launched Google Glass and failed so hard it's become a symbol of product flops. Google built a beautiful device for an idealized tech enthusiast consumer that didn't represent the broader market. That broader market was in a post-recession haze, and Glass was expensive. That broader market was discerning about functionality, and the battery life on the glasses was poor. That broader market cared about privacy in a way that the very idea of the glasses sometimes seemed to violate. They were trying to be a revolution but couldn't bridge the gap between vision and market reality.[1]

One reason for the failure was the team that came together to make it. It was largely composed of engineers and technologists with stellar careers, all of whom likely viewed the tech market from a similar vantage point. Since they were all "on the same page," it was easy, as a group, to explain away or reinterpret the external feedback that signaled potential problems with their approach.[2] They spent enormous sums on development and marketing without sufficient scrutiny of their fundamental assumptions. Some evidence points to one root cause being their like-mindedness and backgrounds making them supremely confident in their assumptions, an echo chamber rather than an environment that harnessed genuine curiosity to innovate for customers.[3]

On its face, this antipattern doesn't seem unreasonable. It's tempting to think that since everyone thinks alike, they can get moving fast and make progress without internal strife, debates, politics, or conflicting opinions. It's *frictionless*, to use a Tin Man term. But this apparent efficiency masks a dangerous reality: missing diverse perspectives leads to groupthink, which creates blind spots about risks and opportunities. Ultimately, like-minded teams are more likely to make bad decisions.

In Tin Man organizational models, "talent" meant finding people who fit seamlessly into existing processes, their diverse ideas largely irrelevant to efficiency; having a different perspective was a heretical proposition. Even as models evolved to take into account some ideas from workers, this premium placed on efficiency and conformity carried forward.

Tin Men still instinctively gravitate toward individuals who mirror their own experiences and perspectives. "Culture fit" becomes a justification for hiring people who think in similar ways. Valuing the perceived efficiency of implicit understanding, working with someone who "gets it" immediately and slots right in feels like a shortcut, avoiding the friction of integrating diverse viewpoints. One revealing study showed that groups joined by an outsider felt less effective and less confident in their decisions than those including only insiders.[4]

But the same study also showed the in-groups were starkly wrong. Adding an outsider doubled their chances of arriving at the correct solution. While the work *felt* harder, outcomes were significantly better. Tin Men don't usually appreciate that diverse teams produce better outcomes *precisely because* it's harder. When information feels difficult to process or unfamiliar, we tend to assume it's wrong versus easier-to-understand data, a bias called the fluency heuristic.

Diversity within teams works, but let's be precise with the word *diversity*. When we think about diversity, we often equate it with demographic diversity—race, gender, and nationality, for example. That kind of diversity is useful—a woman's perspective or an older person's perspective, a man's or younger person's perspective, for example, will likely all be different. But while different backgrounds *may* result in different views, they also may not. When we talk about diversity in teams, we mean *intellectual and cognitive diversity— problem-solving, decision-making*, and *innovation*, including different skills, knowledge, experience, working and thinking styles, and preferences for how individuals gather, process, and assimilate data.[5]

Cognitive diversity naturally leads to *cognitive conflict*, which will be taxing for leaders not trained to handle it constructively. The consequences of cognitively homophilic teams are detrimental. Efficiency and understanding morph into groupthink. Critical analysis is stifled; alternative viewpoints are dismissed. Like-minded teams consider fewer options and are less likely to identify blind spots, yet paradoxically, they carry a higher degree of confidence in their views and approach. They become vulnerable to confirmation bias, mistaking the absence of conflict for productive harmony. For instance, homophilic relationships on corporate boards or between CEOs and directors have been linked to lower levels of monitoring and scrutiny, reducing organizational performance.[6]

In essence, the desire for comfort and control overrides the necessity for adaptability and innovation, prioritizing the smooth operation of the existing machine over the creation of something new and better. Until these organizations shed their rigid armor and embrace the power of difference, they will continue to rust.

What Octopus Organizations Do Instead

Octopus Organizations understand that cognitive diversity is a key for problem-solving, decision-making, and innovation. Broadening perspectives helps overcome stale ways of thinking and sharpens performance.[7] Compared to homophilic teams, diverse teams are more likely to:

- raise facts in debates
- correct errors during deliberations[8]
- reexamine facts and remain objective
- encourage greater scrutiny of each member's actions
- be aware of their own biases that lead them to make decision-making errors[9]

- introduce radical new innovations and new products[10]

- make decisions twice as quickly with half the meetings[11]

- make better decisions 87 percent of the time[12]

Intellectual diversity is at the heart of effective innovation as Harvard professor Linda Hill, a bestselling author on the topic, explained to us. She encourages what she terms *creative abrasion* and three elements that foster it: *intellectual diversity* and the feeling of safety to raise contrarian views; *a marketplace of ideas*, forums where ideas are debated, mixed, and shared to solve problems; and *cognitive conflict*, with clear rules of engagement to improve and elevate ideas without lapsing into interpersonal conflict.

Octopus Organizations harness both individual creativity *and* group dynamics to enable innovation. They recognize that like-minded groups can stifle innovation, as when teams start generating ideas together, many of the best ones never get shared due to the group conformity. Modern organizations recognize that people often generate more and better ideas independently before coming together as a group.[13] At the eyewear retailer Warby Parker employees spend a few minutes weekly writing down innovation ideas that colleagues read and comment on.[14] The company also maintains a shared document where employees can submit requests for new technology. This yields about four hundred new ideas quarterly.

Octopus Organizations actively structure their work to maximize the benefits of diverse thinking. They regularly assemble cross-functional groups to critique solution proposals and ideas, to review prototypes, or to tackle complex problems together. Pixar created "dailies" where work was brought before a diverse team for critique. This process created proximity for diverse thinkers.[15]

Octopus leaders positively amplify cognitive conflict.[16] Team diversity might at first feel more exhausting than hanging out with people like yourself, but good leaders understand that the constructive cognitive conflict is what drives better decisions and problem-solving. Pixar facilitated vigorous task-focused debates by training people to advocate for their point of view and to critically evaluate options. They used ground rules such as:

- Assume positive intent.

- Attack the idea, not the person.

- Listen to understand, not just to respond.[17]

But surely such ways of working can lead to never-ending debates in an environment where speed is valued, you might say. That's why **Octopus**

leaders introduce constraints in debates, such as critical deadlines, like the unyielding film release date and budget at Pixar. Constraints like this force teams to evaluate key assumptions and reframe opportunities, sharpening thinking by requiring teams to find ways to work within limitations. Ideas are tested and refined through experimentation, the same approach used to test and integrate diverse, even opposing, ideas into new and useful solutions rather than forcing compromises or consensus.[18]

Octopus leaders avoid accepting weak compromises that produce suboptimal solutions in order to maintain social cohesion and instead press for better, more integrated alternatives. They are prepared to inject conflict into teams by asking hard questions to ensure the team pushes itself. To avoid creating eternal debates from this process, the leaders introduce constraints such as deadlines to force critical thinking within parameters. Ideas are tested and refined through experimentation, the same approach that is used to test and integrate diverse, even opposing, ideas into new and useful solutions rather than forcing compromises or consensus.[19]

Octopus Organizations reimagine their hiring practices. They don't put such a high premium on "fitting in"; they identify candidates who can bring new perspectives and capabilities while still aligning with organizational values. Structured interviews and bias-mitigation techniques ensure the org isn't falling victim to unconscious biases and candidates aren't succeeding based on superficial similarities to existing team members.

Octopus Organizations monitor teams for like-mindedness. Long-term Amazonian and HR evangelist Stephen Brozovich advises leaders to keep an eye on dynamics that might indicate a team is becoming too like-minded over time. Indicators might include:

- Are new hires consistently rejected from, or leaving, a particular team?
- Is dissent heard in the room, or is agreement reached quickly?
- Is there a diversity of leadership strengths represented within the team, or are the same strengths prevalent?
- Is there sufficient internal movement from and to the team? Is the "dwell time" of individuals in roles and on teams being tracked and managed?

Embracing the varied perspectives of an Octopus Organization might feel challenging at first, but this deliberate nurturing of intellectual diversity is one of the best ways to boost capacity to transform an organization and its products. Organizations with more intellectual diversity are more likely to introduce radical new innovations and new products than those with homo-philic teams.[20]

Levers

^ **Establish clear norms and rules for creative abrasion.** Cocreate principles like "Challenge ideas, not people," "Assume positive intent," "Use data/logic," and "No interrupting." Document these principles in a charter to get buy-in. Agree on conflict-resolution steps (for instance, breaks, reframing, neutral facilitation) for unproductive disagreements. This norm-shaping process itself builds buy-in and shared ownership.

^ **Anchor conflict in shared purpose.** Clearly define and regularly refer-ence collective intent during decision-making to prevent disagreements from becoming personal. Train facilitators to redirect positional debates toward problems to be solved, keeping cognitive friction productive rather than divisive.

^ **Institutionalize constructive dissent.** Create structured debate formats that require exploration of competing solutions, ensuring examination of alternatives. Oxford-style debates have individuals argue both for and against a proposal. Fishbowls are meetings where an inner circle actively debates a topic while an outer circle observes.

^ **Invest in conflict-management development.** Intellectually diverse teams can be more challenging to lead. Formally train people in inclusive communication, team-building methodologies, and conflict management.

^ **Diversify idea generation.** Implement structured idea-generation tech-niques, such as individual written submissions before group discussions or anonymous feedback platforms. These measures ensure all voices are heard and prevent dominant personalities from overshadowing others.

^ **Encourage cross-pollination.** Create opportunities for employees to interact with people from different departments and functional groups, external teams, customers, and external partners to combat like-mindedness. Consider implementing a mandate for individuals to spend time with customers, in a different department, or on a cross-functional project, fostering empathy and broader understanding.

^ **Use "cognitive empathy" programs.** Help team members understand and appreciate different ways of thinking through workshops, personality assessments (used judiciously and ethically), or storytelling sessions where individuals share their unique approaches to problem-solving. The goal is to foster genuine curiosity and respect for diverse cognitive styles.

DISCOVER MORE

ANTIPATTERNS TO READ NEXT

#22: Hiring Poorly

#27: Using Proxies for Customers

#29: Falling in Love with Answers

DEFERRING TO DATA

Data-informed decisions that honor human
experience improve quality of outcomes.

THE TIN MAN BEHAVIOR

Using data, especially easily quantifiable metrics, as a crutch in
complex decision-making and devaluing human experience for data's
supposed "objectivity" in the process

THE RESULTS

- False certainty that leads to bad decisions
- Overreliance on simple metrics that miss context and lead to poor
  decisions
- Ignoring valuable human experience and judgment

How Octopus Organizations Behave Instead

- They invest in data literacy that emphasizes critical thinking about data.
- They balance quantitative and qualitative insights and treat data as
  a tool, not a replacement for judgment.
- They foster collaboration between data scientists and business
  leaders.

The Tin Man Behavior

Data is tricky. It's deeply valuable; modern business couldn't run without it.
Organizations crow about being "data driven," which seems to be a way to say
we've found data that is beyond reproach, data that gives us the right answers.

But it's also difficult for us humans, who are narrative creatures, to understand the limitations of data and properly position it. There are multiple aspects
of this problem. One is that much useful data is probabilistic, and humans are
terrible at probability. Say you take a risk that has an 80 percent chance of success.

What does that mean? What *is* an 80 percent chance? Two people will have vastly different interpretations of what 80 percent represents. And it will be a different feeling than if you tell them it has a "four in five" chance of success.

Anyway, the project fails. You can rightly say to your boss it was the right decision based on the data. And they can rightly say to you it wasn't, because the data shows that it failed.

Another key challenge with data is the high sense of *facticity* that we perceive it to have. That is, we think that because it's numbers and statistics there's some objective truth to it that's unassailable. "In God we trust," said W. Edwards Deming famously. "All others must bring data." This mantra, intended to promote evidence-based decision-making, has morphed into an insidious crutch that replaces critical thinking with an almost blind faith in numbers. Data has become a kind of talisman for justifying decisions, and a way to end deliberation or override challenges.

But data is neither objective nor above reproach. It's highly interpretable, usually incomplete, and only one view of a complex system. In *Weapons of Math Destruction*, Cathy O'Neill warns readers of the consequences of an overreliance on poorly understood data.[1] She points to recidivism-prediction algorithms in American criminal sentencing that end up encoding and amplifying societal biases, using factors like zip code, family criminal history, and employment status to predict the likelihood of reoffending. With a high correlation with race and poverty, someone from a poor neighborhood with high unemployment and crime rates receives a higher risk score regardless of their individual circumstances. In businesses, similar overreliance on data leads to similarly terrible results. One manifestation of this overreliance comes when companies seek assurances from data. Say they create data to determine that customers really do want a new product. There's a paucity of data because the product is new, and customers are notoriously "bad" at being able to articulate what they want. In such a case, data can provide *insight* into preferences but not *assurance* that the product is a good idea.

The ability to easily generate and evaluate data also ironically makes it easy to reinforce subjective biases. Organizations selectively seek and interpret data that confirms their preconceptions, creating a feedback loop that validates their existing worldview while blind spots grow larger. The digital dashboard becomes so alluring that they forget to look out the window. Data is used to kill curiosity rather than foster it. One retailer we worked with had years of decline masked by pandemic-era data on spending. That explained the decline, they thought, and moved on. But it didn't explain it at all, and an ensuing failure to adapt to changing customer needs saw this decline snowball into bankruptcy.

There is also a problem of relying on data that's easy to create or get. Many measures companies rely on are implemented because they're the *fastest and easiest*, not the best way to represent the data. That is, they're low-cost, efficient. Of course, you get what you pay for. A salesperson's sales per quarter is a super simple performance metric. Easy to obtain. Say it's declining. Bad salesperson? Maybe. But what if the decline was due to their investing time in mentorship that increased other team members' flagging performance more than theirs declined, and what if they also spent time learning about a new segment that will inform a strategy pivot that opens up a new market for the company? That's harder to measure and involves statistical modeling. Turns out it's a good salesman held to a bad metric.

No one would argue against the importance of data, but we are often not good at understanding how to use it well, and what it does and does not provide. In short, our data literacy is low while our reliance on data has never been higher.

One fundamental flaw with data is the siloed nature of old-model orgs. The models that generate the crucial business data often come from data scientists isolated from the domains they're attempting to model. This lack of context clouds the full picture. It leads to models that are mathematically sound but missing crucial nuances that experienced practitioners would immediately recognize. For example, a sports team might identify top talent using data models. Most sports have sophisticated models that show how much value a player provides above some mythological "average player" based on past data. And these models don't account for the fact that, while on average they are more valuable in the skills they need, they are a terrible teammate who becomes difficult at the most crucial moments and is bringing overall team performance down.

Just as Tin Man orgs devalue the crucial role of human judgment, experience, and intuition—elements that often provide valuable insights in rapidly changing or ambiguous situations—so does an overreliance on and poor use of data. Innovation and creativity suffer as organizations become risk-averse, unwilling to experiment with approaches that can't be immediately justified by a precise set of numbers.

What Octopus Organizations Do Instead

Octopus Organizations take a nuanced approach to data. They know it plays a crucial role, but it is not the sole arbiter in decision-making. They understand what Amazon's Jeff Bezos articulated: "If you can make a decision with analysis, you should do so. But it turns out in life that your most important decisions are always made with instinct and intuition, taste, heart."[2] As Dutch soccer player and manager Johan Cruyff noted about real-world experience versus data, "If Lionel Messi scores three times out of every ten attempts, he might be criticized by someone who sees only the statistics for being just 30 effective. I'd say: just copy him and see if you can get up to that level. It's practically impossible."[3]

Octopus Organizations reframe data as a tool that provides insight, not answers. It does not replace judgment, experience, and intuition; it supplements them. It means ensuring that machine-learning model builders work closely with domain experts who can provide crucial context and understanding. It means maintaining a healthy skepticism about what data can and cannot tell us.

Octopus Organizations master the art of being data-informed rather than data-driven. This subtle but crucial distinction shapes their entire approach to decision-making. They understand that metrics can be influenced by various contexts and may need to evolve over time. These organizations use data as one voice in a larger conversation. At companies like Spotify and Netflix, data analytics teams work side by side with creative professionals. When Netflix develops new content, they don't just rely on viewing statistics and engagement metrics—they combine these insights with creative judgment and industry expertise to make decisions about future productions. At the online personal styling service Stitch Fix, algorithms drive decisions on what fashions to put in boxes, but there's always a stylist to review this data and make changes based on what that stylist knows and senses that the algorithm doesn't.[4]

Octopus leaders are curious about data. They look for outliers and question if they might be a signal in the noise. They challenge data presented to them. An average call time to the help desk of five minutes might meet service levels, but it also may hide a large number of calls taking twenty minutes. The same leaders pay attention to anecdotes as data points: a single complaint email from a customer or a whispered conversation between employees about poor service should drive more data inquiry rather than being explained away by existing aggregate data. And they respect intuition. Just like the airplane engineer who can unerringly predict when an engine needs servicing due to subtle changes in engine pitch, Octopus leaders stay attuned to their own organization and employees to pick up on their own disturbing vibrations. Jeff said that "when anecdotes contradict data, the anecdotes are usually right"—not because data is wrong, but because you're measuring the wrong thing.[5] He tells a story of metrics that claimed Amazon customer service wait times were under sixty seconds, which seemed good. Customer complaints contradicted this data. During a meeting reviewing the metrics he picked up the phone and called the helpline. Ten minutes passed before his call was answered. The team got curious fast about this uncomfortable disconnect and why the average number was not comporting with experience.[6]

Octopus Organizations respect human experience. They know that behind every data point is a human story, and that some of the most important aspects of business and life—creativity, empathy, innovation, leadership—resist simple quantification. Octopus Organizations harness the power of data while staying deeply connected to human judgment, intuition, and contextual expertise—combining algorithmic insights with the insight of experienced practitioners who understand nuance, relationships, and meaning behind the numbers.

Octopus Organizations develop robust data literacy programs that go beyond teaching employees how to read charts and graphs. These programs focus on critical thinking and context understanding—teaching people not just how to interpret data but how to question it. What's missing from this dataset? What assumptions are we making?

Finally, **modern Octopus Organizations redefine what it means to be strategic with data.** They move away from the traditional approach of pushing endless data and analysis up the hierarchy. Instead, they enable teams closest to the work to make decisions, using data as one of many tools at their disposal. They understand that sometimes the most strategic decision is to trust the experience of a team member who has spent years in the field. This balanced approach doesn't mean these organizations use less data; often they use more. But they use it more effectively for insights rather than as a crutch for decision-making.

Levers

^ **Actively seek counternarratives.** Identify one decision made this past week using data in your organization. Find one person directly affected by that decision (employee or customer) and have a ten-minute chat to understand their perspective without any data present. Listen intently. Ask yourself what new insight came out of the conversation that wasn't reflected in the data. If you didn't get any, ask more questions next time.

^ **Go beyond averages.** Dive into granular data. Look at distributions, not just means. Actively investigate unusual data points, outliers, and clusters.

They might signal emerging trends, hidden problems, or exciting new opportunities that are overlooked when focusing on the overall picture. Implement data visualizations that draw attention to such data points and make it a regular agenda item in data review meetings to identify potential trends.

^ **Elevate data literacy.** Create a data literacy program tailored to employee roles. A short foundational course for everyone would include basic statistics and data visualization, while a longer development plan would add data validation and statistical significance. A hands-on course would have participants manipulating analytics with company data. Back this up with practical tools like a library of real-world examples showing data interpretations. Cement the learning through mentor partnerships between analysts and business leaders.

^ **Rehumanize your data.** Transform abstract data points into human stories by combining quantitative metrics with qualitative feedback, such as pairing customer churn statistics with actual customer interviews. Make it permissible to interject subjective views and intuition into presentations of data. Build customer journey maps that capture emotional responses alongside behavioral data, requiring teams to include customer quotes and stories. Set up regular time between employees and customers ensuring that every major data-driven decision includes a "human impact assessment" that considers how real customers and employees will be affected.

^ **Embed analysts with domain experts.** Break down the structural silo between your data experts and delivery teams. Instead of maintaining a centralized data team that receives "requests," embed analysts and data scientists directly into the business, product, or operational teams they support. Make them part of daily stand-ups, planning sessions, and team goals. A small central team can provide specialized services and maintain standards, while embedded analysts gain deep, firsthand context and are an intrinsic part of the team that solves problems. This transforms them from report-builders into thought partners whose success is measured by outcomes, not dashboard quantity.

DISCOVER MORE

ANTIPATTERNS TO READ NEXT

#5: Misusing Metrics

#20: Seeking Perfect Decisions

#27: Using Proxies for Customers

SEGREGATING TECHNOLOGY

Broad digital fluency bridges divides and unlocks innovation.

THE TIN MAN BEHAVIOR

Separating technology from the remainder of the organization, often unintentionally, and treating tech as a support function, with tech fluency as a specialist's skill

THE RESULTS

- Complexity and technical debt that erodes performance
- Tendency to wastefully chase tech trends
- Failure to translate tech investment into customer impact

How Octopus Organizations Behave Instead

- They cultivate tech fluency for all leaders and invest in bridging knowledge gaps through education.
- They use shared metrics connecting technology to business outcomes.
- They make business leaders co-owners of technology solutions rather than just consumers of IT services.

The Tin Man Behavior

A Sumerian legend has it that King Enmerkar of Uruk wanted to build a great temple for the goddess Inanna but, lacking the right materials, required a vassal, the Lord of Aratta, to provide them. Oral messages from King to Lord, and back, were memorized and relayed across mountain-crossing intermediaries and several languages. The messages, of course, became distorted and led to conflict and escalating tensions. What could have been a straightforward trade negotiation became a prolonged battle between distinct entities, conducted through translators in between.

IT can feel like that distant vassal struggling through intermediaries to translate just what it is they're doing or saying. We have lived this ourselves. For example, imagine that Phil said to Jana: "Paying down our technical debt by decomposing monolithic applications into microservices that represent a logical architecture, and which abstracts the business logic from the underlying database, allows for generative AI capabilities to be integrated to accelerate intelligent automation and enhanced user experiences."

Jana, being tech-savvy, would understand what Phil means. Many leaders outside of IT—including many CEOs—would not. They would hear complex jargon that feels annoyingly not to the point of what they're trying to do: customer value.

Which is strange. Ask the average executive whether they dislike people or don't understand managing money and they'll scoff. Regardless of function, every leader knows the basics of people and financial management.

But technology and data are treated differently than any other major business discipline, separated by language and expertise that reinforce division between "the business" and the technology group that supports "the business." Ask that same executive whether they understand artificial intelligence and they won't scoff. They'll say, "I understand it's important to our future," but they are quite happy to cede understanding beyond that to the technologists. Ask them if they understand what Phil said to Jana above, and they would (probably) admit that they do not, and demand a translation rather than seek to understand.

Out of frustration or a lack of patience, work eventually gets done with "shadow IT" systems—tools users adopt themselves but that IT may have good reason to want them not to use. IT does itself no favors by not communicating in the language of the customers and the business, bristling at users who don't understand. Acrimony ensues.

To be clear, it's neither side's fault here. On the "business" side, senior leadership understanding of technology is a major challenge. Less than 12 percent of board members have a technology background.[1] In the C-suite, digital fluency ranges from a mere 8 percent to 23 percent across critical roles, with less than 10 percent of C-suite teams possessing a sufficient breadth of digital knowledge.[2] This leads to poor value-based technology decisions, ineffective transformation initiatives, poor talent retention, and an inability to integrate technology into organizational strategies.[3]

On the technology side, the group in some ways has self-siloed, partly through speaking its own language. Tech leaders insist on using terms like meshes, bimodal operating models, abstraction layers, microservice architectures, event-driven architectures, polyglot persistence, and DevSecOps. They talk the way Phil talked to Jana in the above example, and then they frown with incomprehension when non-technology colleagues look confused, when in fact Phil could have just said: "We're simplifying our systems: breaking down large, complex software programs into smaller, more manageable ones. This will make it easier and faster to add AI-powered features that can automate tasks and improve user experiences. Imagine it like renovating a house one room at a time, not disturbing the other rooms, instead of gutting the whole house and rebuilding all at once. By doing it this way, we can gradually introduce new capabilities without disrupting operations."

Technologists need to be able to communicate in the lingua franca of their business, focusing on outcomes, value, and risk mitigation. But equally it is important that *all* leaders understand that they require basic technology literacy, and the curiosity to ask questions when they don't understand. After all there is no reason that an executive can't just ask the simple question that starts "Can you help me understand . . . ?"

For what seems like a simple communication issue, the consequences of the chasm are profound. Useless requirements get built due to misunderstandings on the business outcomes expected. More technology gets built than is needed, leading to complexity and cost. Shadow tech increases cost and creates security issues.[4] Existing applications go unused and degrade over time, hindering agility. New technologies are poorly explained, leading to overhype or underselling their value.

Jargon is a symptom of this antipattern, but the root causes lie deeper, embedded within the organizational fabric itself due to:

- **Legacy hierarchies creating power distance.** Tin Man organizations rely heavily on functional specialization. IT, with its complex and rapidly evolving skill sets, becomes the ultimate silo. Traditional structures relegate technology to a support function rather than a strategic driver. Leaders who ascended in a pre-digital era may lack a nuanced understanding of technology's potential. This "power distance" prevents tech from gaining "a seat at the table," resulting in no strategic alignment.[5]

- **Misaligned incentives and metrics.** Business units are typically measured using traditional financial metrics (revenue, costs, and so forth). IT is often evaluated based on operational metrics (uptime, system availability, project delivery timelines). This disconnect incentivizes business leaders to prioritize initiatives that immediately impact their bottom line, while IT focuses on stability and minimizing risk, often at the expense of innovation. IT struggles to justify investments in non-functional requirements or platform health, as well as conflicts in priorities. Urgent business features usually supersede the need to reduce tech debt and maintain system health.

- **A clash of time horizons.** Business units drive change through projects, with defined start and end points, while IT manages evolving product portfolios requiring continuous support, investment, and iterative development. This disconnect creates deep misalignment in funding models (temporary project funding versus ongoing team funding), lifecycle management (build-and-hand-off versus continuous development and evolution), team structure (temporary project teams versus stable product teams), and the fundamental focus (delivering scope on time/budget versus achieving desired business outcomes).

- **Process over people.** Tin Man organizations often prioritize rigid processes and governance over flexible value-driven collaboration. Stage-gated approvals and formal handoffs between "the business" and "IT" create bottlenecks and reinforce the sense of separation, hindering the agility needed for modern technology development.

Beneath all of this misalignment lies a lack of curiosity to build a shared understanding of technology's strategic role, and a lack of incentives for sides (there should be no sides!) to collaborate on creating customer value.

What Octopus Organizations Do Instead

Octopus leaders recognize that technology fluency is a required skill, just as understanding finance and customers is. They achieve this fluency through several reinforcing approaches.

Octopus Organizations champion proactive education on technology's innovation implications, especially emerging technologies like generative AI. This education goes beyond passive briefings; effective methods include hands-on sessions solving real business problems, structured immersion experiences like visiting tech-forward companies, and reverse mentoring—pairing technically fluent employees with senior leaders. Some Octopus Orgs temporarily appoint dedicated "translators" who have hybrid business and technical backgrounds, but the long-term goal is to establish a common language. Job rotations and shadowing further deepen cross-functional empathy and understanding. They also expect their leaders to proactively show curiosity, ask questions, read, and experiment with technology themselves.

Octopus Organizations coach technologists to become effective communicators. It's natural that departments will create jargon within their communities: it saves time. But good communicators adapt to their audience. One supermarket's chief retail and technology officer we spoke to spans both worlds and says, "There is an onus on technology leaders to make technology accessible. There is nothing smart about making it complicated."

Octopus Organizations use metaphors and storytelling to bridge the business-tech gap. Longtime Amazonian and evangelist Stephen Brozovich uses the "currency of leadership" to connect technology initiatives in ways that resonate with individual leaders. One executive demonstrated AI's potential in such a way by showing how it could improve a leader's golf game, making abstract technology tangible and personally relevant, creating genuine engagement rather than perfunctory oversight.

Octopus Organizations redefine ownership and cocreation of technology. Typically in Tin Man orgs, business plans are created and signed off, then handed over to the technologists with the command to go build on time and to budget. Our supermarket technology executive told us how their organization flipped this usual process and got the business owners to participate in debating problems and trade-offs alongside technologists. This process involves defining clear business outcomes and then partnering with product owners and engineers to shape road maps, considering multiple perspectives: benefit optimization, cost reduction, technical stability. By engaging leaders in this joint planning exercise, tech dependencies become transparent, fostering collective understanding and buy-in. Ultimately these organizations dismantle their silos entirely, in favor of persistent, cross-functional teams (often called product teams; at Amazon they're "two-pizza teams").

Octopus Organizations use shared metrics that focus on business outcomes (such as customer lifetime value, speed to market, market share or gain) that both technology and business units contribute to and are accountable for. Shared metrics bridge the silos and ensure that everyone is pulling in the same direction.

Research shows that organizations with digitally fluent leadership outperform their peers significantly in revenue growth, valuations, and margins.[6]

Levers

^ **Establish reverse mentoring.** Pair technically savvy employees with senior executives or any curious person in the organization to ask about and explore technology, specific both to the company and to broader trends. Conversely, pair technologists with non-tech leaders who can provide coaching on effective communication styles to reach those less tech-savvy people and inspire them to get curious.

^ **Schedule regular technology immersion days for executives.** Add regular forty-five-minute slots on boardroom and C-suite agendas to explore tech topics in depth. Use these sessions not just to talk about technology and its relevance, but to bring it to life. Showcase prototypes and new features, guide leaders through writing generative AI prompts, and lead conversations on technology trends and what the organization should do about them.

^ **Create technology feedback loops.** Implement regular surveys and feedback sessions where business users evaluate the clarity of tech communications. Use this feedback to target improvement where clarity lags.

^ **Create technology immersion experiences.** Organize visits to major tech vendors and tech-forward competitors. Follow these visits with "think big" sessions where leaders brainstorm potential applications of the technology to the business. Run quarterly half-day sessions for business leaders focusing on current and emerging technologies like generative AI, cloud computing, and cybersecurity. Include hands-on exercises solving real business problems.

^ **Build tech fundamentals.** Develop a curriculum (cloud basics, AI concepts, cybersecurity awareness, data literacy, product management) using company examples. Use online modules, interactive workshops, and expert Q&A for learning. Take inspiration from Walmart's push to make floor staff tech-savvy and Capital One's training for non-technical stakeholders.[7] Look at ways of encouraging leaders to actively participate in this learning such as adding technology fluency as a criteria for advancement.

^ **Develop a common vocabulary.** Create and maintain a company dictionary that translates technical terms into business language. Create a "living glossary" translating tech terms to business impact. Actively discourage silo-building phrases such as "the business and IT."

^ **Eat your own dog food.** Assign executives ownership of tech products or features. Require them to use these products and participate in development for three months. Document usability issues and feedback directly into the development process. This sort of immersion into the process builds deep empathy for the user experience and grounds decisions in real-world usage.

^ **Communicate!** Send out a one-page update to a wide range of stakeholders weekly on tech topics and how they support customer and business value imperatives. It's a great way to open communications and allows *anyone* to reply to find out more. Start sessions to tech audiences with a state of the customer and business update relating all technology initiatives to the business. Take a leaf from McDonald's SVP Whitney McGinnis's book. She talks about how she wants her team to know how they are impacting the business and to feel they CAN impact it. She talks about the business all the time: how it's going, how it's trending, how the things her team is doing are impacting the business. At every townhall she starts with a "state of the business" update and how her team is contributing to it.

^ **Implement cross-functional pilot teams.** Give the teams business outcome missions and shared metrics, and let them own decision-making. Use these first teams to learn and demonstrate the value of integrated structures. Wrap a protective layer around these teams by including a representative from key organizational functions, like finance and HR.

DISCOVER MORE

ANTIPATTERNS TO READ NEXT

#1: Relying on Jargon

#6: Working Together but Not as a Team

#10: Entrenching Silos

DOWNPLAYING PEOPLE DEVELOPMENT

Weaving development into daily tasks builds tomorrow's critical skills.

THE TIN MAN BEHAVIOR

Neglecting or minimizing people development and treating it as separate from or secondary to "real work"

THE RESULTS

- Critical skills gaps and shortages hinder productivity
- Disengaged workforce and reduced retention
- Reduced innovation leading to competitive vulnerability

How Octopus Organizations Behave Instead

- They view skills and behavior development as a critical, ongoing investment.
- They integrate curiosity and learning into daily work and provide personal paths to growth.
- They role model curiosity and learning and connect it to tangible results.

The Tin Man Behavior

"Wanted: an individual with a GPA of 4.0 who has transformed at least two major Swiss-based health care multinationals using generative AI."

Many job searches feel like a search for a unicorn. You may believe they exist, and even that you've seen one. Perhaps you heard others talk about them. But you can never find them when you need them, so you just find the best person you can, sprinkle them with glitter, and tell them to fly.

What we've seen this kind of search yield are organizations full of capable people whose skills atrophy over time due to a lack of investment in their development. To acquire the skills they need, nearly three-quarters of US companies resort to outside hires.[1] When probed on why they hire from outside instead of training up the capable people already in their buildings—we've probed many—the implied answer (they rarely say it directly) is that employee development is not seen as *real work*, or as something to be done when time and budgets allow, if ever. They might say out loud that budgets are tight so they've suspended that "cost" for the time being.

These are the same organizations that tell us that people are their most important asset.

Organizations we work with are often impatient gardeners when it comes to talent development. They strew seeds across some field, add some of last year's leftover fertilizer, and then water when they think of it, counting on the seeds to take it from there. Perhaps one hardy tomato plant punches through, but disappointment awaits at the end of the season. The gardener blames the seeds rather than the cultivation process.

Learners are left to invest significant time figuring out for themselves how to undertake training while juggling their daily responsibilities.[2] Now and again, employees are subjected to trendy training brought in on an executive's whim rather than identified organizational needs. For Phil in the 1990s, it was a round on "Total Quality Management" in an environment that wasn't nearly ready for it, and for Jana it was "SAFe" in the 2010s.

Despite an estimated $340 billion annual investment in corporate training, its efficacy is frequently questioned.[3] One study indicated that the average employee gets as little as twenty-four minutes weekly for learning.[4] More than half (56 percent) of employees report that their organizations don't encourage skill development to protect against technological disruption.[5]

A lack of serious investment in employee development directly affects every metric organizations care about—from talent acquisition and retention to profitability and innovation. The impact is particularly pronounced at the leadership level and with technology. Research shows that organizations with more than 50 percent digitally fluent leaders outperform peers by 48 percent in revenue growth and valuation, while achieving higher net margins. Yet, internal training integrated into jobs to foster digital literacy across organizations remains low.[6]

Poor talent development stems from a Tin Man idea that if you don't have the talent, you just buy it. In the old industrial economy, leaders could reasonably suspect that the skills they acquired would be useful and unchanging for long periods of time, making learning a luxury *expense* for good times, and one that can be cut when business is tight.

Obviously, it's gotten harder to predict the skills you'll need, even six months from now. (How many people did you have ready to work with large language models [LLMs] when they hit the scene?) We're critically short of the capabilities needed to build thriving workforces that drive success. The most crucial and challenging skills to develop are increasingly in technology, higher cognitive thinking, and social domains—precisely the areas requiring *investment* in continuous training development.[7]

Another reason organizations soft-pedal on training is because they see it as a potential *disadvantage.* The old-model org's adage is that training employees means they might leave, whereas modern organizations *should* worry that not training them means they'll *stay.*

One of the most difficult aspects of this behavior to dismantle is the insistence on treating training as separate from jobs. Learning is viewed as a luxury to bestow when time and budget allow for it. This mindset often leads to training and development being outsourced to HR, which mechanically designs (or buys) and delivers standardized training that violates principles of *andragogy* (adult learning), which emphasize self-direction, relevance, and problem-centered learning.[8]

What Octopus Organizations Do Instead

Octopus Organizations weave learning into the daily fabric of work. It's part of the job. The intelligent octopus's short lifespan means it integrates learning into everything it does to adapt and stay ahead its whole life. Watch an octopus open a jar. It takes just a little trial and error for the octopus to adapt and form associations between stimuli and outcomes. Their curiosity translates into time- and context-relevant learning they take forward. At work, every jar to open comes with learning. As Aaron Dignan notes, crucial knowledge is often "minted on the front lines, in direct contact with reality." Every project retrospective becomes a reflective learning opportunity.[9] Team meetings incorporate knowledge sharing.[10] Peer coaching networks and communities of practice become knowledge exchanges.[11] Status meetings and one-on-ones transform from bureaucratic chores to development dialogues.

Octopus Organizations find inexpensive ways to learn and enable peer-to-peer learning. Learning can be packed into small, simple doses with no HR intervention. It can be as simple as gifting a topical book to a team to read and discuss to stimulate learning and curiosity. At Tesco Bank, Jana created a small ninety-second video about topics like the perils of multi-tasking—a zero-cost approach that any employee could replicate. Google's g2g (Googler-to-Googler) program reports that 80 percent of tracked training is completed employee-to-employee, with a volunteer teaching network of over six thousand Google employees, who gain recognition and develop their own skills.[12] Datadog COO Adam Blitzer embeds individuals with other teams to accelerate learning and break down barriers—a simple reassignment that costs nothing but creates cross-pollination of knowledge. Former Slack and Google executive Brian Elliott sends teams on training together. "The magic is not just that you put your hands on it, but you do it with a team, start sharing, comparing, and contrasting, learning skills together, and having conversations 'how might this be pertinent to our work,' as they know better than anyone else what their work is." Closing the gap between where training happens and its application is paramount to overcoming the *forgetting curve*, which shows how rapidly knowledge fades when not put into practice. Ninety percent of new skills not used within a year after learning are forgotten.[13]

Octopus Organizations recognize that effective learning also requires unlearning. As Alphabet X's Moonshot Factory CEO Astro Teller pointed out to us, "I'm trying to train people to unlearn all the things that have been piled on top of them since they were six years old." He argues that we've been conditioned since childhood to seek correct answers, avoid mistakes, and focus on short-term outcomes—habits that directly oppose innovation. Author and adviser Barry O'Reilly simply argues that the greatest challenge is unlearning the very mindsets that once made us successful but now limit our potential.[14] He advocates for a continuous cycle: consciously "unlearning" an outdated approach, "relearning" a new one through experimentation, and ultimately achieving a breakthrough in thinking and performance.

Octopus leaders regularly map current capabilities against future needs rather than throwing up training regimens to close immediate skills gaps. In doing so they can create skills matrices showing which skills they have in an organization and what they will need in the future. This informs strategic reskilling programs that help those with skills of diminishing importance to gain new skills with a clear understanding of the "why." It proactively prevents costly talent scrambles when new technologies emerge, reduces dependency on expensive external hires, and positions the organization to capitalize on opportunities.

When acquiring talent, forward-thinking Octopus Organizations prioritize candidates who are hungry to learn, solve problems, and enhance customer experiences over credentials. Jessica Hall, Chief Product Officer at Just Eat Takeaway, lets these hungry learners move through the organization, changing positions every eighteen months or so, and learn wherever they go. She credits this plan with improved retention in her own organization.

Also, development doesn't just take the form of upward mobility into management. Octopus Orgs create career lattices—webs of growth that move sideways, diagonally, or even temporarily down for valuable experience that aligns individual interests with opportunities.[15] These "boundary spanners" become connectors across silos, harvesting ideas through their broader organizational understanding and creating the cross-functional connections that drive innovation.

Lastly, **Octopus Organizations measure progress.** Werner Swane-poel, SVP at Sibanye-Stillwater, measures people's development using a "digital dipstick" at every town hall meeting, drawing from a catalog of questions in three categories: the team's level of excitement, self-rating of skills and knowl-edge, and ability to apply skills. This approach provided a popular measure of progress with training and development. Modern learning experience plat-forms and AI-driven analytics offer new possibilities for tracking engage-ment, skill acquisition, and correlating learning with performance indicators, providing richer data for continuous improvement.

Levers

^ **Make learning the work.** Instead of separate training, embed learning into work as training. This could be a two-to-three-day focused sprint at the beginning of an initiative to learn new tools or techniques. Think "We need to use this AI tool. Let's spend two days playing with it and figuring out how it connects to this project." Guide teams through Kolb's Experien-tial Learning Cycle (Experience -> Reflect -> Conceptualize -> Experi-ment).[16] Or give time and processes for *reflective practice* such as structured debriefs, after-action reviews, and journaling prompts to extract and so-lidify learning from experiences. Airbus VP of Artificial Intelligence Fab-rice Valentin uses such methods and tells us that this kind of ownership coupled with direct practical impact accelerates learning.

^ **Create micro-learning content.** Shift away from expensive omnibus programs to short DIY training like focused videos, articles, or interactive exercises, many of which can be developed by employees for employees.

Imagine a three-minute video on a new feature in your software, a five-minute quiz to test your understanding of a new process, or a seven-minute podcast from a leader on how they apply a leadership principle. Emulate Ferrari CEO Benedetto Vigna's process of sending out "management pills"—doses of wisdom—to stimulate curiosity and learning.

^ **Strategically plan skills development.** Proactively identify near-future skills needed based on organizational goals and conduct regular skills-gap analyses. Link the acquisition of skills to career progression opportunities. Incorporate skills development goals into performance reviews. Enable, or require, employees to move into different roles to learn new skills. Ensure that skills taught are closely aligned in time to the opportunity to practice them.[17]

^ **Support metacognitive skill development.** Help employees learn and improve their ability to think how to become more effective learners. Focus on teaching people how to learn by addressing what might limit a team's learning, such as assumptions, mental models, learning styles, or emotional regulation. Encourage them to create learning plans before starting a task, provide reflection journals, identify existing assumptions and mindsets about a task, facilitate quizzing to identify knowledge gaps, and promote peer feedback that emphasizes learning strategies.

^ **Enable self-organized curiosity groups.** Encourage employees to create groups and guilds around topics of shared interest with no management required. The groups can discuss how they are learning and experimenting with, for instance, AI tools or design thinking. Recognize and reward people who contribute as internal trainers or mentors.

^ **Create space for regular development conversations.** Use regular one-on-one meetings as dedicated development conversations. Equip leaders with questions like: "What skill are you trying to build, and how can I help you get practice?" or "What part of your work energizes you most, and how can we do more of that?" This shifts the leader's role from taskmaster to coach, making development a continuous part of the work rhythm.

^ **Create "skill swaps" marketplaces** where employees can list skills they have and skills they want to learn. Think "Airbnb for skills." It encourages cross-pollination and informal knowledge sharing. If you need to learn how to use a data visualization tool, you connect to your colleague in the marketing department who already knows it.

^ **Set up a "curiosity budget,"** a small budget to spend on learning, whether it's buying a book, taking a course, attending a conference, or starting a side project. Give people the autonomy to choose what they want to learn and how.

DISCOVER MORE

ANTIPATTERNS TO READ NEXT

#22: Hiring Poorly

#24: Mismanaging Incentives

#26: Evading Failure

PRETENDING TO INNOVATE

Ideas of any size, from anyone, anywhere create real value.

THE TIN MAN BEHAVIOR

Treating innovation as a bolt-on, separate, and structured activity in part due to a desire to be seen to have "innovative" capabilities

THE RESULTS

- Flashy ideas fail to meet real customer needs and don't survive contact with the real world.
- Stifled curiosity, untapped innovation potential, and disengagement of those not nominated as "innovators"
- Innovation becomes theater rather than customer value.

How Octopus Organizations Behave Instead

- They encourage innovation in everyone's work and enable frontline staff to act on their ideas.
- They prioritize innovation that solves real customer needs, whether big or small.
- They reward practical solutions that create measurable value over impressive innovation theater.

The Tin Man Behavior

Hardly a week goes by without us being asked to talk about how to establish an innovation center for an organization, whether a bank, manufacturer, government agency, utility company, or, of course, tech company. The rationale seems sound: they want to stay relevant and establish a reputation with customers and employees as an innovative company.

The fundamental issue they face, however, isn't about a lack of desire—it's one of *separation*. Tin Man organizations separate innovation from "real work," real customers, and real problems. A 2024 study found that a record 83 percent of executives rank innovation as a top-three priority, yet only 3 percent of companies are considered "innovation ready" to translate this priority into results—a dramatic drop from the still way-too-low 20 percent in 2022.[1] This inability to infuse innovation across organizations manifests in several ways:

- **Physical separation:** Innovation labs become islands, distant from where the actual business happens. We've seen this pattern fail repeatedly—90 percent of them, according to one report, including those at Walmart, Ford, IKEA, Disney, and many more.[2] They are often born from a mix of FOMO and helplessness about how to otherwise drive innovation, and they close when they fail to demonstrate business returns, leaving innovation nowhere to go.[3] When these expensive hubs inevitably close, the desire for a quick fix doesn't vanish. So, the next go-to solution is to try to engineer those conditions through separate physical events such as design-thinking offsites and hackathons for the chosen few. Those can become fun days that do little more than create neat ideas divorced from operational reality and needs, the results of which rarely make it into the real world. But signals of innovativeness are well received by investors and customers, so they continue regardless.

- **Structural separation:** Innovation becomes the job of "special people" while everyone else does the "real work." This implicitly tells the vast majority of employees that innovation isn't their responsibility. Ideas submitted by "normal" employees to suggestion boxes or competitions wither and die, and eventually, the employees give up on the "small-i" innovations that can come from any seat. This creates an organization full of untapped potential. As Virgin Experience Days CEO Christoph Homann says, "It's like buying all the gym kit for home but doing nothing with it."

- **Process separation:** Innovation gets treated as a structured, predictable process. But as Astro Teller, CEO of Alphabet X, told us, "You can't get there by starting with efficiency and trying to insert magic into the process. It's literally impossible. You have to start on the magic side . . . and then insert rigor very carefully so as to not kill the magic."

This behavior is a classic response to what Clayton Christensen famously termed "the innovator's dilemma."[4] Well-managed companies become so adept at serving their most profitable customers with sustaining innovations that their own processes and values prevent them from pursuing the disruptive, often lower-margin ideas that will define the future. The separate lab or hackathon becomes a well-intentioned but often futile attempt to create a space for disruption that the core business is hardwired to reject.

The result of this separation is "innovation theater," the equivalent of cosplay for corporates, much like the Great and Powerful Wizard of Oz pulling levers behind the curtain—impressive displays that often amount to little more than sophisticated stagecraft. Generating novel ideas is perceived as more glamorous than the hard, messy work of diving deep to understand customers and their context, defining which problems to solve, execution and integration—even though this hard messy work is what will make innovation useful.[5] Innovation theater stems from a fundamental misunderstanding of innovation's nature, equating it only with massive, disruptive breakthroughs. But the most significant cost of this theater is the thousands of small, brilliant ideas that come from connecting with real problems and real customer needs that are never born because the people who have them have been told that innovation isn't their job.

What Octopus Organizations Do Instead

They make innovation everyone's job and recognize that innovation is integration, not separation. They understand that valuable innovation— whether a small process improvement or a transformative new business model— comes from connecting ideas directly to real customer problems and real business operations. They treat innovation as part of everyone's job, not a ritual performed by an elite few. In a 2017 filing with the Securities and Exchange Commission, Amazon stated that it was not possible to separately disclose its R&D spending because its teams are "constantly working to build new . . . and simultaneously maintain current" products and services.[6] In other words, innovation is happening everywhere, all the time. It can't be separated.

The story of Amazon Prime illustrates how this integrated approach can nurture a small, frontline idea into a world-changing innovation. Prime was not born in a lab or from a top-down strategic mandate. It was born from five key Octopus behaviors:

- **They enable the edges.** The initial spark for Prime was credited to one engineer, Charlie Ward, and his frustration with Amazon's clunky free shipping options. He had the agency to surface a radical idea: an "all you can eat" shipping service.[7] The idea emerged from the front lines, close to the reality of the customer.

- **They connect small ideas to durable needs.** When Jeff Bezos encountered Ward's proposal, he didn't just see a new feature. He recognized its connection to a "long-lived customer need"—that customers will *always* want things faster and cheaper. He championed the idea, protecting it as a project code-named "Futurama," because it aligned with this deep, strategic insight.

- **They practice ambidexterity.** Even as Amazon's website was experiencing stability problems during a critical pre-Christmas period, Bezos demonstrated what author Safi Bahcall calls "Loonshot" thinking: the ability to support the fragile, uncertain new thing while simultaneously managing the core business.[8] He sheltered the Futurama team, allowing them to explore without being crushed by the urgencies of the moment.

- **They innovate the organization itself.** As the Prime concept evolved, it created tensions with the existing organization. The supply chain would need to change. The incentive model for retail category managers, measured on quarterly profit, would be threatened. Leaders expressed a concern that customers would abuse the program. A Tin Man organization would have let this orthodoxy kill the idea. Amazon instead changed the metrics to align with the new model, demonstrating that true innovation often requires changing how an organization operates—its incentives, measurements, and mental models—not just the product or service.

- **They play the infinite game.** Prime was not a one-and-done launch. It became a platform for more innovation: integrating third-party merchants, adding Prime Video, Prime Music, and Prime Day. This long-term commitment stands in stark contrast to the "launch and forget" pattern of innovation theater, treating the initial success as a foundation to build upon.

Great, you might think, but we're not Amazon. We don't have those deep pockets. That doesn't matter. We've worked with many Octopus Organizations of different sizes, and while the resources may be different, the *behaviors* are consistent. Octopus leaders at organizations of any size engage in several key behaviors. They:

- *Cultivate builders with local ownership*, trusting cross-functional teams that bring diverse perspectives and skills to the problem.

- *Relentlessly working backward from real customer problems*, not building novel things for their own sake.

- *Lead with context, not control*, setting the vision and strategy, not dictating solutions while enabling teams to determine solutions.

- *Provide tools to everyone*, including frameworks, data, and seed funding to remove barriers to experimentation.

- *Foster a culture of creative abrasion*, making it safe to challenge ideas and to learn from mistakes.

- *Show a bias toward action*, building quickly over perfect presentations to learn fast and setting goals that accelerate experimentation and iteration.

This also doesn't mean every employee needs to, or will want to, be an innovator. As Thoughtworks CEO Mike Sutcliff points out, it's often 10 to 15 percent of an organization who are driving such innovation. The role of an Octopus leader is to enable that passionate group *and* the entire organization to contribute by focusing on small-i innovation and to take others' ideas and execute them.

The innovation theater has had its run. What if, starting tomorrow, you simply asked one team what small, real problem they could tackle with a tiny bit more freedom? That's often enough to begin.

Levers

^ **Enable everyday problem-solving.** Dedicate fifteen minutes in your one-on-ones to ask your people: "What's something you're curious about that might help our customers? What's getting in the way of you trying small things? If we had total freedom and a tiny budget, what's one thing we could try *this month* to make [a specific customer's/our own] life slightly easier?" Then, support their experiment on the most promising small idea (remember to get to "no" quickly and focus on monkeys, not pedestals).

^ **Connect innovation to those closest to the customer.** Create a method whereby *anyone* can propose an innovation of any size or scale. Provide basic templates outlining the hypothesis, measurement, and time frame, and simple training on customer insights and experiment design. Reduce the approval layers needed for small bets. Publicly recognize and reward edge innovations that create tangible impact.

^ **Shift focus from ideas to validation.** Stop celebrating raw idea generation from hackathons or flashy prototypes. Instead, reward *validated learning*. Encourage teams to form hypotheses, build Minimum Lovable Products, test them quickly and cheaply, measure results, and learn whether to pivot or persevere. Make "What did we learn?" a more important question than "What did we build?"

^ **Fund the seeds.** Allocate flexible "micro-budgets" directly to teams or team leads for testing ideas, bypassing complex budget approvals for initial exploration. Define clear, simple criteria for accessing these funds and criteria for making data-informed decisions about whether to stop, pivot, or seek further investment based on results.

^ **Change the language.** Move away from using the word "innovation" as a special, separate thing. Instead, start talking about "improvement," "problem-solving," "experimentation," and "making things better." Amazon uses the leadership principle "Invent and simplify." Use these words constantly in communications. It makes innovation more approachable and a natural part of everyone's job.

^ **Make problem-solving visible (not just polished results).** Create a low-friction, highly visible space—like a dedicated Slack channel or a simple wiki page. Encourage teams to post not their finished solutions but their messy, in-progress work: the customer problem they're exploring, the "ugly" prototype they built in an hour, or the surprising insight they just uncovered. The goal is to shift the cultural currency from "presenting a perfect solution" to valuing curiosity and ownership, to make innovation feel accessible and collaborative rather than a high-stakes performance.

DISCOVER MORE

ANTIPATTERNS TO READ NEXT

#28: Mortgaging the Future

#29: Falling in Love with Answers

#30: Avoiding Hard Problems

BECOMING THE OCTOPUS

Without changing our pattern of thought,
we will not be able to solve the problems we created
with our current pattern of thought.

—Albert Einstein

After thirty-six descriptions of what's broken, the natural question is: "So, what now?" The secret isn't a grand plan to fix everything at once. It's finding the one antipattern that feels most true for your team and using it to start a different kind of conversation. We hope that's exactly what you'll do. Undoubtedly, you'll be able to add a few of your own antipatterns you've experienced, which we'd love to hear about at ideas@theoctopusorganization.com.

But even with all the advice we've offered in these thirty-six entries for starting to shed your tin suit for a more fluid future, you probably want more guidance. Leaders we work with intuitively understand the approach, then immediately pivot to three key questions:

- How do I get started?
- How do I make sure it sticks?
- How do I scale it?

This conclusion will answer the first two questions, then slightly adjust the third question to answer a better version of it.

Here's how we recommend you approach your first steps to becoming the Octopus.

Guided by Three Principles

First, resist your urge to reach for the transformation playbook. The benchmarking, analysis, grand planning for a reorg, army of consultants, top-down dictates—all of it is Tin Man behavior you should now be familiar with.

Then, shift your mindset to that of an Octopus leader, and approach the journey with three principles:

- **Do change *with* people, not *to* them.** Tin Man organizations "put the power of interpretation in the hands of a few."[1] Their leaders believe their job is to design a perfect transformation plan and push it "down" onto the organization. The Octopus leader understands their true leverage comes from acting as an architect of the environment, not the architect of the plan. They obsess over creating the conditions—clarity of purpose, psychological safety, and access to information—that allow emergent solutions to flourish from the people closest to the work. In this model, senior leaders rarely drive change; they cultivate the organization's innate capacity to change itself, enabling their people to solve the problems they know best, organically and continuously from every seat.

- **Entwine learning *and* impact.** A Tin Man organization often mistakes activity for progress. An Octopus Organization knows that progress is activity that generates both value *and* learning. They embed experiments into the daily flow of work, ensuring every initiative provides a chance to create impact for customers and the business while simultaneously challenging core assumptions, mental models, and dependencies. Cutting meeting time in half is just activity; learning how to have more effective meetings and making better decisions as a result is progress. Not every experiment will yield the expected value, but it *must* yield deep learning that will inform the next set of experiments.

- **Do less to achieve more.** A Tin Man's default approach to change is to add something new: a process, a tool, a new layer of oversight. The Octopus leader, by contrast, operates with a subtractive mindset, knowing that true leverage often comes from removing what is in the way—eliminating a process, dissolving a dependency, or removing a gatekeeper. When they do introduce something new, they use constraints to reduce unnecessary procrastination. As AWS's Enterprise Strategist Jake Burns notes, "Work expands to fill the time available for its completion," so by intentionally constricting time and scope, they force a ruthless focus on what truly matters, creating momentum and cultivating a *progress over perfection* mindset.[2] This "less is more" philosophy also applies to the scale of change itself; starting small with a single team or a business unit generates frequent, visible progress, which is far more powerful for building long-term engagement than a single, massive, and infrequent "win."[3]

These three mantras help you shift away from the need for periodic large-scale scarring transformations that are done *to* the organization to a state where people close to the action start taking ownership and showing curiosity to advance your organization from every seat. The shift won't happen everywhere, all at once. You will have Octopus-ish parts of your organization and old Tin Men coexisting, especially in large organizations. The idea of a uniform transformation plan for improvement is unrealistic, but you can look to improve things *anywhere*. Just know it will occur at different levels and speeds. Where the new behaviors take hold, a flywheel effect sets in, as Jim Collins describes in *Good to Great*. Each small push builds momentum, and change perpetuates, underpinned by a sense of positive dissatisfaction with the status quo.[4]

Remember, Tin Man organizations operate with *antipatterns and create plans to address them*. You want to create *patterns (not Tin Man plans)*, habits of continuous evolving and advancing.

Understanding and Using the Levers

For each antipattern entry we provided *levers*, ways to get started combating an antipattern that create the most impact with the smallest "force" while creating learnings. We borrowed here from groundbreaking research at MIT, refined by systems-thinking legend Donella Meadows, who describes *leverage points*—points where a small tweak can ripple out, creating outsize effects on your organization (or any system).[5]

Our levers, like Donella's, come in different strengths, ranging from quick parameter adjustments to fundamental shifts in how organizations operate. We break these into three categories:

- **Small levers adjust parameters** in existing decision-making processes but don't change the system structure. They are inexpensive and quick to apply. For instance, reducing the number of approvers for expenses from eleven people to two. Donella notes that since they're easy, they're the ones we go to first, but they have limited power. "Parameters are last on my list of powerful interventions," Donella says. "Probably 99 percent of our attention goes to [small levers], but there's not a lot of leverage in them."[6]

- **Mid-level levers reshape the system's structure, information flows, and feedback loops**. They require more focus than simple tweaks but create a more lasting behavior change, too. Here are three examples:

- *Restructuring material and information flows.* This involves changing the physical or digital structure of how work moves to eliminate delays. Reducing the number of handoffs in a product development group from 160 to 20 isn't just a process improvement; it's a fundamental restructuring of the system. This single change can dramatically shorten time-to-market, adapting to market changes, by removing the queues and wait-states where work languishes.

- *Strengthen balancing (negative) feedback loops.* While "negative" sounds bad, these loops are crucial for stability and self-correction; they act like a thermostat for your organization. A strong balancing loop detects a problem and triggers corrective action. For instance, when customer complaints spike (the signal), a well-designed system automatically triggers an investigation into the root cause (the response), and the resultant fixes reduce future errors and bring complaints back down (the goal). This creates a system that learns and maintains quality without constant manual intervention.

- *Amplifying reinforcing (positive) feedback loops.* These are the engines of growth and momentum, where success breeds more success. For example, consider a well-designed employee recognition system. When great work is publicly celebrated, it not only motivates the recognized individual but also inspires others, creating a virtuous cycle of engagement, higher performance, and more recognition. Octopus leaders actively look for these reinforcing loops and find ways to amplify them.

- **Profound levers** are the most powerful interventions, requiring the greatest leadership focus, but a small push in the right place can create transformative change. They are presented here in order of increasing impact, moving from the visible structures of the organization to the invisible beliefs that govern it:

  - *Rules of the system.* These include the explicit policies, incentives, constraints, and punishments that govern behavior. Rules dictate who has power and what's possible, with power over the rules being seen as real power. An example of a profound lever here would be changing from bureaucratic approval processes to principles-based decision-making. While changing them can be powerful, it is often met with resistance if the underlying goals and mindset remain the same.

- *Self-organization.* This is not about designing the perfect team structure from the top down; it's about enhancing the system's innate ability to evolve, adapt, and create its own order. Octopus leaders foster this by creating the conditions—like clear goals, rapid feedback, and distributed ownership—that allow cross-functional teams and communities of practice to form and reconfigure themselves to meet emerging needs. This builds true organizational resilience and adaptability.

- *Goals.* This can be a fundamental reset of what the organization optimizes for, which drives corresponding changes in incentives and behaviors. Changing the goal changes the trajectory of the entire system. Shifting a company's primary success metric from "quarterly profit" to "customer lifetime value," for example, is a profound lever, as it forces a corresponding change in all underlying rules, incentives, and behaviors.

- *Mental models—the mindset or paradigm from which a system (your octopus) arises.* This is the most powerful leverage point of all. It is the shared, often unstated, set of beliefs and assumptions that form the very foundation of the culture. Once the core mental model shifts—for instance, from "leaders must command and control" to "leaders must empower and trust"—everything else becomes easier. As Donella observed, a paradigm shift can happen in a millisecond in an individual's mind, requiring no capital investment or complex rollout.[7] This is why Octopus leaders focus so much energy here: changing the shared mindset is the fastest, most effective, and most enduring way to transform an organization. To change mindsets, you don't launch a change campaign; you create dissonance. Octopus leaders do this by constantly pointing out the failures and anomalies of the old way of thinking, showcasing small, undeniable successes from the new paradigm (e.g., celebrating a fast, frugal, autonomous team that delivered incredible value), and amplifying the voices of change agents who already embody the new mindset.[8] This creates a steady drumbeat of evidence that makes the old model feel increasingly obsolete and the new one feel both possible and necessary. Practically, you can start by examining your own biases and assumptions.

Octopus leaders ultimately want to use the profound levers most, but all three levels will be useful as you go on your journey and all three are reflected in most of the levers included with the antipatterns. As you use the levers or consider using them, think about the relative payoff versus effort—and think about classifying new levers you come up with.

Many organizations we work with have done so, as has our own. Jeff Wilkie, former Amazon CEO of the Worldwide Consumer business and twenty-one-year Amazon veteran, put Donella's model into practice as a taxonomy of levers that leaders could pull to effect change at Amazon similar to figure C-1. This might not be the right way for you, but it is a good example to help you think about how you might do it.

Start Small: Change One Antipattern

So, let's start putting our tentacles to work. By now you've found one or two antipatterns that resonate, and you're excited to do something about them. So, just start! Resist the temptation to over-plan. Just go ahead and pull some levers, iteratively experimenting and learning.

Identify the antipattern. Having those closest to the Tin Man behavior identify opportunities for overcoming it is the most powerful way to start, just like those neuroclusters in the octopus's arms that exert their local intelligence. In our experience, the selection of the antipattern to attack is often obvious, as we see aggressively nodding heads in one group or another when we mention some of the antipatterns. Look for nervous laughter, frowning, heavy shoulders, or rolling eyes when talking about your antipatterns. Better still, provide copies of this book to groups who will eagerly dog-ear and highlight the antipatterns that they're excited to go after. Emotional reactions are strong drivers for ownership and change. Other sources of antipatterns to attack are:

- New employees questioning organizational norms

- Frustrations in employee surveys

- Exit interviews

- Employee one-on-ones

- Town hall questions

- Help desk tickets: repetitive issues, long lead-time issues, and customer complaints

Once you've zoomed in on an antipattern, see where ownership of it naturally gravitates, but resist forcing it *on* people. For example, is there a team that is most passionate about fixing the behavior? They may take it on. We've also seen leaders successfully ask individuals who are most strongly opposed to changing an antipattern to own it, ironically. Jessica Hall, Chief Product Officer of Just Eat, points out that these are often long-tenured employees with their own sense of how things should go, perhaps the hardest to convince but the best to get on board. Instead of finding a way around those critics, listen to their explanation of why this change should not happen. Learn from them; make the idea better. If the change works, those critics will become the staunchest advocates for change.

Develop a hypothesis.[9] Whoever takes ownership then defines the hypothesis about which levers to pull to escape the antipattern, and what they propose to try. Make it clear that proving the hypothesis wrong is just as valuable as proving it right. The idea is not to force something to work. If it doesn't work, we will have also learned something.

Don't overengineer hypotheses; set them, test them, and uncover actionable insights one way or the other. Document what you learn to make it visible to all. The intent here is fast learning and forward momentum.

Run an experiment and reflect. Experiments come in multiple forms. You may:

- **Deprecate** a frustrating practice. Yes, an experiment can be as simple as stopping something!

- **Deviate** from an established process, altering it temporarily to see what happens.

- **Design** something new, an experiment around an existing lever in this book, or a new one.

Timescales will vary for experiments based on the scope and levers chosen. Smaller levers like changing a daily meeting from thirty minutes to twenty-five minutes or trying a jargon jar might be tested over the course of a week; more complex ones like moving from an annual to a dynamic budget might take a bit of setting up and might be tried over several quarters. Initial experiments should be as small as possible, making the potential downside feel less scary. And as with any good lab experiment, you should have a fire extinguisher handy if things get out of control. This might be a budget to manage unexpected cost issues, a backup team to step in without judgment and help, and a "we're trying something here" memo to avoid finger-pointing and blaming if things go sideways.

And sometimes they will fail. But remember, for an Octopus Organization, that's great! Learning from failure is not to be avoided. It's a valuable signpost for what to do next, quickly.

Tin Men will be tempted to run the loop once and land on one of two conclusions: Either "It worked! Make *all meetings* twenty-five minutes, immediately!" or "It failed! Let's not try that ever again!" This is where double-loop learning comes in. Octopus Organizations do not take a binary approach to experiments. Just because shorter meetings may help the finance team doesn't mean they won't absolutely throttle a product team. Instead, they reflect on two levels:

- **The single-loop.** Analyze the results of the experiment. What happened? What didn't? Based on this, you identify specific actions to implement, stop, or adjust. This is learning about *what* to do.

- **The double-loop.** Go deeper. Analyze the experiment itself. Why did we choose this experiment? What underlying assumptions, goals, or values led us here? This healthy practice challenges existing mental models, helping to reframe the problem and identify deeper systemic issues like the levers we shared above. This is learning about *how you think*.

You can use the antipattern escape canvas (figure C-1) to guide the conversations and capture the learnings in this double-loop process.

Spread, Don't Scale

Overcoming an antipattern is a great start, often having impact within a pocket of the organization. Our experience working with organizations is that once they run a few successful experiments and see some positively Octopus-like behavior in local spots, senior leaders immediately jump to ask, "So how do we scale this?"

This question betrays a Tin Man view. Scaling becomes shorthand for the implementation of a uniform process or tool organization-wide. But scaling risks turning your experimental successes into broad failures, or into an exercise in compliance and standardization. Former Schneider Electric President and AWS VP Tanuja Randery is adamant that "the idea that things must be perfectly the same everywhere is nonsense. Leaders need to be open to courage for flexibility."

Scaling as a concept runs the risk of robbing people of local ownership. It tends to ignore context, assuming the org is a machine with replaceable cogs. It separates the learning and the doing, as those who weren't part of the initial successful experiment are simply ordered to adopt a new behavior. Scaling assumes what works here will work everywhere.

The scaling mindset also makes organizations miss out on local value because the default posture is that if it doesn't scale, we shouldn't support it. For example, one of the world's leading online retail companies ran an immersive, nomination-based leadership development program that was transformative for every leader who went through it. Years later those who participated still

FIGURE C-1

Antipattern escape canvas

Single-threaded owner: _____   *Time box:* _____

What makes this Tin Man? How does this show up? What are the pain points? Share an anecdote that brings it to life.	**What is your hypothesis to test?** If we try [ACTION], we believe [OUTCOME] will improve because of [REASON]. Describe your experiment. Which Octopus levers can you use?
What resources do you need? Who needs to be consulted, to sponsor, or to approve? What skills, data, or tools and funding do you need?	**How will you know you have advanced toward Octopus (or not)?** What behaviors will you be able to observe? What stories will be told? What metric(s) can you experiment with to test your hypothesis? What kill criteria do you set?
What have you learned? What surprised you? What would you do differently now? What's next—now or later? What feedback did you receive? What assumptions or beliefs were challenged? What mental shortcuts were found to be dated? What sacred cow provide to be untrue? Share data and anecdotes.	**What makes this Tin Man?** What changes have occurred, if any (behaviors, language, tools, process, engagement)? What metrics or kill criteria were met? What unexpected impacts occurred? What needs to change next to increase or unblock impact? Share data and anecdotes.

talked about it as the best training they had ever experienced. They went on to become directors, vice presidents, and leaders of large businesses. But the company killed the program because it didn't scale to more than ninety-six leaders per year, despite the broad impact these leaders went on to have.

Octopus Organizations don't default to scaling. They think about *spreading*, whereby ideas and practices flow organically from team to team and leader to leader based on need and context. A new technology, practice, or process (or the removal of one) works in one team, and now others want to try it, too. Spreading accepts that a solution in one part of the organization *might* be suitable in another part if it is adapted to be context appropriate. Watch which local practices or solutions travel beyond the boundaries of local teams to other parts of your organization and get naturally adopted because they make the work better.

While scaling is *pushed* out to everyone, spreading is *pulled*. A pull model reinforces ownership of change from every seat ("Do I want to take this?") and allows curiosity ("How can I adapt this to meet my needs?"). Adopting the mental model of spreading over scaling reinforces the idea that change is no longer (or only rarely) a top-down plan owned by leaders. The leader's job now is to create the conditions where change is being created locally, and can permeate through the organization, spreading everywhere.

Stephen Brozovich was a web developer working on Amazon's landing page twenty years ago, when web technology was not nearly as mature as it is now. Editors would send him product and promotional images weekly for posting. At the time he could only post these using an arcane command-line interface that required memorizing image names, complex file paths, and other information. There was no way to search the images visually. He got tired enough of doing this and wasting his time re-uploading images that were already on the server that he taught himself just enough programming to build a program that let him search image files visually. The program worked so well that soon, all Amazon web developers, designers, and several other groups were using it, too. Eventually someone created an international version.

There was no mandate. No promotion of the tool. It was just pulled through the organization because it worked. That's spreading in action. For Stephen's work, he received Amazon's "Just Do It" award to recognize someone who showed initiative without asking for permission.[10] The award, a used oversize (size 23) Nike shoe with an old sock, was handed to Stephen by CEO Jeff Bezos in an all-hands meeting.[11]

If you've read even a few antipatterns and the levers you can use to overcome them, you'll see plenty of Octopus behavior in this example. This pull model is how organizations truly sustain change and keep changing—not through mandates and rollouts, but through practices that prove their worth and attract adoption.

We've observed several benefits of spreading over scaling:

- When solutions to antipatterns spread under their own energy, Octopus behaviors are more likely to stick. Ownership and agency are powerful.

- A culture of change becomes embedded and harder to derail as it naturally engages *many* more people than a top-down transformation.

- It fosters more diverse solutions, skills, and teams, which creates more resilience. A positive tension exists between "competing" solutions, fueling new thinking.

A culture of spreading rather than scaling is supported by visibility. Make spreading behavior visible to all to nudge it along. This culture will also benefit from an *appreciative inquiry* approach, looking for those behaviors, practices, and tools that already work well and can be built upon and amplified, rather than just looking to spread fixes for what's not working.[12]

The act of identifying successful patterns helps spread new ones, fostering greater openness to change.[13] When Western Union CIO Ryan Seaman noticed that his South American team had developed a great market solution, he didn't tell them to move on to another problem to fix; he challenged and supported them to continue developing it so it might spread to other markets.

When You Do Scale: Platforms and Mechanisms, Not Practices

This doesn't mean nothing is ever scaled. Octopus Organizations are very deliberate about what gets scaled. They don't try to control the ocean's fluid movement; they focus on building stable coral reef to enable life to flourish. Ishit Vachhrajani, former A+E Networks CTO, advises, "Don't carpet bomb the place. Pick one good fight. Paint a grounded picture of why the change is necessary." They scale foundational platforms to provide enabling, safe structure—not rigid or restrictive—for everyone, like a shared, secure cloud environment or common brand and safety principles. They scale effective mechanisms—the "currents" of the organization—like a robust hiring process to ensure quality with autonomy, or a shared framework for making big bets.

The goal is simply to provide a strong foundation that can accelerate and liberate decentralized teams to navigate, adapt, and innovate freely on it.

Remember as you do this that what you are scaling are *artifacts*, which are only useful if there is successful *behavior* change along with the scale. A tool (artifact) to share lessons across the entire enterprise is a waste unless the *behavior* of sharing is the focus of what the organization wants to accomplish.

Where you decide to implement such scaling, we recommend using *mechanisms*, a very engineering-centric idea Amazon uses but one that applies to any part of the business. Mechanisms are an Octopus's way to scale, using tools and processes that *guide* behavior (they do not mandate it) beyond direct leadership. They shift the focus from trying to achieve outputs to focusing on controllable inputs that can help you achieve the output.

To scale with mechanisms you need *tools*, like a software system, that transform inputs into outputs. You need an *adoption* strategy to ensure the tools are implemented and used, and you need a process for *inspection* to periodically make sure the mechanism is effective or to look for ways to improve it. Each mechanism has an owner.

For example, it might make sense to scale customer acquisition rather than let it spread through levers. But you can't effectively control an output goal of "X amount of customer acquisition." What you can control is the precision of an advertising campaign, the volume of meaningful social media engagement, promotion frequency, and the number of new partnerships to affect the amount of customer acquisition—inputs to reach that goal. Find a way to implement those tools across the organization and then check in on them to make sure they're helping you reach that output goal.

Note that mechanisms don't force behavior change. You don't say, "Buy a software package we tell you to buy that targets ads"—rather, they enable more ownership closer to the customer at scale. "Figure out what software will help you target ads at scale."

The Octopus Organization builds strong, consistent platforms and effective mechanisms that enable teams to develop and spread their own solutions. This is how you get both the benefits of standardization where it matters and the benefits of organization-wide continuous adaptation and evolution.

Lead to Not Lead

OK. You're ready. You know the antipatterns. You have an approach to tackling them. Time to become more Octopus.

Our experience, perhaps not surprisingly, is that leaders struggle with tackling antipatterns and becoming more Octopus-like much more than their people who are enabled by this shift. Teams tend to get it right away and embrace this approach. But for leaders, it means unlearning a career's worth of behaviors that have been assumed to be the right way, the only way, to do things. "There is something paradoxical about what you're about to do," says Aaron Dignan in *Brave New Work*. "You're trying to lead your organization to a place where you're not the leader anymore, at least not in the way you are today."[14]

Your job now is to help people who have been *managed* all their lives to take ownership. Focus on facilitating clarity, removing obstacles to ownership, and celebrating curiosity. At first, it may be as foreign a feeling as it must be for someone jacketed in metal to suddenly feel the flowing, adaptive, distributed intelligence of being an Octopus. You've never moved this way, or thought this way, or been able to do the things you can do with eight smart arms.

Leaders, you create the *conditions* for success in the Octopus Organization, not the success itself. You will be less involved in everyday operational decisions, but more involved in setting and reinforcing strategy and purpose, ensuring there is clear ownership for outcomes across the organization, and creating the conditions that value learning and experimentation. The successful leaders we speak to, from Ferrari CEO Benedetto Vigna, to Dynafit CEO and extreme mountaineer Benedikt Böhm, to former PepsiCo CEO and Chairperson Indra Nooyi, London Stock Exchange CEO Dame Julia Hoggett, and so, so many others, dedicate what Tin Man leaders would consider a disproportionate amount of their time to refining and revisiting their "why." They communicate it, and communicate it again, consume customer insights, and colleagues' feedback, refine their messages, and communicate some more.

Leadership in the Octopus world could be a book unto itself (and maybe it will be), but what struck us in interviews and in working with Octopus Organizations is that leadership emerges at every level of the organization. Some of the common, enduring characteristics we found in people who lead in an Octopus way, whether or not they have formal authority, include:

- **They lead with humility.** Octopus leaders think beyond their tenure, seeing themselves as temporary caretakers of something valuable that existed before them and will continue after them. This frees them from the need to have all the answers, allowing them to subjugate their ego, genuinely listen, and focus on bringing out the best ideas in others.

- **They practice voracious curiosity.** They replace "commanding" with "questioning," making it their primary role to learn. This is most visible in how they listen—redirecting their own mental energy away from forming a reply and toward fully understanding what the other person is saying, and more broadly listening to what trends and technologies are emerging.

- **They act as system architects.** They work *on*, not *in* the system. Instead of micromanaging tasks, they focus on designing the organizational environment and removing the friction that prevents talented people from doing their best work.

- **They default to trust.** Octopus leaders start with the fundamental belief that their people are capable and want to do good work. This allows them to grant the real ownership needed to solve problems, replacing top-down control with shared context and purpose.

- **They provide stability.** Their consistency comes not from rigid adherence to plans, but from an unwavering commitment to the organization's purpose and values. Their actions and words stay consistent over time, changing only when their convictions change. They create the stability that enables teams to take risks with confidence.[15]

- **They are a source of positive energy and belief.** They genuinely believe in their people's ability to solve hard problems and overcome challenges, getting better each time. They actively look for and celebrate progress, no matter how small, fueling a sense of possibility and resilience throughout the organization.

We are certain most people possess the capacity for these leadership qualities. Our sense from working with so many of them is that they also *want* to embrace this expanded view of what leadership means. They just need to learn how to amplify these natural abilities and shift their mental models of what it means to lead. This book is the first step.

. . .

If you see a real octopus in the wild, one of the first things you'll notice are its huge, inquisitive eyes looking into the distance. At the same time, its tentacles are experiencing, exploring, and manipulating their immediate surroundings. If it needs to, the octopus will change its color or texture, or reshape itself based on what it's learned about its immediate environment and what's out beyond.

The intelligence and fluidity of an octopus's behavior are beautiful and inspiring. Becoming an Octopus Organization will allow you to look across the business landscape while you nimbly and fluidly adapt to what's happening right now in your organization. The octopus and the Octopus Organization are both built to learn and adapt. As we support organizations in their Octopus journeys, we find time and again that the problems they face are known and the answers are within reach, if they just create clarity, provide ownership, and foster curiosity. With a little practice, you, too, can achieve the same beautiful existence as our eight-legged friend.

GRATITUDE (BECAUSE NO ONE MAKES OCTOPUS WAVES ALONE)

This book exists because people showed up.

To our families: You gave us the runway. The late nights, the missed holidays: you saw the glimmer and fanned the flame. Your own remarkable curiosity and grit are woven into these pages. Thank you for the trust, the patience, and for reminding us what truly matters.

To the brilliant minds—colleagues, customers, thinkers—who wrestled with these ideas alongside us: This is your wisdom, distilled. You challenged, you shared, you made it better. The best parts of this book likely started as a question you asked or a story you told.

And to the chorus of thinkers who generously lent their red pens, sharp eyes, and precious time to make these ideas better: A special thank you to Adam Blitzer, Adrian Cockcroft, Alicia Greenwood, Amy Edmondson, Andrew Linn, Professor Andrew Stephen, Annie Duke, Astro Teller, Axel Hefer, Barry O'Reilly, Benedetto Vigna, Benedikt Böhm, Brian Elliott, Brittany Anderson, Chris Butler, Chris Henessey, Chris Jones, Chris-Markus Kratz, Christoph Homann, Coté, Craig Suckling, Dang Ly, Darren Bowling, Deb Hall-Lefevre, Deepak Sondar, E. A. Rockett, Emma Soane, Emma Stace, Fabrice Valentin, Fernando Jana Vergara, Hannah Foxwell, Helena Yin Koeppl, Hilary Tam, Howard Behar, Ian Millar, Indra Nooyi, Ishit Vachhrajani, Jessica Hall, 9Jonathan Allen, Dame Julia Hoggett, Kiki van den Berg, Kim Atherton, Kyle Bird, Leo Martinez, Liam Maxwell, Linda Hill, Luc Hennekens, Manuel Bohnet, Mark Preston, Mark Schwartz, Martin Bishop, Marty Cagan, Max Spoto, Melanie McGrory, Michael Newton, Michael Sutcliff, Miriam McLemore, Peter Hinssen, Rich Hua, Richard Murphy, Robert Barrios, Rob Carr, Rob Hodges, Robbie Clutton, Robert Werner, Ryan Seaman, Shaun Braun, Tom Soderstrom, Sophie Seiwald, Stephen Heidari-Robinson, Stephen Brozovich, Sue Pittacora, Tanuja Randery CBE, Thilina Gunasinghe, Thomas Blood, Tom Godden, Walter Gruener, Werner Swanepoel, Whitney McGinnis, Will Thomas, Will Venters, Allison Peter and the entire production team at HBR Press, and anyone we missed.

Your fingerprints are on these pages, and the work is immeasurably stronger because you showed up for it.

To the leaders who let us peek behind the curtain: Your candor about the messy, human work of change was a gift. Your stories are the proof.

To Suzanne Heywood: You opened the door. Thank you.

To Scott Berinato at HBR Press: You're the kind of editor who doesn't just fix sentences; you help find the soul of the work. You saw what our manuscript could become and helped us get there with generosity and insight. A true Octopus leader.

To everyone who whispered "keep going": Your cheers mattered more than you know.

And finally, to you—the reader, the leader, the instigator already fighting the good fight against the status quo: This book is for you. You're building something better, something more human, something that works. Keep making waves. The world needs it.

NOTES

Introduction

1. In writing this book we drew on our experience working with *Fortune* 500 organizations and their leadership teams; we were also privileged to interview a diverse set of over seventy leaders ranging from former and current CEOs and other leaders in some of the world's most recognizable brands and governments along with academics, other experts, and practitioners, all leaders in their fields. While not everyone is quoted directly in the book, each provided nuanced insights into what really propels organizations toward becoming more Octopus-like.

2. Steve Armbruster, "Large-Scale Transformations for Long-Term Impact," McKinsey & Company, 2023, https://www.mckinsey.com/capabilities/implementation/our-insights/how -to-implement-transformations-for-long-term-impact.

3. Laura LaBerge et al., "Digital Transformation Survey Results," McKinsey & Company, 2022, https://www.mckinsey.com/capabilities/mckinsey-digital/our-insights /three-new-mandates-for-capturing-a-digital-transformations-full-value; Nagesh Ramesh and Dursun Delen, "Digital Transformation: How to Beat the 90% Failure Rate?" *IEEE Engineering Management Review* 49, no. 3 (April 19, 2021): 22–25; Patrick Forth et al., "Flipping the Odds of Digital Transformation Success," Boston Consulting Group, October 29, 2020, https://www.bcg.com/publications/2020/increasing-odds-of-success-in -digital-transformation.

4. Greg Kihlstrom, "CX Quality Is Falling—Forrester Says Total Experience Can Fix It," CMSWire Insights, June 27, 2025; https://www.cmswire.com/customer-experience/cx-quality -is-fallingforrester-says-total-experience-can-fix-it/.

5. "Wealth Management Digitalization Changes Client Advisory More Than Ever Before," Deloitte, 2017, https://www2.deloitte.com/content/dam/Deloitte/de/Documents /WM%20Digitalisierung.pdf.

Part 1

1. Stanley A. McChrystal et al., *Team of Teams: New Rules of Engagement for a Complex World* (New York: Portfolio, 2015).

2. David T. Bastien and Todd J. Hostager, "Jazz as a Process of Organizational Innovation," *Communication Research* 15 (1988): 582–602.

3. Patrick Lencioni, *The Advantage: Why Organizational Health Trumps Everything Else in Business* (San Francisco: Jossey-Bass, 2012).

Antipattern #1

1. Scott Galloway, "Yogababble. No Mercy. No Malice," 2019, https://www.profgalloway .com/yogababble/.

2. Noel Carroll et al., "Transform or Be Transformed: The Importance of Research on Managing and Sustaining Digital Transformations," *European Journal of Information Systems* 32, no. 3 (May 25, 2023); Michael Gale and Chris Aarons, *The Digital Helix: Transforming Your Organization's DNA to Thrive in the Digital Age* (Austin, TX: Greenleaf Book Group, 2017).

3. John P. Kotter, "Words Matter: Getting Rid of Business Jargon," *Forbes*, December 14, 2011, https://www.forbes.com/sites/johnkotter/2011/12/14/words-matter-getting-rid-of-business-jargon/.

4. Adrian Chiles, "We Need to Get Rid of Business Jargon. Do I Have Your Buy-in?," *The Guardian*, July 1, 2021, https://www.theguardian.com/commentisfree/2021/jul/01/we-need-to-get-rid-of-business-jargon-do-i-have-your-buy-in.

5. André Spicer, "Shooting the Shit: The Role of Bullshit in Organisations," M@n@gement 16, no. 5 (2013): 653–666, 10.3917/mana.165.0653.

Antipattern #2

1. Reed Hastings and Erin Meyer, *No Rules Rules: Netflix and the Culture of Reinvention* (New York: Penguin Press, 2020).

2. Ranjay Gulati, *Deep Purpose: The Heart and Soul of High-Performance Companies* (New York: Harper, 2022).

3. Daniel Coyle, *The Culture Code: The Secrets of Highly Successful Groups* (New York: Bantam, 2018).

4. "Work in Progress: How the Future of Work Depends on Us," Accenture, 2022, https://www.accenture.com/content/dam/accenture/final/capabilities/strategy-and-consulting/talent-and-organization/document/Accenture-Work-In-Progress-How-The-Future-Of-Work-Depends-On-Us.pdf.

5. Jonathan Knowles et al., "What Is the Purpose of Your Purpose?," *Harvard Business Review*, March–April 2022, https://hbr.org/2022/03/what-is-the-purpose-of-your-purpose.

6. Paul Campbell and Mark Milward, "Power of Purpose," Deloitte.com, 2022, https://www.deloitte.com/global/en/our-thinking/insights/topics/business-strategy-growth/mind-the-purpose-gap.html.

7. "State of the Global Workplace Report," Gallup, 2025, https://www.gallup.com/workplace/349484/state-of-the-global-workplace.aspx.

8. "State of the Global Workplace Report."

9. Scott Galloway, "Yogababble. No Mercy. No Malice," 2019, https://www.profgalloway.com/yogababble/.

10. Robert E. Quinn and Anjan V. Thakor, "Creating a Purpose-Driven Organization," *Harvard Business Review*, July–August 2018.

11. Quinn and Thakor, "Creating a Purpose-Driven Organization."

12. Simon Sinek, "How Great Leaders Inspire Action," TED Talk, September 2009, https://www.ted.com/talks/simon_sinek_how_great_leaders_inspire_action?language=en; Simon Sinek, *The Infinite Game* (New York: Portfolio, 2019).

13. Alex Edmans, *Grow the Pie* (Cambridge, UK: Cambridge University Press, 2020).

14. Sally Blount and Paul Leinwand, "Why Are We Here?," *Harvard Business Review*, November–December 2019.

15. Daniel H. Pink, *Drive: The Surprising Truth about What Motivates Us* (New York: Penguin, 2011).

16. Stephanie Santos, "Make Purpose Real for Employees," Harvard Business Impact, https://www.harvardbusiness.org/make-purpose-real-for-employees/.

17. Anish Shah, "The Ideas That Inspire Us," *Harvard Business Review,* November–December 2022.

18. Darrell Rigby et al., "What Successful Purpose Statements Do Differently," hbr.org, March 1, 2024, https://hbr.org/2024/03/what-successful-purpose-statements-do-differently.

19. Blount and Leinwand, "Why Are We Here?"

20. Jonathan Knowles et al., "What Is the Purpose of Your Purpose?," *Harvard Business Review,* March–April 2022.

Antipattern #3

1. Donald Sull et al., "No One Knows Your Strategy—Not Even Your Top Leaders," *MIT Sloan Management Review,* February 12, 2018, https://sloanreview.mit.edu/article/no-one-knows-your-strategy-not-even-your-top-leaders/.

2. Gary Hamel, "Killer Strategies That Make Shareholders Rich: The Top Companies Thrive, Says Our Author—a Leading Strategy Guru—by Changing the Rules of the Game," *Fortune,* June 23, 1997; https://money.cnn.com/magazines/fortune/fortune_archive/1997/06/23/228085/index.htm.

3. "PwC's 27th Annual Global CEO Survey—Thriving in an Age of Continuous Reinvention," PwC, 2024, https://www.pwc.com/gx/en/ceo-survey/2024/download/27th-ceo-survey.pdf.

4. Shane Parrish, "Signal without Static," *Farnam Street,* June 22, 2025; https://fs.blog/brain-food/june-22-2025/.

5. Seth Godin, *This Is Strategy: Make Better Plans (Create a Strategy to Elevate Your Career, Community and Life)* (New York: Authors Equity, 2024).

6. Peter Westberg, "Netflix: How a Subscription Price Cut Boosted Free Cash Flow!," HighRadius, May 17, 2024, https://www.highradius.com/finsider/netflix-financial-strategy/.

7. Kate O'Flaherty, "The Netflix Password Sharing Crackdown Is Working," *Forbes,* October 27, 2023, https://www.forbes.com/sites/kateoflahertyuk/2023/10/25/the-netflix-password-sharing-crackdown-is-working-and-others-will-certainly-follow/.

8. Rita McGrath, *Seeing Around Corners: How to Spot Inflection Points in Business Before They Happen* (New York: HarperCollins, 2021).

9. James B. Stewart, "Amazon Says Long Term and Means It," *New York Times,* December 16, 2011, https://www.nytimes.com/2011/12/17/business/at-amazon-jeff-bezos-talks-long-term-and-means-it.html.

10. Jerome Barthelemy, "All Business Strategies Fall into 4 Categories," hbr.org, May 23, 2024, https://hbr.org/2024/05/all-business-strategies-fall-into-4-categories.

11. Bill Murphy Jr., "If You Can Answer Yes to These 5 Unexpected Questions, You're a Much Better Leader Than Most People," *Inc.,* April 23, 2023, https://www.inc.com/bill-murphy-jr/can-you-answer-yes-to-these-5-unexpected-questions-youre-a-much-better-leader-than-most.html.

Antipattern #4

1. Finbarr Toesland, "How Five Brands Learned from Digital Transformation Failure," *Raconteur,* September 26, 2018, https://www.raconteur.net/digital-transformation/digital-transformation-failure.

2. Blake Morgan, "Companies That Failed at Digital Transformation and What We Can Learn from Them," *Forbes,* December 10, 2021, https://www.forbes.com/sites/blakemorgan/2019/09/30/companies-that-failed-at-digital-transformation-and-what-we-can-learn-from-them/.

3. Richard P. Rumelt, *Good Strategy, Bad Strategy: The Difference and Why It Matters* (New York: Crown, 2011).

4. Morgan W. McCall, *High Flyers: Developing the Next Generation of Leaders* (Boston: Harvard Business School Press, 1998); Michael R. Wade, "The Five Stages of the Chief Digital Officer—and Why They Often Fail," IMD Business School, February 2020, https://www.imd.org/research-knowledge/digital/articles/the-five-stages-of-the-chief-digital-officer-and-why-they-often-fail/.

5. Satya Nadella et al., *Hit Refresh: The Quest to Rediscover Microsoft's Soul and Imagine a Better Future for Everyone* (New York: HarperCollins, 2017).

6. "Our Business Model and Growth Strategy," McDonald's Corporation, accessed May 28, 2025, https://corporate.mcdonalds.com/corpmcd/our-company/who-we-are/business-model-and-growth-strategy.html.

7. Andrew S. Grove, *High Output Management* (New York: Random House, 1983); John Doerr, *Measure What Matters: How Google, Bono, and the Gates Foundation Rock the World with OKRs* (New York: Portfolio, 2018).

8. See "Antipattern #5: Misusing Metrics."

Antipattern #5

1. Richard Chataway, *The Behaviour Business: How to Apply Behavioural Science for Business Success* (Petersfield, UK: Harriman House, 2020).

2. Simon Caulkin, "The Rule Is Simple: Be Careful What You Measure," *The Guardian*, February 9, 2008, https://www.theguardian.com/business/2008/feb/10/businesscomment1.

3. George Mack, "12 Thoughts on Incentives," X.com, December 23, 2023, https://x.com/george__mack/status/1738533937343803439.

4. Micah Solomon, "Tony Hsieh Reveals the Secret to Zappos' Customer Service Success in One Word," *Forbes*, November 30, 2017, https://www.forbes.com/sites/micahsolomon/2017/06/12/tony-hsieh-spills-the-beans-the-one-word-secret-of-zappos-customer-service-success/.

Antipattern #6

1. John P. Kotter, "The Disastrous Effects of a 'Mostly Aligned' Executive Team," *Forbes*, December 5, 2012, https://www.forbes.com/sites/johnkotter/2012/11/28/the-disastrous-effects-of-a-mostly-aligned-executive-team/.

2. Natasha Bergeron et al., "Improve Your Leadership Team's Effectiveness through Key Behaviors," McKinsey & Company, January 27, 2020, https://www.mckinsey.com/capabilities/people-and-organizational-performance/our-insights/the-organization-blog/improve-your-leadership-teams-effectiveness-through-key-behaviors.

3. "Can Organisational Alignment Boost Profitability?" PwC, 2023, https://www.pwc.com/gx/en/issues/c-suite-insights/the-leadership-agenda/can-organisational-alignment-boost-profitability.html.

4. Patrick Lencioni, *The Five Dysfunctions of a Team: A Leadership Fable* (San Francisco: Jossey-Bass, 2011).

5. Laurent-Pierre Baculard et al., "Orchestrating a Successful Digital Transformation," Bain & Company, https://www.bain.com/insights/orchestrating-a-successful-digital-transformation/.

6. Michael Gale and Chris Aarons, *The Digital Helix: Transforming Your Organization's DNA to Thrive in the Digital Age* (Austin, TX: Greenleaf Book Group, 2017).

7. Ranjay Gulati and Jeffrey Huizinga, "Lyft 2023: Roads to Growth and Differentiation," Case 424-060 (Boston: Harvard Business School, 2024), https://www.hbs.edu/faculty/Pages/item.aspx?num=65633#:~:text=Confronted%20with%20declining%20market%20share,differentiation%20and%20rebuilding%20investor%20confidence.

Antipattern #7

1. Thomas J. Peters and Robert H. Waterman, *In Search of Excellence: Lessons from America's Best-Run Companies* (New York: Harper and Row, 1982).

2. Jay B. Barney et al., "Create Stories That Change Your Company's Culture," *Harvard Business Review*, September–October 2023; Robert I. Sutton and Huggy Rao, *The Friction Project: How Smart Leaders Make the Right Things Easier and the Wrong Things Harder* (New York: St. Martin's Press, 2024).

3. "Leadership Principles," Amazon, 2024, https://www.amazon.jobs/content/en/our-workplace/leadership-principles.

4. Marco Quiroz-Gutierrez et al., "Microsoft CEO Satya Nadella Calls Two CEOs a Day—Here's What He Asks," *Fortune*, October 11, 2024, https://fortune.com/2024/10/11/microsoft-ceo-satya-nadella-calls-two-ceos-a-day/.

5. Reed Hastings and Erin Meyer, *No Rules Rules: Netflix and the Culture of Reinvention* (New York: Penguin Press, 2020).

6. "Company Culture's Role in Hiring," Robert Half, 2018, https://www.roberthalf.com/us/en/insights/hiring-help/company-cultures-role-in-hiring?utm_campaign=Press_Release&utm_medium=Link&utm_source=Press_Release; Kyla Dewar, "Organizational Culture: Definition, Importance, and Development," *Achievers*, March 25, 2025, https://www.achievers.com/blog/organizational-culture-definition/.

7. These examples of the language of principles are modeled on the Amazon leadership principles (see note 3).

Antipattern #8

1. Stephen R. Covey, *The 7 Habits of Highly Effective People* (New York: Simon & Schuster, 1989).

2. "From Tech Investment to Impact: Strategies for Allocating Capital and Articulating Value," *Deloitte Insights*, 2023; https://www.deloitte.com/us/en/insights/topics/leadership/maximizing-value-of-tech-investments.html.

3. Aaron Dignan, *Brave New Work: Are You Ready to Reinvent Your Organization?* (New York: Portfolio, 2019).

4. Chris Argyris and Donald A. Schön, *Organizational Learning: A Theory of Action Perspective* (Reading, MA: Addison-Wesley, 1978).

5. Daniel Coyle, *The Culture Code: The Secrets of Highly Successful Groups* (New York: Bantam, 2018).

6. Donald Sull et al., "No One Knows Your Strategy—Not Even Your Top Leaders," *MIT Sloan Management Review*, February 12, 2018, https://sloanreview.mit.edu/article/no-one-knows-your-strategy-not-even-your-top-leaders/.

7. Adam Grant, *Think Again: The Power of Knowing What You Don't Know* (London: Ebury Publishing, 2023).

8. Patrick Sanders, "Chief of the General Staff Speech at RUSI Land Warfare Conference," GOV.UK, June 28, 2022, https://www.gov.uk/government/speeches/chief-the-general-staff-speech-at-rusi-land-warfare-conference.

9. "The Truth About Setting Priorities: Five Is Probably the Wrong Number," *Business and Society*, Columbia Business School, December 23, 2022, https://business.columbia.edu/insights/business-society/truth-about-setting-priorities-five-probably-wrong-number.

10. Greg McKeown, *Essentialism: The Disciplined Pursuit of Less* (New York: Crown, 2014).

11. "The Truth About Setting Priorities."

12. Laura Beck, "Warren Buffett's Key to Success: 'Say No to Almost Everything,'" Yahoo Finance, March 7, 2024, https://finance.yahoo.com/news/warren-buffett-key-success-no-161048764.html.

13. Jason Fried and David H. Hansson, *Rework: Change the Way You Work Forever* (New York: Crown, 2010).

14. Ranjay Gulati and Jeffrey Huizinga, "Lyft 2023: Roads to Growth and Differentiation," Case 424-060 (Boston: Harvard Business School, 2024), https://www.hbs.edu/faculty/Pages/item.aspx?num=65633#:~:text=Confronted%20with%20declining%20market%20share,differentiation%20and%20rebuilding%20investor%20confidence.

15. Eric Ries, *The Lean Startup: How Constant Innovation Creates Radically Successful Businesses* (New York: Portfolio, 2011).

Antipattern #9

1. "BBC's Digital Media Initiative a Complete Failure," UK Parliament, April 10, 2014, https://committees.parliament.uk/work/4279/bbc-digital-media-initiative/news/183139/bbcs-digital-media-initiative-a-complete-failure/.

2. "Reinventing Tech Finance: The Evolution from IT Budgets to Technology Investments," Deloitte, January 7, 2020, https://www2.deloitte.com/us/en/insights/focus/cio-insider-business-insights/tech-finance-technology-investment-budgeting-processes.html.

3. Ellen Huet and Olivia Zaleski, "Silicon Valley's $400 Juicer May Be Feeling the Squeeze," *Bloomberg*, 2017, https://www.bloomberg.com/news/features/2017-04-19/silicon-valley-s-400-juicer-may-be-feeling-the-squeeze.

4. "Enterprise Resource Planning to Optimize Operations," Gartner, 2014, https://www.gartner.com/en/information-technology/topics/enterprise-resource-planning.

5. Louron Pratt, "Users Engage with Only 6% of Product Features: Product Benchmark Findings," *Mind the Product*, October 2, 2024, https://www.mindtheproduct.com/users-engage-with-6-of-product-features-product-benchmark-findings/?utm_source=substack&utm_medium=email; Saffa Faisal, "Core Feature Adoption Rate: Benchmark Report 2024," *Userpilot*, 2024, https://userpilot.com/blog/core-feature-adoption-rate-benchmark-report-2024/.

6. Lou Powell, "Why Your Enterprise Keeps Failing at Digital Transformation," *Forbes*, November 1, 2019, https://www.forbes.com/councils/forbestechcouncil/2019/11/01/why-your-enterprise-keeps-failing-at-digital-transformation/.

7. John F. Love, *McDonald's: Behind the Arches* (New York: Bantam, 1988).

8. John Hamburger, "Ray Kroc, Not the Founder, but a Financial Engineer," *Restaurant Finance Monitor*, November 2, 2020, https://www.restfinance.com/restaurant-finance-across-america/ray-kroc-not-the-founder-but-a-financial-engineer/article_a3d94b01-60db-5a81-9ac9-6e1ec10d8d28.html.

9. Ranjay Gulati and Jeffrey Huizinga, "Lyft 2023: Roads to Growth and Differentiation," Case 424-060 (Boston: Harvard Business School, 2024), https://www.hbs.edu/faculty/Pages/item.aspx?num=65633#:~:text=Confronted%20with%20declining%20market%20share,differentiation%20and%20rebuilding%20investor%20confidence.

10. For more on MLPs, see Antipattern #27, "Using Proxies for Customers."

Antipattern #10

1. Nicole Forsgren, Jez Humble, and Gene Kim, *Accelerate: The Science of Lean Software and DevOps: Building and Scaling High Performing Technology Organizations* (Portland, OR: IT Revolution Press, 2018).

2. Jonathan Smart et al., *Sooner, Safer, Happier: Antipatterns and Patterns for Business Agility* (Portland, OR: IT Revolution, 2020).

3. Jeff Atwood, "The Multitasking Myth," *Coding Horror*, September 27, 2006, https://blog.codinghorror.com/the-multi-tasking-myth/; Ashley Faus and Christine D. Rosa, "5 Diagrams That Show How Context Switching Saps Your Productivity," Atlassian, January 8, 2022, https://www.atlassian.com/blog/productivity/context-switching; Rohan N. Murty et al., "Do You Know How Your Teams Get Work Done?," hbr.org, December 1, 2021, https://hbr.org/2021/12/do-you-know-how-your-teams-get-work-done.

4. John Seddon, *Freedom from Command and Control: A Better Way to Make the Work Work* (New York: Productivity Press, 2005).

5. Pim de Morree, "Bayer's Bold Bet: How a 160-Year-Old Giant Is Liberating 100,000 People," Corporate Rebels, November 17, 2024, https://www.corporate-rebels.com/blog/how-bayer-transitions-to-self-management-with-100-000-employees.

Antipattern #11

1. Aaron Dignan, *Brave New Work: Are You Ready to Reinvent Your Organization?* (New York: Portfolio, 2019).

2. Dignan, *Brave New Work.*

3. Robert Pear, "Democrats Demand Inquiry into Charge by Medicare Officer," *New York Times*, March 14, 2004.

4. Ron Westrum, "Thinking by Groups, Organizations, and Networks: A Sociologist's View of the Social Psychology of Science and Technology," in Barry Gholson et al., *Psychology of Science: Contributions to Metascience* (Cambridge, UK: Cambridge University Press, 1989), 329–342.

5. Westrum, "Thinking by Groups, Organizations, and Networks."

6. Dignan, *Brave New Work.*

7. Stanley McChrystal, "The Military Case for Sharing Knowledge," TED Talk, March 2014, https://www.ted.com/talks/stanley_mcchrystal_the_military_case_for_sharing_knowledge.

Antipattern #12

1. Mark Cruth, "The Spotify Model for Scaling Agile," Atlassian, accessed April 8, 2025, https://www.atlassian.com/agile/agile-at-scale/spotify.

2. Philip M. Rosenzweig, *The Halo Effect: How Managers Let Themselves Be Deceived* (New York: Simon & Schuster, 2008).

3. Ethan Bernstein et al., "Beyond the Holacracy Hype," *Harvard Business Review*, July–August 2016.

4. Richard M. Cyert and James G. March, *Behavioral Theory of the Firm,* 2nd ed. (Malden, MA: Blackwell, 1992).

5. Patrick Guggenberger et al., "The State of Organizations 2023: Ten Shifts Transforming Organizations," McKinsey & Company, April 26, 2023, https://www.mckinsey.com/capabilities/people-and-organizational-performance/our-insights/the-state-of-organizations-2023.

6. Stephen Heidari-Robinson and Suzanne Heywood, *ReOrg: How to Get It Right* (Boston: Harvard Business Review Press, 2016).

7. John P. Kotter, "Leading Change: Why Transformation Efforts Fail," *Harvard Business Review*, March–April 1995, 59–67.

Part 2

1. "State of the Global Workplace: 2024 Report," Gallup, 2024; https://www.gallup.com /file/workplace/645608/state-of-the-global-workplace-2024-download.pdf.

2. Daniel H. Pink, *Drive: The Surprising Truth about What Motivates Us* (New York: Penguin, 2011).

3. Pink, *Drive*.

4. Edward L. Deci et al., "Self-Determination Theory in Work Organizations: The State of a Science," *Annual Review of Organizational Psychology and Organizational Behavior* 4, no. 1 (April 2017); 10.1146/annurev-orgpsych-032516-113108.

5. Neel Doshi and Lindsay McGregor, *Primed to Perform: How to Build the Highest Performing Cultures Through the Science of Total Motivation* (New York: Harper Collins, 2015).

6. Peter Warr, "Decision Latitude, Job Demands, and Employee Well-Being," *Work and Stress* 4, no. 4 (1990), 285–294; 10.1080/02678379008256991.

7. Aaron De Smet and Brooke Weddle, "Gen AI Talent: Your Next Flight Risk," McKinsey & Company, 2024; https://www.mckinsey.com/capabilities/people-and -organizational-performance/our-insights/gen-ai-talent-your-next-flight-risk.

Antipattern #14

1. Jack Zenger and Joseph Folkman, "The 3 Elements of Trust," hbr.org, February 5, 2019, https://hbr.org/2019/02/the-3-elements-of-trust.

2. Timo O. Vuori and Quy N. Huy, "Distributed Attention and Shared Emotions in the Innovation Process: How Nokia Lost the Smartphone Battle," *Administrative Science Quarterly* 16, no. 1 (September 2015); https://doi.org/10.1177/0001839215606951.

3. Amy C. Edmondson and Michaela J. Kerrissey, "What People Get Wrong About Psychological Safety," *Harvard Business Review*, May–June 2025.

4. Simon Sinek, "Landing Moonshots with Google's Innovation Chief Dr. Astro Teller," *A Bit of Optimism*, https://www.youtube.com/watch?v=uKJvSfCqHNM&start=1761.

5. Sinek, "Landing Moonshots with Google's Innovation Chief Dr. Astro Teller."

6. Amy Edmondson et al., "Reimagining the Employee Experience at the LEGO Group," Case 625-088 (Boston: Harvard Business School, 2025), https://www.hbs.edu/faculty/Pages /item.aspx?num=66780.

7. Amy C. Edmondson, *The Fearless Organization: Creating Psychological Safety in the Workplace for Learning, Innovation, and Growth* (Hoboken, NJ: Wiley).

Antipattern #15

1. Simon Sinek, "Simon Sinek: Leader versus Manager," YouTube, 2019; https://www .youtube.com/watch?v=nSUJwmPQEyg.

2. Ann Kulow, "Qualitative Study of the Relationship between the Employee Engagement of Certain Employees and the Emotional Intelligence of Their Respective Leaders," College of Professional Studies Professional Projects, Spring 2012; https://epublications .marquette.edu/cps_professional/21/.

3. Emmanuel T. Ampofo and Osman M. Karatepe, "The Effect of Abusive Supervision on Turnover Intentions: On-the-Job Embeddedness versus Traditional Attitudinal

Constructs," *Journal of Management and Organization* 30, no. 6 (2022): 1772–1789; 10.1017/jmo.2022.80.

4. "State of the Global Workplace Report," Gallup, 2025; https://www.gallup.com/workplace/349484/state-of-the-global-workplace.aspx.

5. Linda A. Hill et al., *Collective Genius: The Art and Practice of Leading Innovation* (Boston: Harvard Business Review Press, 2014).

6. Peter M. Senge, *The Fifth Discipline: The Art and Practice of the Learning Organization*, rev. ed., (New York: Doubleday/Currency, 2006).

7. Marshall Goldsmith and Mark Reiter, *What Got You Here Won't Get You There: How Successful People Become Even More Successful* (New York: Hyperion, 2007).

8. Goldsmith and Reiter, *What Got You Here Won't Get You There.*

Antipattern #16

1. Andrew Chakhoyan, "Is the Era of Management Over?," World Economic Forum, December 7, 2017, https://www.weforum.org/agenda/2017/12/is-management-era-over/.

2. Reed Hastings and Erin Meyer, *No Rules Rules: Netflix and the Culture of Reinvention* (New York: Penguin Press, 2020).

3. Aaron Dignan, *Brave New Work: Are You Ready to Reinvent Your Organization?* (New York: Portfolio, 2019).

4. Phil Le-Brun, "Tenets: Supercharging Decision-Making," AWS, June 1, 2023, https://aws.amazon.com/blogs/enterprise-strategy/tenets-supercharging-decision-making/.

5. For more details, see Antipattern #19, "Fetishizing Process."

Antipattern #17

1. Ken Rubin, "Effectively Managing Dependencies with Ken Rubin," *Agile Mentors* podcast, February 12, 2024; https://sites.libsyn.com/405140/website/effectively-managing-dependencies-with-ken-rubin.

2. Diane E. Strode and Sid L. Huff, "A Taxonomy of Dependencies in Agile Software Development," *Proceedings of the 23rd Australasian Conference on Information Systems*, December 2012; https://www.researchgate.net/figure/A-taxonomy-of-dependencies-in-agile-software-development-projects_fig1_267706181.

3. Siying Liu et al., "Analyzing the Strategic Impact of Zara's Branding Strategies on Consumer Engagement and Market Position," *SHS Web of Conferences* 185 (2024); https://www.shs-conferences.org/articles/shsconf/pdf/2024/05/shsconf_iclcc2024_03018.pdf.

4. Sarah Zimmerman, "P&G Shifts Suppliers, Product Formulas to Avoid Supply Chain Issues," *Supply Chain Dive*, October 22, 2021; https://www.supplychaindive.com/news/procter-gamble-alternate-suppliers-reformulate-products/608625/.

5. Matthew Skelton and Manuel Pais, *Team Topologies: Organizing Business and Technology Teams for Fast Flow* (Portland, OR: IT Revolution Press, 2019).

6. Domenica DeGrandis, *Making Work Visible: Exposing Time Theft to Optimize Work and Flow* (Portland, OR: IT Revolution Press, 2022).

Antipattern #18

1. Larry Barrett and Sean Gallagher, "McBusted," *Baseline* 20 (July 2003).

2. Roland Robertson, "Globalisation or Glocalisation?" *Journal of International Communications* 18, no. 2 (2012): 191–208; https://doi.org/10.1080/13216597.2012.709925.

3. Phil Le-Brun, "Organising for Data," *AWS Cloud Enterprise Strategy* (blog), September 25, 2020, https://aws.amazon.com/blogs/enterprise-strategy/organising-for-data/.

4. Adam Cohen, *The Perfect Store: Inside eBay* (New York: Little, Brown: 2002).

Antipattern #19

1. Marty Cagan, "Scaling with Process vs. People," Silicon Valley Product Group, 2022, https://www.svpg.com/scaling-with-process-vs-people/.

2. Steve Blank, "Why Companies Do 'Innovation Theater' Instead of Actual Innovation," hbr.org, October 7, 2019; https://hbr.org/2019/10/why-companies-do-innovation-theater-instead-of-actual-innovation.

3. Bradley Brownell, "Remember When a Dutch Airline Put 440 Squirrels into a Giant Shredder?" *Jalopnik*, 2024, https://www.jalopnik.com/remember-when-a-dutch-airline-put-440-squirrels-into-a-1851573516/.

4. Brownell, "Remember When a Dutch Airline Put 440 Squirrels into a Giant Shredder?"

5. C. Northcote Parkinson, *Parkinson's Law, and Other Studies in Administration* (Boston: Houghton-Mifflin, 1965).

6. "2025 Global Human Capital Trends," Deloitte, https://www2.deloitte.com/us/en/insights/focus/human-capital-trends.html.

7. Gary Hamel and Michele Zanini, "The $3 Trillion Prize for Busting Bureaucracy," MLab, https://www.garyhamel.com/sites/default/files/uploads/three-trillion-dollars.pdf.

8. "2025 Global Human Capital Trends."

9. Robert I. Sutton and Huggy Rao, *The Friction Project: How Smart Leaders Make the Right Things Easier and the Wrong Things Harder* (New York: St. Martin's Press, 2024).

10. Sutton and Rao, *The Friction Project*.

11. Jennifer A. Chatman and Sandra Cha, "Leading by Leveraging Culture," *California Management Review* 45, no. 4 (July 2003); 10.2307/41166186.

12. Julie Makinen and Hayagreeva Rao, "AstraZeneca: Scaling Simplification," Graduate School of Business, Stanford University, https://stanford.edu/dept/gsb-ds/Inkling/AstraZeneca_Scaling_Simplification/index.html.

13. Reed Hastings and Erin Meyer, *No Rules Rules: Netflix and the Culture of Reinvention* (New York: Penguin Press, 2020).

14. Ed Catmull and Amy Wallace, *Creativity, Inc.: Overcoming the Unseen Forces That Stand in the Way of True Inspiration* (New York: Random House, 2014).

15. Peter Economy, "17 Powerfully Inspiring Quotes from Southwest Airlines Founder Herb Kelleher," *Inc.*, January 4, 2019, https://www.inc.com/peter-economy/17-powerfully-inspiring-quotes-from-southwest-airlines-founder-herb-kelleher.html.

16. Laszlo Bock, *Work Rules! Insights from Inside Google That Will Transform How You Live and Lead* (New York: Twelve, 2015).

17. Nick van der Meulen, "The Four Guardrails That Enable Agility," *MIT Sloan Management Review*, September 10, 2024; https://sloanreview.mit.edu/article/the-four-guardrails-that-enable-agility/.

18. Shreya Garg, "Amazon's 'Bureaucracy Mailbox' Is a Good Example of Integrating Employees' Feedback; Know Why It's a Good Move," *Times Now*, September 17, 2024, https://www.timesnownews.com/lifestyle/relationships/amazons-bureaucracy-mailbox-is-a-good-example-of-integrating-employees-feedback-know-why-its-a-good-move-article-113414996; "Amazon CEO Andy Jassy Shares 3 Steps Plan to Cut Bureaucracy at Companies," *Times of India*, May 1, 2025, https://timesofindia.indiatimes.com/technology/tech-news/amazon-ceo-andy-jassy-shares-3-steps-plan-to-cut-bureaucracy-at-companies/articleshow/120757629.cms.

19. Gary Hamel and Michele Zanini, *Humanocracy: Creating Organizations as Amazing as the People Inside Them* (Boston: Harvard Business Review Press, 2020).

20. Sutton and Rao, *The Friction Project*.

21. Sutton and Rao, *The Friction Project*.

Antipattern #20

1. Amos Tversky and Daniel Kahneman, "Loss Aversion in Riskless Choice: A Reference-Dependent Model," *Quarterly Journal of Economics* 106, no. 4 (November 1991): 1039–1061.

2. Mike Parsons, "Intel and the Innovator's Dilemma: A Case Study in Market Disruption," Apollo Advisors, August 14, 2024, https://www.apolloadvisor.com/intel-and-the -innovators-dilemma-a-case-study-in-market-disruption/.

3. "Netflix Ad-Supported Tier Has Launched, Here Is Its Price, What's Missing, and More," *Nerdist*, July 19, 2023, https://nerdist.com/article/netflix-launching-ad-supported-tier -earnings-interview/.

4. Annie Duke, *Thinking in Bets: Making Smarter Decisions When You Don't Have All the Facts* (New York: Portfolio, 2018).

5. For more details, see Antipattern #19, "Fetishizing Process."

6. J. S. Lerner and P. E. Tetlock, "Bridging Individual, Interpersonal, and Institutional Approaches to Judgment and Decision Making: The Impact of Accountability on Cognitive Bias," in S. L. Schneider and J. Shanteau, eds., *Emerging Perspectives on Judgment and Decision Research* (Cambridge, UK: Cambridge University Press, 2003), 431–457.

7. Ray Dalio, *Principles: Life and Work* (New York: Avid Reader Press, 2017).

8. Duke, *Thinking in Bets.*

Antipattern #21

1. Vinciane Beauchene and Molly Cunningham, "The End of Management as We Know It," Boston Consulting Group, 2020; https://www.bcg.com/publications/2020/end -management-as-we-know-it; Adam Waytz, "Beware a Culture of Busyness," *Harvard Business Review*, March–April 2023; "The State of Meetings in 2019," *Doodle*, March 24, 2025, https://doodle.com/en/resources/research-and-reports-/the-state-of-meetings-2019/.

2. Jason Fried and David Heinemeier Hansson, *Rework: Change the Way You Work Forever* (London: Vermilion, 2010).

Antipattern #22

1. Joshua H. Katz et al., "Implicit Impressions of Creative People: Creativity Evaluation in a Stigmatized Domain," *Organizational Behavior and Human Decision Processes* 169 (March 2022); https://doi.org/10.1016/j.obhdp.2021.104116.

2. Richard Sheridan, *Joy, Inc.: How We Built a Workplace People Love* (New York: Portfolio, 2015).

3. Rohan N. Murty et al., "Do You Know How Your Teams Get Work Done?" hbr.org, December 2021, https://hbr.org/2021/12/do-you-know-how-your-teams-get-work-done.

4. Roy Maurer, "Onboarding Key to Retaining, Engaging Talent," *Society for Human Resources Management*, April 16, 2015; https://www.shrm.org/resourcesandtools/hr-topics /talent- acquisition/pages/onboarding-key-retaining-engaging-talent.aspx.

5. Larry Stybel, "Why 33 Percent of New Employees Quit in 90 Days," *Psychology Today*, March 3, 2019; https://www.psychologytoday.com/gb/blog/platform-success/201903/why-33 -percent-new-employees-quit-in-90-days.

6. Devlin Peck, "Employee Onboarding Statistics: Top Trends & Insights (2025)," https://www.devlinpeck.com/content/employee-onboarding-statistics.

7. Peck, "Employee Onboarding Statistics."

8. Jason Fried and David H. Hansson, *Rework: Change the Way You Work Forever* (London: Vermilion, 2010).

9. Jennifer A. Chatman and Sandra Cha, "Leading by Leveraging Culture," *California Management Review* 45, no. 4 (July 2003); 10.2307/41166186.

10. Marc Marchese and Paul M. Muchinsky, "The Validity of Job Interviews," *International Journal of Selection and Assessment* 1, no. 1 (April 2007): 18–26.

11. Alison Beard, "X's Astro Teller on Managing Moonshot Innovation," in *HBR IdeaCast*, March 28, 2023, https://hbr.org/podcast/2023/03/xs-astro-teller-on-managing -moonshot-innovation.

12. Francesca Gino, "The Business Case for Curiosity," *Harvard Business Review*, September–October 2018.

13. Ray Dalio, *Principles: Life and Work* (New York: Avid Reader Press, 2017).

14. Tony Fadell, *Build: An Unorthodox Guide to Making Things Worth Making* (New York: Harper, 2022).

15. Beth Galetti, "How Amazon Is Built to Try and Learn," McKinsey & Company, February 18, 2020, https://www.mckinsey.com/capabilities/mckinsey-digital/our-insights /fasttimes/interviews/beth-galetti.

16. Colin Bryar and Bill Carr, "The Bar Raiser Process," Working Backwards, https:// workingbackwards.com/concepts/bar-raiser-hiring/.

17. Patrick Lencioni, *The Five Dysfunctions of a Team: A Leadership Fable* (San Francisco: Jossey-Bass, 2011); Reed Hastings and Erin Meyer, *No Rules Rules: Netflix and the Culture of Reinvention* (New York: Penguin Press, 2020).

18. Tim Cochran and Premanand Chandrasekaran, "Bottleneck #06: Onboarding," MartinFowler.com, https://martinfowler.com/articles/bottlenecks-of-scaleups/06 -onboarding.html.

19. Maurer, "Onboarding Key to Retaining, Engaging Talent"; Peck, "Employee Onboarding Statistics: Top Trends & Insights (2025)."

20. Jean Decety, ed., *The Social Brain: A Developmental Perspective* (Cambridge, MA: MIT Press, 2020); Robert I. Sutton and Huggy Rao, *The Friction Project: How Smart Leaders Make the Right Things Easier and the Wrong Things Harder* (New York: St. Martin's Press, 2024).

21. Richard Sheridan, *Joy, Inc.: How We Built a Workplace People Love* (New York: Portfolio, 2015).

22. Sheridan, *Joy, Inc.*

Antipattern #23

1. J. V. Craig and William M. Muir, "Selection for Reduction of Beak-Inflicted Injuries Among Caged Hens," *Poultry Science*, https://www.sciencedirect.com/science/article/pii/ S0032579119338520.

2. Michael Housman and Dylan Minor, "Toxic Workers," working paper 16-057, Harvard Business School, Boston, October 2015 (revised November 2015).

3. "The ROI of Respect: Why Incivility Costs Companies Millions," *Rely*, March 24, 2025, https://relyplatform.com/the-roi-of-respect-why-incivility-costs-companies-millions/; "State of the Global Workplace," Gallup, 2025; https://www.gallup.com/workplace/349484 /state-of-the-global-workplace.aspx.

4. Michael Lewis, "The No-Stats All-Star," *New York Times*, February 13, 2009; https://www.nytimes.com/2009/02/15/magazine/15Battier-t.html.

5. Patrick M. Lencioni, *The Ideal Team Player: How to Recognize and Cultivate the Three Essential Virtues* (New York: Jossey-Bass, 2016).

6. "Google re:Work—Guides: Understand Team Effectiveness," Google re:Work, accessed May 11, 2025; https://rework.withgoogle.com/en/guides/understanding-team -effectiveness.

7. Matthew Skelton and Manuel Pais, *Team Topologies: Organizing Business and Technology Teams for Fast Flow* (Portland, OR: IT Revolution, 2019).

8. Gary Hamel and Michele Zanini, *Humanocracy: Creating Organizations as Amazing as the People Inside Them* (Boston: Harvard Business Review Press, 2020).

9. Laszlo Bock, *Work Rules! Insights from Inside Google That Will Transform How You Live and Lead* (New York: Twelve, 2015).

10. Alexa Robles-Gil, "Watch Octopuses Team Up with Fish to Hunt—and Punch Those That Don't Contribute," *Smithsonian,* September 25, 2024; https://www.smithsonianmag.com/smart-news/watch-octopuses-team-up-with-fish-to-hunt-and-punch-those-that-dont-contribute-180985134/.

11. Robert I. Sutton and Huggy Rao, *The Friction Project: How Smart Leaders Make the Right Things Easier and the Wrong Things Harder* (New York: St. Martin's Press, 2024).

12. Rob Preston, "Sir Richard Branson: Life, Business Lessons from a Half Century of Shaking Things Up," *Forbes,* January 19, 2017; https://www.forbes.com/sites/oracle/2017/01/19/sir-richard-branson-life-business-lessons-from-a-half-century-of-shaking-things-up/.

13. Daniel Coyle, *The Culture Playbook: 60 Highly Effective Actions to Help Your Group Succeed* (New York: Bantam, 2022).

Antipattern #24

1. Alfie Kohn, *Punished by Rewards: The Trouble with Gold Stars, Incentive Plans, A's, Praise, and Other Bribes* (Boston: Houghton Mifflin Harcourt, 1993).

2. Daniel H. Pink, *Drive: The Surprising Truth about What Motivates Us* (New York: Riverhead, 2011).

3. Pink, *Drive.*

4. Jennifer McMillan, "How Slack Built a People First Company Culture," *Lattice,* February 28, 2019, https://lattice.com/library/how-slack-built-a-people-first-company-culture.

5. Allan Schweyer, "Academic Research in Action: Individual or Team-Based Incentives?" Incentive Research Foundation, September 2021; https://theirf.org/research_post/academic-research-in-action-individual-or-team-based-incentives/.

6. Amy Edmondson et al., "Reimagining the Employee Experience at the LEGO Group," Case 625-088 (Boston: Harvard Business School, 2025); https://www.hbs.edu/faculty/Pages/item.aspx?num=66780.

7. Ranjay Gulati et al., "Netflix: A Creative Approach to Culture and Agility," Case 420-055 (Boston: Harvard Business School, 2019); https://www.hbs.edu/faculty/Pages/item.aspx?num=56185.

8. AJ Hess, "What Airbnb Learned After a Year of Letting Employees Work from Anywhere," *Fast Company,* July 24, 2023; https://www.fastcompany.com/90921228/what-airbnb-learned-after-a-year-of-letting-employees-work-from-anywhere.

Antipattern #25

1. Of course, if they are doing something you genuinely believe is wrong, turn it into a coaching conversation, or be directive if necessary.

2. "Shonda Rhimes on Saying Yes to What Scares You," *ReThinking* with Adam Grant, April 22, 2025; https://www.ted.com/pages/shonda-rhimes-on-saying-yes-to-what-scares-you-transcript.

3. Michael Bungay Stanier, *The Coaching Habit: Say Less, Ask More, and Change the Way You Lead Forever* (Page Two Books, 2016).

4. Reed Hastings, "How Netflix Changed Entertainment—and Where It's Headed," TED Talk, April 2018; https://www.ted.com/talks/reed_hastings_how_netflix_changed _entertainment_and_where_it_s_headed/transcript.

5. For an explanation of "chicken behavior," see Antipattern #21, "Diluting Accountability."

Part 3

1. "A Talk with Indra Nooyi, Amazon Board Member and Former PepsiCo CEO," YouTube, 2024, https://www.youtube.com/watch?v=eP25p_oO60w.

2. Mary Kingston Roche, "Creating a Curiosity-Inspired Life and World," TEDxOcala," https://www.youtube.com/watch?v=bTojPc7uJmw.

3. "Global Education Monitoring Report, 2020: Inclusion and Education: All Means All," UNESCO, https://gem-report-2020.unesco.org/; Gerald C. Kane et al., *Technology Fallacy: How People Are the Real Key to Digital Transformation* (Cambridge, MA: MIT Press, 2022).

4. "2024 Global Human Capital Trends," Deloitte, https://www2.deloitte.com/xe/en /insights/focus/human-capital-trends.html.

5. "Be Curious: State of Curiosity Report 2016," Merck, https://www.merckgroup.com /company/curiosity/Curiosity_Full-Report_English.pdf.

6. Matt Richtel, "We Have a Creativity Problem," *New York Times*, April 16, 2022, https://www.nytimes.com/2022/04/16/science/creativity-implicit-bias.html.

Antipattern #26

1. "The Third Annual State of Agile Culture Report," JCURV, Truth Sayers, and Agile Business Consortium, 2023, https://www.agilebusiness.org/resource-report/state-of-agile -culture-report-2023.html.

2. Dan Pilat and Sekoul Krastev, "Prospect Theory," The Decision Lab, 2025, https:// thedecisionlab.com/reference-guide/economics/prospect-theory.

3. See Antipattern 29, "Falling in Love with Answers."

4. Ray Dalio, *Principles: Life and Work* (New York: Avid Reader Press, 2017).

5. Astro Teller, "Secrets to Building a Diverse Dream Team," Grace Hopper Conference Keynote, October 2016, www.astroteller.net. https://www.astroteller.net/talks/secrets-to -building-a-diverse-dream-team.

6. Amy C. Edmondson, "Strategies for Learning from Failure," *Harvard Business Review*, April 2011.

7. Jeffrey Shupack et al., *How to Thrive (or Fail) in Building a Learning Culture* (Portland, OR: IT Revolution, 2023).

8. Eric Ries, *The Lean Startup: How Constant Innovation Creates Radically Successful Businesses* (New York: Portfolio, 2011)

9. "A Fireside Chat with X's Captain of Moonshots, Astro Teller (Google I/O'19)," YouTube, https://www.youtube.com/watch?v=HC2EMDL4EVo.

10. Edmondson, "Strategies for Learning from Failure"; Teller, "Secrets to Building a Diverse Dream Team."

Antipattern #27

1. Sam Oches, "Inside the Plan to Fix McDonald's," *QSR*, May 1, 2018, https://www .qsrmagazine.com/reports/inside-plan-fix-mcdonalds/; "Financial Information," McDonald's Corporation, https://corporate.mcdonalds.com/corpmcd/investors/financial-information. html.

2. Barry O'Reilly, *Unlearn: Let Go of Past Success to Achieve Extraordinary Results* (New York: McGraw-Hill Education, 2018).

3. "80% of Customers Said They Have Switched Brands Because of Poor Customer Experience," Qualtrics, December 14, 2021, https://www.qualtrics.com/blog/qualtrics -servicenow-customer-service-research/.

4. "2016 Letter to Shareholders," Amazon, https://www.aboutamazon.com/news /company-news/2016-letter-to-shareholders.

5. O'Reilly, *Unlearn*.

6. Indra Nooyi, *My Life in Full: Work, Family, and Our Future* (New York: Little, Brown, 2001); and "A Talk with Indra Nooyi," AWS, 2024, https://aws.amazon.com/executive -insights/podcast/a-talk-with-indra-nooyi/.

7. Eric Ries, *The Lean Startup: How Today's Entrepreneurs Use Continuous Innovation to Create Radically Successful Businesses* (New York: Crown, 2011).

8. Aaron Holmes "Nadella's Network: How Microsoft's CEO Avoids Getting Disrupted," *The Information*, 2024, https://www.theinformation.com/articles/nadellas-network-how -microsofts-ceo-avoids-getting-disrupted.

Antipattern #28

1. "From Amazon to Space—Jeff Bezos Talks Innovation, Progress and What's Next," *New York Times*, December 20, 2024, https://www.nytimes.com/2024/12/20/podcasts/jeff -bezos-amazon-space-washington-post.html.

2. "Waymo Safety Impact," Waymo, https://waymo.com/safety/impact/.

3. "Loon," The Moonshot Factory, https://x.company/projects/loon/.

4. David Robertson and Bill Breen, *Brick by Brick: How LEGO Rewrote the Rules of Innovation and Conquered the Global Toy Industry* (New York: Crown, 2014); Duncan Wardle, "Corporate Learning Is Boring—But It Doesn't Have to Be," hbr.org, April 5, 2024, https://hbr.org/2024/04/corporate-learning-is-boring-but-it-doesnt-have-to-be.

5. "How Generative AI Helps Amazon Eliminate Checkout Lines and Revolutionize the Shopping Experience," Amazon, September 26, 2023, https://www.aboutamazon.com/news /retail/how-does-amazon-just-walk-out-work.

6. See Antipattern #27, "Using Proxies for Customers."

7. James Carse, *Finite and Infinite Games* (New York: Free Press, 2013).

8. "The Ideas That Inspire Us," *Harvard Business Review*, November–December 2022, https://hbr.org/2022/11/the-ideas-that-inspire-us.

9. "Interview: Amazon CEO Jeff Bezos," *Business Insider*, 2014, YouTube, https://www .youtube.com/watch?v=Xx92bUw7WX8.

10. Astro Teller, "Innovation Is Rule Breaking," *Bit of Optimism* podcast, https://www .astroteller.net/talks/landing-moonshots-with-googles-innovation-chief.

11. Eric Ries, "Methodology," The Lean Startup, accessed April 27, 2025, https:// theleanstartup.com/principles.

12. Teller, "Innovation Is Rule Breaking."

13. "Leadership Principles," Amazon, https://www.amazon.jobs/content/en/our -workplace/leadership-principles.

Antipattern #29

1. Nathan Mattise, "General Magic—How Tech Superfriends Assembled, Dreamt Up Smartphones, and Failed," *Ars Technica*, August 12, 2018; https://arstechnica.com/gaming /2018/08/general-magic-how-tech-superfriends-assembled-dreamt-up-smartphones-and -failed/.

2. Tony Fadell, *Build: An Unorthodox Guide to Making Things Worth Making* (New York: Harper, 2022).

3. Fadell, *Build*.

4. Fadell, *Build*.

5. David A. Hofmann, "Overcoming the Obstacles to Cross-Functional Decision Making: Laying the Groundwork for Collaborative Problem Solving," *Organizational Dynamics* 44, no. 1 (January–March 2015): 17–25; https://doi.org/10.1016/j.orgdyn.2014.11.003.

6. Richard M. Cyert and James G. March, *Behavioral Theory of the Firm*, 2nd ed. (Malden, MA: Blackwell, 1992).

7. See Antipattern 27.

8. Edward Capaldi, "Toyota's 5 WHYS," YouTube, https://www.youtube.com/watch?v=HxqKy1HACmA.

9. Ryan Singer, *Shape Up: Stop Running in Circles and Ship Work That Matters* (Chicago: Basecamp, 2019).

10. Duncan Wardle, "Corporate Learning Is Boring—But It Doesn't Have to Be," hbr.org, April 5, 2024; https://hbr.org/2024/04/corporate-learning-is-boring-but-it-doesnt-have-to-be.

11. Alison Beard, "X's Astro Teller on Managing Moonshot Innovation," HBR IdeaCast, March 28, 2023; https://hbr.org/podcast/2023/03/xs-astro-teller-on-managing-moonshot-innovation.

12. Simon Sinek, "Landing Moonshots with Google's Innovation Chief Dr. Astro Teller," *A Bit of Optimism*, 2024; https://www.youtube.com/watch?v=uKJvSfCqHNM&start=1761.

13. Adam Grant, "How to Build a Culture of Originality," *Harvard Business Review*, March 2016.

14. Clayton M. Christensen et al., "Know Your Customers' 'Jobs to Be Done,'" *Harvard Business Review*, September 2016.

15. Fernanda Arreola, "Extreme Users: Understanding Their Role in Innovation and Design," *European Business Review*, March 12, 2025, https://www.europeanbusinessreview.com/extreme-users-understanding-their-role-in-innovation-and-design/.

16. A brainstorming technique that takes a systematic approach to generating alternatives. SCAMPER stands for "Substitute, Combine, Adapt, Modify, Put to other uses, Eliminate, Reverse"; and Dan Pilat and Sekoul Krastev, "SCAMPER," The Decision Lab, accessed April 27, 2025; https://thedecisionlab.com/reference-guide/philosophy/scamper.

17. Teresa Torres, *Continuous Discovery Habits: Discover Products That Create Customer Value and Business Value* (Bend, OR: Product Talk, 2021).

Antipattern #30

1. Shana Lebowitz, "Why 'Monkey First' Perfectly Sums Up How People Work at Google X," *Inc.*, October 13, 2017; https://www.inc.com/business-insider/alphabet-google-x-moonshot-labs-how-people-work-productivity-monkey-first.html.

2. Shana Lebowitz, "People at Alphabet's 'Moonshot' Lab Have a Saying About Productivity: #MonkeyFirst—Here's What It Means," *Business Insider*, October 13, 2017; https://www.businessinsider.com/monkeyfirst-google-x-productivity-success-2017-10.

3. Lebowitz, "People at Alphabet's 'Moonshot' Lab Have a Saying About Productivity."

4. Simon Sinek, "Landing Moonshots with Google's Innovation Chief Dr. Astro Teller," *A Bit of Optimism*, 2024; https://www.youtube.com/watch?v=uKJvSfCqHNM&start=1761.

5. "Taara," X, the Moonshot Factory, accessed February 27, 2025; https://x.company/projects/taara/.

Antipattern #31

1. Maurice Switzer, *Mrs. Goose, Her Book* (Classic Reprint) (London: FB&C, 2015).

2. Margaret Heffernan, "Dare to Disagree," TED Talk, June 2012; https://www.ted.com /talks/margaret_heffernan_dare_to_disagree?subtitle=en.

3. Solomon E. Asch, "Studies of Independence and Conformity: I. A Minority of One against a Unanimous Majority," *Psychological Monographs: General and Applied* 70, no. 9 (1956): 1–70; https://doi.org/10.1037/h0093718.

4. Jeff Dyer et al., "Why Innovation Depends on Intellectual Honesty," *MIT Sloan Management Review*, January 17, 2023; https://sloanreview.mit.edu/article/why-innovation -depends-on-intellectual-honesty.

5. Frans Johansson, *The Medici Effect: Breakthrough Insights at the Intersection of Ideas, Concepts, and Cultures* (Boston: Harvard Business School Press, 2004).

6. Robert Kegan and Lisa L. Lahey, *Immunity to Change: How to Overcome It and Unlock Potential in Yourself and Your Organization* (Boston: Harvard Business Press, 2009).

7. Roger Fisher et al., *Getting to Yes* (Boston: Houghton Mifflin Harcourt, 1991).

8. Robert P. Vecchio et al., "The Influence of Leader Humor on Relationships between Leader Behavior and Follower Outcomes," *Journal of Managerial Issues* 21, no. 2 (July 2009): 171–194.

9. Julia A. Minson and Francesca Gino, "Managing a Polarized Workforce," *Harvard Business Review*, March–April 2022.

10. Dyer et al., "Why Innovation Depends on Intellectual Honesty."

11. Linda A. Hill et al., *Collective Genius: The Art and Practice of Leading Innovation* (Boston: Harvard Business Review Press, 2014).

12. Annie Duke, *Thinking in Bets: Making Smarter Decisions When You Don't Have All the Facts* (New York: Portfolio, 2019).

Antipattern #32

1. Umair Haque, "Google Glass Failed Because It Just Wasn't Cool," hbr.org, January 30, 2015; https://hbr.org/2015/01/google-glass-failed-because-it-just-wasnt-cool.

2. "Smart Glasses Raise Privacy Concerns, Harvard Students Show in Study," NBC10 Boston, 2024, YouTube, https://www.youtube.com/watch?v=aqrolPymsFw.

3. Tyler Labiak, "Analysis of the Google Glass Failure and Why Things May Be Different Now" (research paper, University of Virginia, 2021); https://libraetd.lib.virginia.edu /downloads/dv13zt950?filename=Labiak_Tyler_2021_STS_Research_Paper.pdf.

4. David Rock et al., "Diverse Teams Feel Less Comfortable—and That's Why They Perform Better," hbr.org, September 22, 2016; https://hbr.org/2016/09/diverse-teams-feel-less -comfortable-and-thats-why-they-perform-better.

5. David Rock and Heidi Grant, "Why Diverse Teams Are Smarter," hbr.org, November 4, 2016; https://hbr.org/2016/11/why-diverse-teams-are-smarter.

6. Gokhan Ertug et al., "What Does Homophily Do? A Review of the Consequences of Homophily," *Academy of Management Annals* 16, no. 1 (January 26, 2022); doi.org/10.5465 /annals.2020.0230.

7. Rock and Grant, "Why Diverse Teams Are Smarter."

8. Georgi Karadzhov et al., "The Effect of Diversity on Group Decision-Making," Arxiv, February 2, 2024, https://arxiv.org/html/2402.01427v1.

9. Rock and Grant, "Why Diverse Teams Are Smarter."

10. Alison Reynolds and David Lewis, "Teams Solve Problems Faster When They're More Cognitively Diverse," hbr.org, March 30, 2017, https://hbr.org/2017/03/teams-solve-problems -faster-when-theyre-more-cognitively-diverse; Ishani Aggarwal and Anita Williams

Woolley, "Team Creativity, Cognition, and Cognitive Style Diversity," *Management Science* 65, no. 4 (April 20, 2018): 1586–1599, https://doi.org/10.1287/mnsc.2017.3001; Steven H. Cady and Joanne Valentine, "Team Innovation and Perceptions of Consideration: What Difference Does Diversity Make?" *Small Group Research* 30, no. 6 (December 1999): 730–750; https://doi .org/10.1177/104649649903000604.

11. Erik Larson, "Research Shows Diversity + Inclusion = Better Decision Making at Work," *Cloverpop*, September 25, 2017; https://www.cloverpop.com/blog/research-shows -diversity-inclusion-better-decision-making-at-work.

12. Larson, "Research Shows Diversity + Inclusion = Better Decision Making at Work."

13. Brian Mullen et al., "Productivity Loss in Brainstorming Groups: A Meta-Analytic Integration," *Basic and Applied Social Psychology* 12, no. 1 (June 7, 2010): 3–23, https://doi.org /10.1207/s15324834basp1201_1.

14. Max Chafkin, "Warby Parker," *Fast Company*, February 9, 2015; https://www .fastcompany.com/3039573/warby-parker.

15. Linda A. Hill et al., *Collective Genius: The Art and Practice of Leading Innovation* (Boston: Harvard Business Review Press, 2014).

16. Hill et al., *Collective Genius*.

17. Hill et al., *Collective Genius*.

18. Hill et al., *Collective Genius*.

19. Hill et al., *Collective Genius*.

20. Reynolds and Lewis, "Teams Solve Problems Faster When They're More Cognitively Diverse"; Aggarwal and Williams Woolley, "Team Creativity, Cognition, and Cognitive Style Diversity"; Cady and Valentine, "Team Innovation and Perceptions of Consideration: What Difference Does Diversity Make?"

Antipattern #33

1. Cathy O'Neill, *Weapons of Math Destruction: How Big Data Increases Inequality and Threatens* Democracy (New York: Crown, 2016).

2. Isobel A. Hamilton, "This Is How Jeff Bezos Makes Decisions," *Business Insider*, September 14, 2018; https://www.businessinsider.com/how-jeff-bezos-makes-decisions-2018-9.

3. Shane Parrish, "The Loudest Signals," *Fs*, April 6, 2025, https://fs.blog/brain-food /april-6-2025/.

4. Thomas Davenport, "The Future of Work Now: AI-Assisted Clothing Stylists at Stitch Fix," *Forbes*, March 21, 2021.

5. Roger Dooley, "A Two-Minute Masterclass from Jeff Bezos—Five Powerful Insights," *Forbes*, December 9, 2024, https://www.forbes.com/sites/rogerdooley/2024/12/09/a-two -minute-masterclass-from-jeff-bezosfive-powerful-insights/.

6. Lex Fridman, "Jeff Bezos: Amazon and Blue Origin," Lex Fridman Podcast #405," YouTube, https://www.youtube.com/watch?v=DcWqzZ3I2cY.

Antipattern #34

1. Hugo Sarrazin and Paul Willmott, "Adapting Your Board to the Digital Age," McKinsey & Company, July 13, 2016; https://www.mckinsey.com/capabilities/mckinsey -digital/our-insights/adapting-your-board-to-the-digital-age; Eve Tahmincioglu, "Is Your Board Tech-Ready?" *Directors and Boards*, October 30, 2018; https://www.directorsandboards .com/articles/is-your-board-tech-ready/.

2. Peter Weill et al., "Does Your C-Suite Have Enough Digital Smarts?" *MIT Sloan Management Review*, March 3, 2021; https://sloanreview.mit.edu/article/does-your-c-suite -have-enough-digital-smarts/.

3. J. Yo-Jud Cheng et al., "Is Your C-Suite Equipped to Lead a Digital Transformation?," hbr.org, March 12, 2021; https://hbr.org/2021/03/is-your-c-suite-equipped-to-lead-a -digital-transformation; Gerald C. Kane et al., "Achieving Digital Maturity," *MIT Sloan Management Review*, July 13, 2017; https://sloanreview.mit.edu/projects/achieving-digital -maturity/.

4. Christopher Mims and Bill Curtis, "The Invisible $1.52 Trillion Problem: Clunky Old Software," *Wall Street Journal*, March 1, 2024; https://www.wsj.com/tech/personal-tech/the -invisible-1-52-trillion-problem-clunky-old-software-f5cbba27.

5. Mark Schwartz, *A Seat at the Table: IT Leadership in the Age of Agility* (Portland, OR: IT Revolution, 2017).

6. "Honing Your Digital Edge," Accenture, 2020, https://www.accenture.com/content/dam /accenture/final/a-com-migration/pdf/pdf-141/accenture-honing-your-digital-edge-pov.pdf.

7. "A Walmart Case Study: How Software Agencies Drive Digital Transformation for Businesses," Alabama Solutions, 2024, https://alabamasolutions.com/a-walmart-case-study -how-software-agencies-drive-digital-transformation-for-businesses; "Capital One on AWS," AWS, 2018," https://aws.amazon.com/solutions/case-studies/innovators/capital-one/.

Antipattern #35

1. Peter Cappelli, "How Financial Accounting Screws Up HR," *Harvard Business Review*, January–February 2023.

2. Bruce C. Rudy, "Build Learning into Your Employees' Workflow," hbr.org, July 11, 2022; https://hbr.org/2022/07/build-learning-into-your-employees-workflow.

3. Josh Bersin, "The $340 Billion Corporate Learning Industry Is Poised for Disruption," JoshBersin.com, April 6, 2024; https://joshbersin.com/2024/03/the-340-billion -corporate-learning-industry-is-poised-for-disruption/; Jonathan Deller, "Training Evaluations Models: The Complete Guide," Kodo Survey, April 30, 2020; https://kodosurvey .com/blog/training-evaluations-models-complete-guide.

4. Josh Bersin, "A New Paradigm for Corporate Training: Learning in the Flow of Work," JoshBersin.com, June 3, 2018; https://joshbersin.com/2018/06/a-new-paradigm-for -corporate-training-learning-in-the-flow-of-work/.

5. Stacia Garr and Priyanka Mehrotra, "Don't Sacrifice Employee Upskilling for Productivity," *MIT Sloan Management Review*, July 10, 2024; https://sloanreview.mit.edu /article/dont-sacrifice-employee-upskilling-for-productivity/.

6. Peter Weill et al., "Does Your C-Suite Have Enough Digital Smarts?" *MIT Sloan Management Review*, March 3, 2021; https://sloanreview.mit.edu/article/does-your-c-suite -have-enough-digital-smarts/; David Shaw and Emma McGuigan, "Global Digital Fluency Study," Accenture, 2020, https://www.accenture.com/gb-en/insights/consulting/honing -digital-edge.

7. Anu Madgavkar et al., "Help Wanted: Charting the Challenge of Tight Labor Markets in Advanced Economies," McKinsey Global Institute, June 26, 2024; https://www.mckinsey .com/mgi/our-research/help-wanted-charting-the-challenge-of-tight-labor-markets-in -advanced-economies.

8. Malcolm S. Knowles et al., *The Adult Learner: The Definitive Classic in Adult Education and Human Resource Development* (Waltham, MA: Butterworth-Heinemann, 2025).

9. Mark K. Smith, "Donald Schon (Schön): Learning, Reflection and Change," infed.org; https://infed.org/mobi/donald-schon-learning-reflection-change/.

10. Aaron Dignan, *Brave New Work: Are You Ready to Reinvent Your Organization?* (New York: Portfolio, 2019).

11. Etienne Wenger, *Communities of Practice: Learning, Meaning, and Identity* (Cambridge, UK: Cambridge University Press, 1999).

12. "Create an Employee-to-Employee Learning Program," Google re:Work, accessed January 20, 2025; https://rework.withgoogle.com/en/guides/learning-development-employee -to-employee#make-learning-part-of-the-culture.

13. Rachel Emma Silverman, "So Much Training, So Little to Show for It," *Wall Street Journal*, October 26, 2012; https://www.wsj.com/articles/SB100014240529702044259045780 72950518558328.

14. Barry O'Reilly, *Unlearn: Let Go of Past Success to Achieve Extraordinary Results* (New York: McGraw-Hill Education, 2018).

15. Forbes Human Resources Council, "Council Post: Lattice or Ladder? 10 Best Ways for Professionals to Advance Their Careers," *Forbes*, February 12, 2019; https://www.forbes.com /councils/forbeshumanresourcescouncil/2019/02/12/lattice-or-ladder-10-best-ways-for -professionals-to-advance-their-careers/.

16. David A. Kolb, *Experiential Learning: Experience as the Source of Learning and Development* (Upper Saddle River, NJ: Prentice-Hall, 2015).

17. "Learning Emerging Skills Doesn't Always Pay Off," *Harvard Business Review*, January–February 2025, https://hbr.org/2025/01/learning-emerging-skills-doesnt-always -pay-off.

Antipattern #36

1. Justin Manly et al., "Innovation Systems Need a Reboot," Boston Consulting Group, June 4, 2024; https://www.bcg.com/publications/2024/innovation-systems-need-a-reboot.

2. Anderee Berengian, "It's Time to Ditch Your Innovation Lab," *VentureBeat*, March 22, 2017; https://venturebeat.com/business/its-time-to-ditch-your-innovation-lab/.

3. Cristian Granados et al., "Is It Substantive or Just Symbolic? Understanding Innovation Theater in Organisations: The Case of Technology-Based Innovation," *Technovation* 129 (January 2024), 10.1016/j.technovation.2023.102880; and Isabelle Bousquette, "Where Does the Best Innovation Happen? Not in Stand-Alone Labs, Some Companies Say," *Wall Street Journal*, April 10, 2024, https://www.wsj.com/articles/where-does-the-best-innovation -happen-not-in-stand-alone-labs-some-companies-say/.

4. Clayton M. Christensen, *The Innovator's Dilemma: When New Technologies Cause Great Firms to Fail* (Boston: Harvard Business Review Press, 2016).

5. Vijay Govindarajan and Chris Trimble, *The Other Side of Innovation: Solving the Execution Challenge* (Boston: Harvard Business School Press, 2010).

6. "Securities and Exchange Commission Response," correspondence between Amazon and US Securities and Exchange Commission, July 28, 2017; https://www.sec.gov/Archives /edgar/data/1018724/000101872417000133/filename1.htm.

7. Jason Del Rey, "The Making of Amazon Prime, the Internet's Most Successful and Devastating Membership Program," *Vox*, May 3, 2019; https://www.vox.com/recode/2019/5/3 /18511544/amazon-prime-oral-history-jeff-bezos-one-day-shipping.

8. Safi Bahcall, *Loonshots: How to Nurture the Crazy Ideas That Win Wars, Cure Diseases, and Transform Industries* (New York: St. Martin's Press, 2019).

Conclusion

1. Aaron Dignan, *Brave New Work: Are You Ready to Reinvent Your Organization?* (New York: Portfolio, 2019).

2. Jake Burns, "Jake Burns' Post," LinkedIn, 2025; https://www.linkedin.com/feed /update/urn:li:activity:7264445377251016704/.

3. Teresa M. Amabile and Steven J. Kramer, "The Power of Small Wins," *Harvard Business Review*, May 2011; https://www.hbs.edu/faculty/Pages/item.aspx?num=40244.

4. Jim Collins, *Good to Great: Why Some Companies Make the Leap . . . and Others Don't* (New York: Random House Business, 2001).

5. Jay W. Forrester, *World Dynamics* (Pegasus Communications, 1971); Jay W. Forrester, *Urban Dynamics* (Pegasus Communications, 1969); Donella Meadows, "Leverage Points: Places to Intervene in a System," The Donella Meadows Project, https://donellameadows.org /archives/leverage-points-places-to-intervene-in-a-system/.

6. Meadows, "Leverage Points."

7. Meadows, "Leverage Points."

8. Thomas S. Kuhn, *The Structure of Scientific Revolutions*, 2nd ed. (Chicago: University of Chicago Press, 1970).

9. See Antipattern #26, "Evading Failure."

10. Danny Sheridan, "Just Do It Award," Fact of the Day 1, February 13, 2020; https:// www.factoftheday1.com/p/just-do-it-award-ed4951f54d0c.

11. Beth Galetti, "How Amazon Is Built to Try and Learn," McKinsey & Company, February 18, 2020; https://www.mckinsey.com/capabilities/mckinsey-digital/our-insights /fasttimes/interviews/beth-galetti.

12. David Cooperrider and Suresh Srivastva, "Appreciative Inquiry in Organizational Life," *Research in Organizational Change and Development* 1, no. 1 (1987): 129–169.

13. *Curiosity (HBR Emotional Intelligence Series)* (Boston: Harvard Business Review Press, 2024).

14. Dignan, *Brave New Work.*

15. Ashley Goodall, *The Problem with Change: The Essential Nature of Human Performance* (New York: Little, Brown, 2024).

INDEX

ABOUT THE AUTHORS

PHIL LE-BRUN is an enterprise strategist at Amazon Web Services and a former corporate VP and international CIO at McDonald's Corporation. At McDonald's he co-led the consolidation and modernization of technology across thirty-eight thousand restaurants globally. In his current role, Phil engages with *Fortune* 500 executives and their teams and with public-sector customers to mentor, advise, and guide them on their journeys to become more adaptable organizations. He is a sought-after speaker and has been featured in *Harvard Business Review*, the *Wall Street Journal*, and *The Guardian*.

JANA WERNER is an enterprise strategist at Amazon Web Services, where she guides the executive teams of *Fortune* 500 companies in building adaptive customer-centric organizations. Her insights are forged from a career at the intersection of business strategy and technology: leading major digital transformations in financial services, guiding and scaling tech startups to growth and acquisition, and advising on complex global change at DHL. Her academic background in uncertainty dynamics grounds her practical advice for leaders navigating complex environments and building resilient organizations.